The Flow of Gifts

The Flow

of Gifts

Reciprocity and
Social Networks
in a Chinese Village

Yunxiang Yan

STANFORD UNIVERSITY PRESS
Stanford, California ⁓ 1996

Stanford University Press
Stanford, California
©1996 by the Board of Trustees of the
Leland Stanford Junior University
Printed in the United States of America

CIP data are at the end of the book

Stanford University Press publications are distributed
exclusively by Stanford University Press within the United
States, Canada, Mexico, and Central America; they are
distributed exclusively by Cambridge University Press
throughout the rest of the world

Acknowledgments

This book would not have been completed without the help and support of many people and institutions. The first individual to whom I would like to express my gratitude is James L. (Woody) Watson, my principal advisor and good friend. Working with Woody since 1989, I have enjoyed a student-teacher-friend relationship completely unknown in Chinese academic circles. Woody is warm, caring, and untiring in his support. His thoughtful guidance, valuable comments, and consistent appreciation of my work enabled me to overcome the cultural and academic barriers between Chinese and Western traditions in my intellectual journey at Harvard University.

I have been more than lucky to have many professors at Harvard University who care for me and my work. I owe special thanks to Arthur Kleinman for providing theoretical inspiration, methodological guidance, and critical advice. I have received generous help and support from Kwang-chih Chang ever since I was fortunate enough to be his student in 1986. Although not sitting on my committee as supervisors, Andrew Walder and Rubie Watson are also my teachers and mentors. Myron Cohen at Columbia University was among the first to read my research proposal on gift giving in 1989; since then he has continued to offer me comments and advice, which have contributed much to the growth of this study. Ezra Vogel is another "unofficial" advisor to whom I owe special thanks.

For my intellectual development, thanks are also due many people in and out of Harvard who guided me on my way into the Western academic tradition. To name only a few: Thomas Gold, Kathleen Hartford, Jean Oi, Wei-ming Tu, Jonathan Unger, Robert Weller, Mayfair Yang, and David Zweig. I would particularly like to thank Nur Yalman and Thomas Barfield for the generous help they gave me during the first (and most difficult) two years of my stay at Harvard. Equally important, I have learned a lot from my student peers and I missed them very much after my graduation.

I am also grateful to Nancy Hearst at Harvard for her skillful editorial assistance and to Muriel Bell at Stanford Press for her enthusiastic support for this book as well as her editorial expertise.

Because of the support of the villagers and my friends in the local government, my fieldwork in Xiajia village, Heilongjiang province, was pleasant and fruitful. I am especially grateful to Mr. Hu Yanjun and Mr. Guo Hengwen, who worked with me throughout my fieldwork. They are extremely decent and knowledgeable fellows, with great senses of humor. My research would have been much more difficult, if not impossible, without their help.

My graduate study benefited greatly from the generosity of the Harvard-Yenching Institute. The Institute sponsored my study during the first three and a half years and offered another year of fellowship for dissertation writing. My fieldwork in 1991 was supported by the National Science Foundation (grant number BNS-9101369). I also received scholarships from the Department of Anthropology and the Council on East Asian Studies, Harvard University. I am grateful to all these institutions for their financial support.

My final words of gratitude go to Xiaoxia Gong. For the past fourteen years she has been the firmest supporter of my professional pursuits, the toughest critic of my work, and the most valuable "sharpener" of my thought.

Yunxiang Yan

Contents

Maps, Figures, and Tables

The Flow of Gifts

Introduction: The Gift in Anthropology and Chinese Society

This book offers an ethnographic account of the system of gift exchange and the patterns of interpersonal relations in a north China village. It has been widely recognized that gift giving is one of the most important modes of social exchange in human societies. The obligatory give-and-take maintains, strengthens, and creates various social bonds—be they cooperative, competitive, or antagonistic. A study of gift exchange, therefore, provides us with a means of understanding and interpreting various cultural rules and the structure of social relations in a given society.

Although I probably never would have been able to comprehend the theoretical significance of everyday gift-giving behavior had I not received graduate training in anthropology, my interest in this subject is rooted in my personal experience of rural life. Born and reared in Beijing, I later lived in farming villages in two provinces of north China from 1966 to 1978. During the early phase of the Cultural Revolution, my father, like many citizens at that time, was falsely accused of being a "class enemy of the people"; as a consequence, my family was forced to leave Beijing and settle in my father's natal village in Shandong province. I was twelve at the time and had yet to learn what it meant to be disengaged from urban life. Instead, I was enthralled by the new environment, which offered things I had never seen before, such as open fields, domestic animals, and strange customs. One of my most memorable experiences was watching our neighbors exchange gifts with their relatives during the lunar New Year.

Throughout the first week of the festival, the villagers were busy visiting one another, and I soon noticed that everyone carried a small basket or bag filled with home-made steamed buns. I was surprised to learn that these buns were "gifts" (*liwu*) to be exchanged among the villagers. In Beijing, I had thought of a gift as something unusual and lovely—a cute toy, beautiful cloth, or a box of candy. How could these steamed buns be considered gifts? They were just ordinary food. And why did everyone give and receive the same kind of gift? I asked my mother, and she, who had no more rural experience than I, told me that this was the practice in rural areas.

When I witnessed my uncle (my father's brother) and aunt (my uncle's wife) receiving a guest (and his gift), I became even more confused. The visitor, who was my aunt's sister's son, first kowtowed to my aunt and uncle; he then offered up a basket to them, telling them it was a gift from his family and it brought all best wishes to my aunt and uncle. When the two men began talking and drinking, I followed my aunt to the kitchen and discovered that under the red cloth cover were two bottles of wine on top of several steamed buns. My aunt took one bottle of wine and half the buns out of the basket, and then, strangely enough, she put a dozen of her own recently steamed buns in the gift container. Perhaps noticing my curious expression, my aunt told me that on such occasions one usually took only half the gift and offered some additional goods to the gift giver. "You can't let your guest return home with an empty basket," she said. Later, when the guest was leaving, my aunt returned the basket to him while thanking him for his nice gift. The guest in turn complimented my aunt on her gift, telling her that she should have taken the other bottle of wine and the rest of the steamed buns. My aunt replied, "We have received your good feelings conveyed by the gift, and we are very happy. Please take the rest back for your family."

They argued back and forth for a while and repeatedly expressed gratitude to each other before the guest finally went home.

In 1971 I left my father's natal village and moved alone to Xiajia village in Heilongjiang province. (Twenty years later I would return to Xiajia to conduct the fieldwork that resulted in this book.) When I settled in Xiajia I was seventeen years old and thus had to participate in the local system of gift exchange as an adult member of the community. I soon began to understand the obligations of offering gifts to mark a fellow villager's wedding or a neighbor's funeral, and I felt a strong sense of shame when I did not have enough money to fulfill these obligations. I also discovered that, in addition to the regular, ritualized occasions of gift giving, there were many instances where individuals exchanged special gifts. I recall one case when several villagers challenged a young man to show his tobacco container to a group of farm workers. After the young man furiously denied that he had such a container, his friends threw him down to the ground, searched his pockets, and discovered a silk tobacco bag embroidered with a pair of mandarin ducks—a symbol of lovers in Chinese culture. Under his peers' interrogation, the captive finally admitted that the bag was a gift from his fiancée. It was an exciting and happy moment for his friends: all of us admired the beautiful gift and congratulated him on finding such a wonderful fiancée.

The longer I lived in the village, the more I came to appreciate how interesting these episodes of gift exchange could be. I soon learned of a case that occurred in 1962 during a wedding in which three guests engaged in a public contest of gift giving; they happened to be married to the groom's three elder sisters. To simplify matters, let me label the three men A, B, and C. Both A and B were farmers, whereas C was a worker in the city of Ha'erbin. During the period in question workers in China enjoyed a much higher status than farmers, both economically and socially, in the socialist hierarchy. When presenting his gift to the host, C made a point of giving more money than A or B in an obvious attempt to flaunt his generosity. Naturally, both A and B, being senior in age, were offended and immediately worked out a plan to dishonor C publicly.

Weddings are the most important occasions for gift exchange in rural life, and gifts are given at various periods of the ritual to different recipients (see Cohen 1976; and R. Watson 1985). In addition to the main gift-giving rite when the groom's father (or senior household head) receives all the gifts, there is a small rite when the groom and bride kowtow to the groom's closest relatives and receive some extra gifts. In this case, A offered a cash gift of 80 yuan to the bride and groom (which at that time was an unusually large gift). Following this example, B gave 100 yuan to the couple. The ritual reached its climax when the specialist in charge announced loudly: "Now the new couple are going to kowtow to the groom's third sister's husband. Mr. C please take the seat of honor and prepare to receive the new couple's respects." As he had exhausted his money on the first round, C could do nothing but lower his head and pretend that he had not heard this announcement. All eyes were fixed on him; unable to bear the embarrassment, he ran away.

When I interviewed C in 1991, he denied that he was driven out of the ritual by shame. In his version of the story, his father-in-law (the groom's father) saved him from embarrassment by saying: "Mr. C is too young to receive the kowtow, so please leave him alone." Nonetheless, C admitted to me that this episode was still a nightmare for him and that he regretted challenging A and B in the first place.

This case has become a local legend in Xiajia and it was brought up in public discussion many times when I lived in the village during the 1970's. Years later when I read about the potlatch among the Kwakiutl Indians on the American northwest coast, I immediately recalled the gift-giving contest in Xiajia village; hence my interest in the general topic of gifts and gift giving grew. When the time came for me to do my own anthropological research, it seemed logical to dig deeper into this subject. It is important, however, to place this study in the context of previous research on gift exchange. As I shall argue in the concluding chapter, the unique character of the Chinese style of gift giving sets it apart from other systems described in the anthropological literature.

The Gift in Anthropological Discourse

Anthropological theories of gift exchange draw heavily on Marcel Mauss's well-known essay *The Gift*, which raises one central question: "In primitive or archaic types of society what is the principle whereby the gift has to be repaid? What force is there in the thing given which compels the recipient to make a return?" (1967: 1). Mauss finds his answer in the Maori concept of *hau*—a mystic power that lies in the forest and in the valuables (*taonga*) given by one person to another. The *hau* always wishes to return to its place of origin, but can only do so through the medium of an object given in exchange for the original gift. Failure to return a gift, therefore, can result in serious trouble, including the death of the recipient. It is the *hau* in the gift, Mauss asserts, that forces the recipient to make a return, and he calls this "the spirit of the gift" (1967: 8–9). As a result, "one gives away what is in reality a part of one's nature and substance, while to receive something is to receive a part of someone's spiritual essence. To keep this thing is dangerous, not only because it is illicit to do so, but also because it comes morally, physically and spiritually from a person" (1967: 10).

The bonds created by gifts (inalienable objects) are thus the mutually dependent ties between persons. Here we can see that the fundamental issue in Mauss's analysis of the gift is to determine how people relate to things and, through things, to each other. As John Liep notes, both Marx and Mauss are concerned with the alienation of people from the products of their labor, which correlates to the development of a world capitalist market economy (1990: 165). But, unlike Marx, who focuses on the system of commodity exchange in modern societies and discovers the secret of surplus value (1976), Mauss concentrates on gift exchange in "primitive" societies and seeks answers from indigenous belief systems. To compare the "primitive," personalized gift economy with the modern, impersonalized system of commodity exchange, Mauss draws a three-stage evolutionary scheme: Human exchange begins with "total prestations," in which the materials transferred between groups are only part of a larger range of noneconomic transfers. The second stage is gift exchange between moral persons who represent groups, leading finally to commodity exchange between independent individuals in modern societies (see Mauss 1967: 68–69).

The spirit of the gift and the opposition between gifts and commodities—two themes elaborated by Mauss—continue to be of central interest to modern anthropologists. In fact, it is not an exaggeration to say that anthropology itself, as a distinct field of study, has emerged from a long series of controversies regarding the nature of "gifts" in various societies. Fortunately for our discipline, the controversy shows no sign of abating.

Motivations for Returning a Gift: The Norm of Reciprocity

Prior to the appearance of Mauss's classic, Bronislaw Malinowski had already published his ethnographic account of exchange in Melanesian society, describing in detail the local system of transactions, ranging from the "pure gift" to "real barter" (1984). Rejecting Mauss's interpretation of the spirit of the gift, Malinowski retracts his category of the pure gift in a later book (1926) and articulates the principle of reciprocity to explain the local system of economic transactions. He argues that the binding force of economic obligations lies in the sanction either side may invoke to sever the bonds of reciprocity. One gives because of the expectation of return and one returns because of the threat that one's partner may stop giving. All rights and obligations are "arranged into well-balanced chains of reciprocal services" (1926: 46). He thus arrives at the conclusion that reciprocity, or "the principle of give-and-take," is the foundation of Melanesian social order (1926: chaps. 3, 4, 8, and 9).

Inspired by Malinowski's example, Raymond Firth argues that the concept of reciprocity (locally called *utu*) is a fundamental drive to action among the Maori in New Zealand. The Maori attach great importance to the notion of "compensation" or "equivalent return" (1959: 412ff.). With regard to the anthropological theory of the gift, Firth offers the most detailed and influential criticism of Mauss's treatment of the Maori *hau*. According to Firth, Mauss misinterprets the *hau* by imputing active qualities to its social construction, which Maori people do not recognize; he also confuses the *hau* of the gift with the *hau* of the gift giver; and finally, he neglects the third party in a given transaction, which is crucial to comprehend the original Mauri meaning of the *hau* (see Firth 1959: 419–20; and MacCormack 1982: 287).

Challenged by Malinowski's rational model of reciprocity and Firth's powerful criticism, Mauss's interpretation of the spirit of the gift was subject to yet more criticism by Claude Lévi-Strauss in

the 1960's and Marshall Sahlins in the 1970's. Although partially at-
tributing the original inspiration for his structuralist approach to
Mauss's concept of "total prestation," Lévi-Strauss does not accept
Mauss's interpretation of the spirit of the gift. According to Jonathan
Parry, Lévi-Strauss regards "the discussion of the *hau* as a regrettable
instance of the anthropologist allowing himself to be mystified by
the native, whose culturally specific rationalizations cannot possibly
explain a general structural principle" (Parry 1986: 456; see also Weiner 1992: 46). While viewing social life as a system of transactions
between groups and individuals, Lévi-Strauss develops a theory of
cousin marriage based on the distinction between the restricted exchange and the generalized exchange of women (1969: 61–68). In
other words, the principle of reciprocity still dominates Lévi-
Strauss's theory of exchange, even though it has been reinterpreted
as a projection of universal mental structures.

Sahlins (1972) criticizes Mauss's preoccupation with the spiritual
significance of the *hau* and concomitant neglect of its economic significance. According to Sahlins, "The meaning of hau one disen-
gages from the exchange of taonga is as secular as the exchange itself.
If the second gift is the hau of the first, then the hau of a good is its
yield, just as the hau of a forest is its productiveness" (1972: 160).
Sahlins thus demystifies the spirit of the gift and reinforces the ac-
countability of the principle of reciprocity. He identifies three variables as critical to determining the general nature of gift giving
and exchange: kinship distance, sociability, and generosity. To demonstrate the universality of reciprocity, Sahlins also introduces a
tripartite division of exchange phenomena: generalized reciprocity, balanced reciprocity, and negative reciprocity (1972: 191–210).
Thanks to Sahlins's sophisticated disentanglement of the mechanisms of reciprocity, the gift remains at the center of anthropological
debate.

Today many ethnographic accounts deal broadly with gift giving
and reciprocity. In fact, the notion of reciprocity is so frequently employed to generalize about social patterns that it has become something of a cliché. As Geoffrey MacCormack warns, "The description of all types of exchanges as reciprocal easily leads to an obscuring of the significant differences between them" (1976: 101).

Melanesian and Polynesian societies are the heartland of anthropological studies of the gift. Among the many anthropologists who have worked in New Guinea, nearly all have commented on the significance of gift giving and other forms of social exchange. In a study of ceremonial interclan exchange, R. F. Salisbury describes the balanced exchange of ritual valuables as a case of "the ideology of reciprocity" (1962: 104). Andrew Strathern pays more attention to the superiority of the gift giver over the recipient in a hierarchical context and notes that "whether this superiority implies political control over the recipient or whether it merely indicates a gain in prestige on the part of the giver are matters in which individual systems vary" (1971: 10). K. Burridge makes a distinction between siblingship that is governed by the obligation of reciprocity and filiate relations that do not involve direct reciprocal returns. Thus, gifts are presentations made by a parent to a child with no expectation of return (1969: xix).

In African studies, P. Bohannan (1955) helped to establish the modern field of economic anthropology by analyzing three distinct spheres of exchange among the Tiv: the first sphere (in order of moral ranking from lowest to highest) consists primarily of foodstuffs associated with the market; the second sphere consists of prestige items, such as cattle or metal bars; and the last sphere is restricted to the exchange of women through marriage. M. Fortes (1949) emphasizes the political function of gift exchange and reciprocity in maintaining social equilibrium between potentially conflicting sectors in Tallensi society. He maintains that stability among the Tallensi is achieved through a rendering of mutual services between different sections of a clan. In the long run, each section receives roughly the equivalent of what it gave (1949: 135). The formal exchange of gifts, according to Fortes, is carried out mainly between affines (1949: 120). The significance of gift exchange is emphasized by many other Africanists, and reciprocity is regarded as a way to distinguish kin from non-kin (see, e.g., Krige and Krige 1943; and Gulliver 1969).

The potlatch, found among indigenous peoples of the northwest coast of North America, is a particular type of gift exchange that has continued to be the subject of keen debate ever since Franz Boas introduced it to a broad circle of scholars (Boas 1897). The Kwakiutl Indians developed the potlatch to its most elaborate form during the early twentieth century (see Codere 1950). The exaggerated generosity and perceived wastefulness displayed at potlatches served to highlight the personal wealth of chiefs; competition took the form of a symbolic struggle for supremacy in giving, as opposed to receiving. Mauss regards the potlatch as a typical example of what he calls "the total prestation," where the exchange of gifts subsumes religious, economic, social, and legal aspects of social life (see Mauss 1967: 36–37).

Turning to Asian societies, we find that most studies of the Indian caste system refer to intracaste prestations and intercaste transactions through the exchange of food, services, and marriage partners (see, e.g., Appadurai and Breckenridge 1976; Dumont 1980; Marriott 1976; and S. Vatuk 1975). Research has also been done on Japanese gift exchange (e.g., Befu 1966–67; Johnson 1974; and Smith 1974). According to Harumi Befu, gift giving in modern Japan is characterized by its function of cementing previously established social relations; with the rapid modernization of Japanese society, gift-giving activities have become more and more individualized and instrumentalized (1966–67: 173–75). By contrast, Colleen Johnson argues that among Japanese Americans in Honolulu, the balanced exchange of gifts helps minimize the increasing differentiation resulting from social mobility, and "the obligation to give and to receive perpetuates relationships which otherwise might lapse because of the pressures for assimilation into the wider society" (1974: 306).

It is interesting to note that rules of gift exchange derived from relatively "simple" societies, such as the obligation of return and the superiority of the gift giver, do not always fit the social reality of more complex, differentiated societies where there is an advanced division of labor and a significant commercial sector. The universality of the principle of reciprocity, which has dominated studies of the gift since Malinowski's, is challenged by ethnographic evidence from Asia. For instance, Takie Sugiyama Lebra (1969) questions the "equivalent return" in reciprocal relations by examining the repayment of Japanese *on* gifts (benevolent favors from superiors). She demonstrates that, given the hierarchical context of Japanese society, the gift donor in a subordinate position can never balance the gift received from a superior. Lebra (1975) further argues that the exchange aspect of reciprocity is characterized by two strains, one toward symmetry and the other toward asymmetry, and she offers a more inclusive model of reciprocity that includes extradyadic relations. In South Asian studies, several anthropologists have explored the Indian notion of giving without expectation of material return. Ved Prakash Vatuk and Sylvia Vatuk observe the asymmetric gift-giving relationships in the context of caste hierarchy: "Persons of low castes, particularly if they are also in an economically subordinate position *vis-à-vis* the donor, are generally not expected to return the gifts they receive from their superiors, and in such cases these gifts may be classified as *dan* and thus meritorious" (1971: 217). Both Parry (1986) and Gloria Raheja argue that because the gift of *dan* transfers the dangerous and demanding burden of death and the impurity of the donor to the recipient, the institutionalized pattern of gift flow from the dominant caste to subordinate castes creates a mode of cultural domination (Raheja 1988: 28, 31, 248). These findings constitute a serious challenge to the generalized model of reciprocity, leading Parry (1986: 463, 466) to rethink Mauss's notion of the spirit of the gift.

The Inalienability of the Gift: A New Perspective

A new approach to the study of the gift gradually emerged in the 1980's, emphasizing the inalienability of objects from their owners. It is not surprising that this new approach emerged mainly among Pacific specialists, particularly those who work on the Kula exchange. In a provocative paper, F. H. Damon examines the Muyuw *kitoum*—a kind of Kula valuable that is individually owned. He argues that because the objects in question represent the "congealed labor" of the individual owner, "no matter where a *kitoum* is . . . it can be claimed by its owner" (1980: 282). All Kula valuables are brought into the exchange by the labor of specific individuals and, therefore, constitute one's inalienable *kitoum* (1980: 284). C. A. Gregory developed similar views in an analysis of the difference between gift-debt relations and commodity-debt relations. According to Gregory, gift debts involve a transfer of inalienable objects between mutually dependent persons, whereas commodity debts result from the exchange of alienable objects between independent transactors: "A gift is like a tennis ball with an elastic band attached to it. The owner of the ball may lose possession of it for a time, but the ball will spring back to its owner if the elastic band is given a jerk" (1980: 640). These provocative essays by Damon and Gregory have led to a new wave of interest in what might be called the inalienability of gifts (see, e.g., Damon 1983; Gregory 1982; Keesing 1990; J. Leach 1983; Liep 1990; and Weiner 1980, 1985). The most intriguing point to arise from this discussion is that the inalienability of certain valuables may explain not only the motivation to return but also the original motivation for participation in competitive systems such as the Kula (see Feil 1982: 340–42; Damon 1982: 342–43; and Gregory 1982: 344–45).

The inalienability of the gift is at the core of a new theory of gift exchange recently elaborated by Annette Weiner. Weiner is critical of standard anthropological studies that rely on the principle of reciprocity. She argues that the norm of reciprocity is deeply rooted in Western thought and has been used to justify theories of a free-market economy since Thomas Hobbes (see Weiner 1992: 28–30). Continuing in this tradition, anthropologists take for granted that there is an innate, mystical, or natural autonomy in the workings of reciprocity. Weiner maintains: "What motivates reciprocity is its reverse—the desire to keep something back from the pressures of give and take. This something is a possession that speaks to and for an individual's or a group's social identity and, in so doing, affirms the difference between one person or group and another. Because the ownership of inalienable possessions establishes difference, ownership attracts other kinds of wealth" (1992: 43). There is, according to Weiner, an elementary principle of keeping-while-giving, and it is this principle, rather than the norm of reciprocity, that explains the obligation to return a gift—the central issue raised by Mauss (Weiner 1992: 46). Interestingly, Weiner suggests Mauss is right about the Maori *hau*: "The hau as a life force embedded in the person is transmitted to the person's possessions" and thus adds inalienable value to the objects (Weiner 1992: 63; see also D. Thompson 1987). Thus, anthropology has come full circle. The spirit of the gift has been reintroduced to the center stage of our discipline in the guise of a new discourse.

Gifts Versus Commodities

Mauss's original distinction between personalized gift giving and impersonalized commodity exchange has been widely accepted and, until recently, rarely criticized. Based on Karl Polanyi's theory of three modes of exchange (1957), Sahlins suggests that the distinction between gift exchange and commodity exchange should not be seen as a bipolar opposition, but rather as extreme points of a continuum (Sahlins 1972: 191–97). The most important determinant is kinship distance: "Reciprocity is inclined toward the generalized pole by close kinship, toward the negative extreme in proportion to kinship distance" (1972: 196). In other words, people tend to exchange gifts among kin and commodities among non-kin. Because so-called primitive societies are regarded as kinship-based communities, Sahlins's scheme implies the opposition between gift exchange in clan-based societies and commodity exchange in class-based societies, a proposition further developed by Gregory a decade later (Gregory 1980, 1982).

Following Marx's definition of commodities and Mauss's characterization of gifts, Gregory offers a binary formulation of a gift economy versus a commodity economy: "In a class-based society the objects of exchange tend to assume the alienated form of a commodity and, as a consequence, reproduction in general assumes the particular form of commodity reproduction. In a clan-based society the objects of exchange tend to assume the non-alienated form of a gift; reproduction assumes the particular form of gift reproduction" (1982: 41). Gregory further notes that "commodity exchange establishes objective quantitative relationships between the objects transacted, while gift exchange establishes personal qualitative relationships between the subjects transacting" (1982: 41).

During the 1980's many anthropologists questioned the sharp contrast between gift exchange and commodity exchange as elaborated by Gregory. For instance, Damon points out that although the Kula is not a system of commodity exchange, it does lead to an expansion or accumulation of valuables among individual participants (1982: 343). Citing historical evidence, Ian Morris argues that in state societies, such as ancient Greece, gift exchange also functioned as a primary form of exchange both within and between communities: "After 700 B.C., in spite of the increasing volume of commodity trade which was probably taking place, the *ideal* still remained personalized gift exchange. . . . Aristotle again tells us that even in the fourth century generosity in gift giving was still a central feature in the definition of a nobleman" (Morris 1986: 6–7). Several scholars have pointed out that the radical opposition between gifts and commodities is actually a result of the ideological construction of the pure gift in the West and the romanticization of gift relations in non-Western societies (Appadurai 1986a: 11–13; Carrier 1990: 20–25; Parry 1986: 465; and Parry and Bloch 1989: 8–12). Using ethnographic findings reported in their edited volume on money (1989), Parry and Bloch propose a new approach to understanding the difference between gift and commodity. In their view most societies have two related but separate transactional orders: in most societies, "on the one hand transactions concerned with the reproduction of the long-term social or cosmic order; on the other, a 'sphere' of short-term transactions concerned with the arena of individual competition" (1989: 24).

For those who emphasize the inalienable features of the gift, however, the distinction between gifts and commodities remains essential. M. Strathern (1992) insists that gift exchange differs from barter or commodity exchange because the value of the gift is judged qualitatively and not quantitatively, as in the case of commodities. Melanesian gift exchange, for example, is based on "the capacity for actors (agents, subjects) to extract or elicit from others items that then become the object of their relationship" (1992: 177). Similarly, Weiner maintains that "inalienable possessions attain absolute value that is subjectively constituted and distinct from the exchange value of commodities or the abstract value of money" (1992: 191, n. 2). It is probable that such debates, like those concerning motivations to return gifts, will continue in the future.

Gift Giving and Interpersonal Relations in Chinese Society

Let us now turn to the Chinese practice of gift exchange. When Western observers talk about gift giving in China, they almost always refer to another set of social phenomena—interpersonal relations, or personal connections. Discussions of gift giving and personal connections have even become routine in popular travel guidebooks for Westerners touring who visit China (see, e.g., Storey 1990: 17).

The Significance of Gift Exchange in China

From an academic point of view, a systematic study of gift exchange in rural China is justifiable for several reasons. First, gift exchange, while existing in all societies, appears to be central to Chinese culture throughout its long history. Among the Chinese there is a high degree of consciousness regarding the importance of gift behavior. In contrast to many other societies, the structure of social relations in China rests largely on fluid, person-centered social networks, rather than on fixed social institutions. Gift giving and other reciprocal exchanges therefore play a leading role in social life, especially in maintaining, reproducing, and modifying interpersonal relations (see, e.g., Jacobs 1979; Walder 1986; M. Yang 1989). A number of Chinese scholars (see, e.g., Hwang 1987; King 1988a, 1991; Qiao 1988) have recently made efforts to establish an analytic framework based on indigenous Chinese categories, drawing on *guanxi* (personal networks), *renqing* (moral norms and human feelings), *mianzi* (face), and *bao* (reciprocity). This explicitly defined Chinese perspective, which emphasizes the importance of interpersonal relations, should provide insights for a comparative study of gift giving and social exchange.

Second, gift exchange in China is embedded in a process anthropologists have called the "cultural construction of personhood": individuals are required to learn how to deal with different categories of people through the practice of gift exchange. Gift exchange not only defines the boundaries of the socially recognized person (Vogel 1965; L. Yang 1957) but also helps to create experiences that are "the intersubjective medium of social transactions in local moral worlds" (Kleinman and Kleinman 1991: 277). It is axiomatic, therefore, that by studying gift exchange one should begin to understand the core features of Chinese culture. Moreover, the Chinese version of gift exchange is characterized by features that make it different from practices common in other societies. For example, in China gifts are often given by people of lower social status to those of higher status, and the former always remain inferior to the latter. This outcome violates the general rule deriving from classic anthropological literature, wherein the gift giver is deemed to be superior to the recipient. This issue is discussed at length in Chapter 7.

Third, in contemporary Chinese society, gift exchange remains an important mode of exchange in economic and political life, both as part of the state system of redistribution and, recently, as part of the market system for commodities. The fact itself is significant, considering the state's unrivaled control over various aspects of Chinese social life. An inquiry into the survival and transformation of gift relations during the past four decades may help explain how Chinese cultural traditions have persisted despite attacks by state socialism. (For an interesting discussion of the processes involved, see M. Yang 1986, 1989.) Moreover, gift exchange has been used, to an extent, as a means of pursuing political and economic interests (see Chan and Unger 1983; Oi 1985). Thomas Gold (1985) argues, for example, that personal relations have become more instrumental and utilitarian during the reform era (Gold 1985). This, in turn, has led to a heightened concern about corruption in post-Mao China. Hence the study of gift exchange might also contribute to our understanding of the political economy of state socialism.

Finally, gift exchange has yet to be the subject of a full-scale ethnographic investigation in China. This is surprising, considering its overarching significance in Chinese culture. In the field of Chinese studies, one can find only a handful of works concerning gift exchange, most of which deal with gifts as a means of making particularistic ties (*guanxi*) between individuals. These studies have focused primarily on personal connections and individual strategies in urban contexts rather than on the rules of exchange governing social behavior in small-scale community settings.

A Characterization of Personal Relations in China

According to Weber, the "personalist principle" was the core of Confucian ethics (1968: 236). Building on Weber's argument, Parsons proposes that the "whole Chinese social structure accepted and sanctioned by the Confucian ethic was a predominately 'particularistic' structure of relationships" (1949: 551). Responding to these views, Shu-ming Liang suggests that Chinese society was neither individual-based nor group-based, but relation-based: "The focus is not fixed on any particular individual, but on the relations between individuals who are engaged in social exchange with each other" (Liang 1963: 94). Xiaotong Fei makes a similar comparison between the West and China and concludes that, structurally, Chinese society is composed of numerous personal networks defined by dyadic social ties and without explicit boundaries. The moral content of behavior in such a network-based society is contextually determined, and the ego is always the most important concern in every situation. Therefore, Fei characterizes Chinese society as egocentric, as opposed to Western society, which he sees as individualistic (1947: 22–37). It is interesting to note that the value of personal networks, especially family relations in private enterprises, has in recent years attracted the attention of scholars studying the development of the so-called four dragons in industrial East Asia (see, e.g., Hamilton and Kao 1990; Kao 1991; Vogel 1991; and S. Wong 1985, 1988). The primacy of personal relations, previously characterized as an unhealthy element of Chinese culture (following Weber's thesis), has been reappraised as a positive feature of the Chinese model of capitalism (Redding 1990).

According to Ezra Vogel (1965), the Chinese Communist Party (CCP) succeeded to a great extent in transforming the traditional pattern of particularistic ties to a universalistic morality under the name of "comradeship." This transformation of personal relations was achieved primarily through a combination of intimidation and the promotion of a socialist economy that diminished the importance of personal connections. However, follow-up studies in the 1980's argue that this transformation was not as successful as outside observers had assumed. In the 1980's particularism and instrumentalism came to dominate behavior, and gift exchange became the primary means by which people gained access to desirable resources (Chan and Unger 1983; Gold 1985; Oi 1985; and Walder 1986).

Among many others, three studies of personal relations in China are particularly noteworthy; all examine the well-known social phenomenon of *guanxi*. Defining *guanxi* as "particularistic ties" (1979: 238), Bruce Jacobs develops a preliminary model, which includes a typology of personal strategies in the construction of particularistic ties (1979: 238). Applying this model to the political system of a Taiwan township, Jacobs reveals the important role that the manipulation of particularistic ties plays in local politics, especially in the context of making political allies and securing votes.

While Jacobs regards *guanxi* as the personal basis of Chinese politics, Andrew Walder views *guanxi* as an informal aspect of the institutional culture in socialist factories, "an exchange relationship that mingles instrumental intentions with personal feeling" (1986: 179). Translating *guanxi* as "instrumental-personal ties," Walder distinguishes these ties across a continuum, with particularism at one end and "ceremonialized bribery" at the other, in accordance with the presence or absence of personal affection. The granting and receiving of favors of various kinds is the motivating force behind these personal ties, which help workers obtain desirable resources that otherwise would be inaccessible. Because workers must pursue their interests without challenging authority, Walder argues that "these ties have a certain stabilizing effect on authority relations" (1986: 186).

Taking a Foucauldian perspective, M. Yang offers a systematic study of gift exchange and personal relations in urban China (1989, 1994). Yang argues that the gift economy and *guanxi* networks in China constitute an informal power in opposition to the power of the socialist state. In her text, the terms "gift economy" and the "art of *guanxi*" are used interchangeably (1989: 35). She examines in detail the extensive networks of personal loyalty, obligation, and mutual assistance both within and between work units (*danwei*). She also analyzes the five mechanisms by which the inalienability of the gift and its donor enables the donor to force the recipient to give a return favor, thus obtaining desirable resources. During such a process of exchanging gifts for favors, the gift economy redistributes what the state economy has already distributed and also substitutes "a discourse of relational ethics for the dominant discourse of universalistic ethics that pervades the state redistributive mode of exchange" (M. Yang 1989: 50). Unlike those scholars who emphasize the negative results of the exchange of gifts for favors (cf. Gold 1985; Oi 1989), Yang argues that "while the immediate goal of the art of *guanxi* is to acquire some material utility, it exerts a subversive effect on the microtechniques of administrative power" (1989: 38) and thus constitutes an "oppositional power" (1989: 49). Under certain circumstances, these personal networks may serve as the basis of a Chinese version of a civil society, or a second society, as she puts it. "I propose that in China, an area to watch for in the development of civil society, is that art of guanxi, a dynamic element of the second society" (1994: 295). And this Chinese civil society based on *guanxi*, according to Yang, is characterized by two "between" statuses: between the individual and society, and between the individual and formal, voluntary associations (1994: 295–305).[1]

In contrast to the aforementioned scholars, who tend to emphasize the instrumental role of *guanxi* in specific social contexts, some Chinese scholars have made efforts to take *guanxi* and other indigenous notions—such as *renqing*, *mianzi*, and *bao*—as conceptual tools to understand Chinese society and culture in general. Liensheng Yang (1957) was perhaps the first to examine the role of reciprocity in interpersonal relations. According to Yang, the concept of *bao* (*pao*), which means "to respond" or "to return," is the Chinese expression of the principle of reciprocity, and it serves as the basis for social relations. "The Chinese believe that reciprocity of actions (favor and hatred, reward and punishment) between man and man, and indeed between men and supernatural beings, should be as certain as a cause-and-effect relationship, and therefore, when a Chinese acts, he normally anticipates a response or return" (L. Yang 1957: 291).

So far the most elaborate interpretations of interpersonal relations in Chinese society have been offered by Ambrose King (1985, 1988a, and 1991) and Kwang-kuo Hwang (1987). Based on Confucian social theory, King's analysis emphasizes the relative autonomy of the individual in Chinese society, especially interpersonal relations (King 1991: 67): "The individual self is . . . capable of shaping, if not fixing, what kinds of relationships to have with others" (1985: 64). King also introduces the notion of *renqing* as the main conceptual tool to study patterns of personal relations (1988a: 76–77). Another important contribution is King's balanced view of the prevalence of particularism and the existence of universalistic norms in Chinese society (1988a, 1991). While recognizing the significant role of personal networks, King argues that "in the very Chinese cultural system, there are also cultural mechanisms to neutralize or to freeze the practice of *jen-ch'ing* [*renqing*] or *kuan-hsi* [*guanxi*] in order to carve out room for instrumental rationality which is necessary to maintain economic and bureaucratic (in the Weberian sense) life" (1991: 75–76).

Applying exchange theories in sociology and social psychology, Hwang proposes a framework of personal relations in an effort to depict not only social behavior in Chinese society but also "a general model for illustrating the process of social interactions in most cultures" (1987: 945). Like King, Hwang regards the notions of *guanxi*, *renqing*, and *mianzi* as keys to understanding social behavior among Chinese. He pays special attention to the strategies individuals use to influence others and discovers that "doing face work" and seeking personal networks are the most common power games in Chinese society. He concludes that, in Chinese society, in contrast to Western society, the norms of reciprocity are largely shaped by the hierarchically structured network of social relations and are always being negotiated through "face work" (1987: 968).

The Framework of the Present Study

The preceding review of the literature on Chinese society reveals several interesting points. First, with the exception of the work by M. Yang (1989, 1994), the complex of gift exchange in China has not been analyzed as an independent subject nor has it been compared with gift-giving institutions in other societies. Second, most Western scholars' studies of personal relations in Chinese society have focused on the utility of gift giving and the cultivation of personal networks while overlooking the cultural meanings of these social interactions. Third, the conceptual analyses offered by King and Hwang, which touch on the fundamental issue of the relationships between persons and things, are heavily influenced by Confucian social theories and thus need to be tested by empirical studies.

The present study was conceived as an effort to examine the process of gift exchange and network cultivation in a north China village. Since the activity of gift exchange pervades social life, this study will not be limited to special rituals such as weddings, funerals, and ancestral rites. On the contrary, a systematic study of gift exchange must embrace all categories of social activity that involve gift giving in daily life, such as mutual visiting between relatives, the exchange of food and labor between neighbors, and gift giving among friends. I thus present gift exchange in China as a total social institution, and provide an empirical account of customs related to gift exchange, that can be used to test established theories and concepts.

Unlike previous studies, which emphasize individual motivations and strategies in gift-giving behavior, my analysis focuses on the cultural rules and operative logic of gift exchange. Sahlins observes that "a material transaction is usually a momentary episode in a continuous social relation" (1972: 185–86); the same is certainly true of gift giving. In my research, I attempt to go beyond earlier studies and examine the networks of social relations expressed in the process of continuous exchange among people who live in a close-knit community. This approach is particularly useful for studying rural society in China, where norms and rules of social behavior are not highly institutionalized. Furthermore, in rural China social relations appear to be contextually defined, and egocentric social groups—or "non-groups," as Jeremy Boissevain calls them (1968: 542)—play an important role in social life. It would be impossible to study the social structure of rural China through an examination of static institutionalized social relations and social actions. I believe it is more fruitful to examine the dynamic process of social interactions between individuals and groups.

Chapter 2 traces the historical background of Xiajia village in Heilongjiang province, where I conducted the fieldwork for this study. Chapter 3 describes the system of gift exchange in the community. Using local categories of gifts, I identify 21 kinds of gift-giving activities and present a preliminary classification of both expressive gifts and instrumental gifts exchanged by the villagers.

Chapters 4 and 5 are devoted to the complex social phenomenon of personal networks (*guanxi*). By studying the endless process of gift exchange and the moral constraints that obligate villagers to participate in this process, I explore the interlocking relationship between gift giving and network building. I then examine the villagers' reliance on personal networks during social and economic crises, which in turn helps us to understand the significance of gift exchange in village life. An analysis of the structural features of these personal networks reveals that Xiajia residents have established networks far more complex than existing theories in sinological anthropology can explain.

The cultural meanings of gift exchange and network cultivation are discussed in Chapter 6, which focuses on the notion of *renqing*. The local rules of gift giving provide an excellent means of understanding the complexity, flexibility, and contextuality of interpersonal experience. I analyze both the moral and emotional aspects of personal relations, interpreting *renqing* as a system of ethics based on commonsense knowledge in village society.

Chapter 7 is concerned with the asymmetrical flow of gifts in the hierarchical context of social relations. Data from Xiajia reveal a sharp contrast to previous generalizations, which maintain that unilateral giving usually generates power and prestige on the side of the gift giver. In Xiajia gift receiving rather than gift giving is the symbol of prestige; in some contexts gifts flow only up the social status hierarchy, with the recipient always superior in status to the giver. Further analysis reveals numerous social-cultural mechanisms that sustain this kind of unilateral gift giving and help to reproduce the existing social hierarchy.

Chapter 8 deals with the impact of social change on patterns of gift giving, with special emphasis on the most popular types of gift: bridewealth and dowry. A diachronic examination of these two local practices over the past four decades demonstrates that, in response to social changes in the larger environment, the custom of bridewealth has evolved from a form of gift giving to a means of wealth allocation.

I conclude with a discussion of the three themes that dominate this study: (1) the features of the Chinese system of gift exchange and their implications for the ongoing discourse of the gift in anthropology; (2) the complexity of personal networks (*guanxi*) and moral norms of interpersonal behavior (*renqing*) in Chinese culture; and (3) the relationship between the gift economy and social changes in the larger environment.

Gift giving as a social phenomenon exists in all societies. The form it takes, however, varies from one society to another depending on the cultural matrix. The significance of the present study lies in its articulation of the Chinese position in the universe of the gift.

Xiajia Village: A Sketch of the Field Site

The fieldwork for this study was conducted in Xiajia village, Heilongjiang province, a place I have known for more than twenty years. I lived in Xiajia as an ordinary farmer for seven years (1971–78) and have maintained a correspondence with several village friends since that time. In the spring of 1989 I carried out a short-term survey in Xiajia, which enabled me to chart patterns of social changes. In 1991, I returned to conduct six months of fieldwork on the subject of gift exchange, and then in 1993 I visited the village for a follow-up field survey.

Located on the southern edge of Heilongjiang province, 50 kilometers south of the provincial capital Ha'erbin and 24 kilometers southeast of the county seat, Shuangcheng, Xiajia village is a farming community that grows mostly maize and soybeans. The village is encircled by farming land on the north and by grass marshlands on the south. Neighboring villages are no more than one to three kilometers away. Five kilometers south of Xiajia, the Lalin River separates Heilongjiang from Jilin province. As in other villages scattered along the river, most of the land in Xiajia is constantly threat-

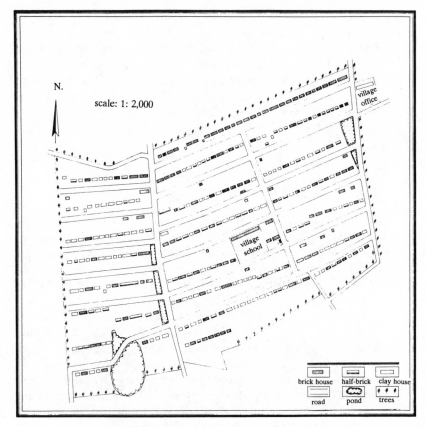

MAP 1. Street map of Xiajia village

ened by floods. During the dry years, however, the village enjoys fertile, black soil.

According to the household register of 1990, Xiajia has a population of 1,564 in 365 households. As shown in Map 1, house construction in Xiajia has been well organized, such that today the village consists of seven rows of houses, which form six streets from east to west, and two north-south avenues. As an administrative unit, Xiajia also officially incorporates a neighboring community of 416 people in 97 households. My research was confined to the core community of Xiajia and did not include this neighboring village.

Because the present study focuses on the specific subject of gift exchange and social networks, it is impossible to introduce every aspect of social life in Xiajia village in a single chapter. Rather, I will briefly review the village's history in both the precommunist and communist periods in an attempt to draw the social boundaries of the community. I will then describe the local systems of social stratification and kinship organizations, which are directly related to the endless process of social exchange and patterns of interpersonal relations.

The Origin of Xiajia Village

In comparison to other villages in many parts of China south of the Great Wall, Xiajia is a relatively young community, with a history of little more than 100 years. This newness is, however, quite common for villages in Shuangcheng, since the whole region was only opened for settlement in the early nineteenth century by the Qing government.

According to historical documents and local gazetteers (the following historical account is based on ECSG 1990; S. Li 1990; and Zhang 1926), until 1815 the vast land in Shuangcheng county, where Xiajia village is now located, remained uncultivated. To resolve financial burdens and other social problems created by the increasing number of professional Manchu soldiers, who were known as bannermen (qiren), the Qing emperor decided to mobilize a large-scale migration of these men to their original base: northeast China. From 1815 to 1827, a total of 3,000 bannermen, later followed by their families, were sent by the Qing state to be stationed in the Shuangcheng area. These Manchu homesteaders were selected from the different units of Manchu troops—known as the eight-banner system.[1] One thousand came from Beijing and the rest came from other areas in Shenyang city and Jilin province. Each Manchu homesteader was allocated 300 mu of land, for which no tax was claimed by the state for the first three years (Li 1990; Zhang 1926).

When these homesteaders arrived at Shuangcheng, they established villages exactly in accordance with the eight-banner system. For each banner unit, five residential subunits were built, which

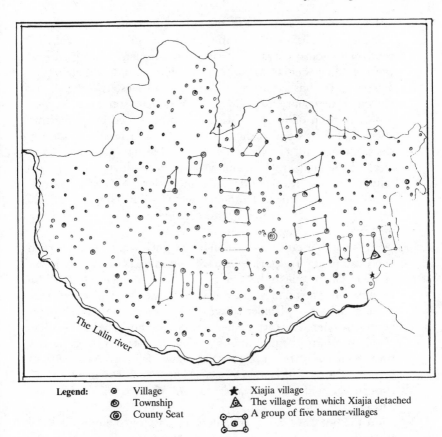

Legend:
◎ Village
◉ Township
◎ County Seat
★ Xiajia village
⬢ The village from which Xiajia detached
A group of five banner-villages

MAP 2. Villages in Shuangcheng county

were called *tun*, originally meaning "military camp." One village
(*tun*) was located in the center and consisted of 28 households. The
other four were set up respectively in the northwest, southwest,
southeast, and northeast directions of the central camp, at a distance
of 2.5 kilometers from the center, each of which contained 24 families. The villages were named after their banner unit. For instance,
in the Plain Yellow Banner, the five villages were named First Camp
of Plain Yellow Banner, Second Camp of Plain Yellow Banner, and
so on.

It is interesting to note that the villages built after the initial settlement project have been stratified into three ranks. These ranks depend on the social status of the early homesteaders. During the first wave of official migration in 1815, forty villages under the eight banners were established along the eastern and western sides of the Shuangcheng county seat, which was then a garrison town (see Map 2—each group of banner villages is distinguished by connecting lines), and they stood at the top level of the hierarchy of locales. These banner villages were called the "old camps" (*lao yingzi*) and were inhabited mainly by ethnic Manchus from the Beijing area, locally called *jingqi* (the bannermen from Beijing). Nowadays the residents in the old camps refer to themselves as "the Dragon's followers" and maintain that their ancestors settled in this area by following the steps of the Qing emperor.

At the middle rank, there are another eighty banner villages called "new camps" (*xin yingzi*), which were established during the 1820's or later. The people in these villages came from Shenyang and Jilin province. As shown in Map 2, the new villages lie at the outer circle of the original forty banner villages and are thus exposed to the dangerous frontier. The early Manchu settlers in both the old and new camps were given equal amounts of land protected by Qing law from being cultivated or purchased by non-Manchus. As a result, 83 percent of the arable land in Shuangcheng was still owned by Manchus in 1925, fifteen years after the end of the Qing dynasty (see Zhang 1926: 10).

At the bottom rank, there are villages scattered along the Lalin River in the southern and southwestern parts of Shuangcheng county, far away from the banner villages. The residents in these villages were and still are mainly ethnic Han immigrants from the central plains of China, hence they are called *minren* (meaning "civilians," mostly Han immigrants), as opposed to *qiren* (bannermen). To protect the Manchu settlers' interests, the Qing state built a defense line of mounds along the outer circle of the cluster of banner villages, which separated them from these Han villages. Nevertheless, both outside and inside this dividing line, many Han farmers worked for Manchu landowners from the very beginning of the official settlement, because the early Manchu homesteaders did not know how to farm their land. As a result of the demand for skilled tenants, Han villagers migrating to the area soon outnumbered the Manchu landowners. In addition to the villages of *minren* along the Lalin River, many tenant villages were set up around the original 120 banner villages within the dividing line; residents in this area were both Manchu and Han. By the late 1920's, there were 346 villages outside the system of banner camps, and by 1982, this number increased to 527.

Xiajia is one of these later-established villages along the dividing line. According to older villagers, several dozen Xia families migrated to a banner village called Fourth Camp of Bordered White Banner, located three kilometers north of present-day Xiajia (see Map 2), and rented land from the Manchu landlords. Two brothers of a Xia family, however, decided to stay closer to the land they had rented and built a small shanty in a place which is now the center of Xiajia village. During the next several years, the two brothers were joined by their families and some agnates from the old banner village. Permanent houses were built up, and a small hamlet gradually emerged in the midst of the farming land. During the following decades, many more villagers moved there from nearby counties and remote provinces like Shandong and Hebei. The landowners finally found it in their interest to move into the new settlement. Xiajia was first officially recognized as an administrative village in the late 1930's.

Compared to the residents of the old banner villages, Xiajia settlers had access to less arable land, for they had missed the earlier opportunity to claim huge amounts of uncultivated land granted by the state. Within the village, landownership was concentrated in the hands of a few Manchu landlords and some rich Han farmers; less than 25 percent of the land was cultivated by independent small landholders. Most villagers worked as long-term tenants or short-term, contract workers for big landowners.[2] As land was legally not transferable from Manchus to non-Manchus until the 1911 Revolution, it is not surprising that two out of the three richest agnatic groups in Xiajia were of Manchu descent.

In the first half of the twentieth century, the dominant lineage in Xiajia was the Wang, a small Manchu agnatic group that controlled more than half the land in Xiajia and other neighboring villages. The Wang lineage also maintained political connections in the local gov-

ernment; one of the Wang gained an imperial degree a few years before the fall of the Qing empire and subsequently became a government official in a neighboring county during the republican era. The
five Wang families lived in a large compound encircled by high walls
and protected by security guards with guns. The strength and influence of the Wang families protected Xiajia from local bandits, who
were extremely active along the riverbanks. According to a well-
known story, bandits once surrounded the village and tried to make
their way into the Wang compound. One of the Wangs who was
brave and a very good shot, demanded a one-on-one fight with the
bandit leader. During the exchange of fire, he fooled the bandit by
using a hat to disguise his position and then shot the bandit to death.
After that battle, no bandit ever bothered Xiajia again.[3] Some older
villagers also claimed that, although the Wangs were rich and powerful, they always treated their tenants fairly and were careful to cultivate good relations with fellow villagers. For instance, they participated in ceremonial activities and maintained gift-giving relations with most families in Xiajia, including the poor tenants. For
this reason, the Wangs suffered less than other landlords after the
communists took power.

Social Change and Economic Development Under Socialism

Land reform was launched by the communists in the Shuangcheng
area during 1946 and 1947. The prior social hierarchy was completely altered during this radical attempt at social transformation.
Landlords were brought to struggle sessions, and most of their
property was confiscated and redistributed among the poor. Citizens were assigned a class label in accordance with their economic
status and occupation at the time of the land reform. The labels
included "poor peasant," "middle peasant," "rich peasant," and
"landlord." The latter two, plus "counterrevolutionary" and "rotten element" (reserved for those who challenged the communist re-
gime), were assigned to class enemies, also known as the "four bad
elements." To a great extent these class labels determined people's
life chances during the 1960's and 1970's when class struggle was
stressed.[4] But at the early stage of land reform, Xiajia villagers did

not understand much about the meaning of such labels. Villagers were required to determine their own economic status, to label themselves, and then to report their self-evaluations to the cadres for final examination. An informant told me his mother had reported that his family should be assigned to the rich peasant category and had argued with the cadres when her request was turned down; she believed it was better under any circumstance to be rich rather than to be poor.

Villagers soon learned, however, that being poor was a critical resource for social mobility and that all the formerly rich villagers were discriminated against in this new society. A shepherd and two short-term (landless) tenants from the poorest families were chosen by the local CCP to be cadres in the village. For several years these new leaders were called "the head of the poor" (qiongtou) by villagers, and, encouraged by CCP ideology, they began to regard their poverty as political capital. It was said that during one of the struggle sessions, the shepherd who had become the village head stated, in all seriousness: "Thanks to the Party, it is now those of us who lay green shit who have the final say." The expression "lay green shit" was his way of describing villagers so poor that before the 1949 Revolution they had to subsist on wild herbs.

Because of their previous marginality in village society, these cadres were extremely loyal to their party superiors. Accordingly, during the subsequent collectivization campaigns, Xiajia was subject to most, if not all, of the irrational social experiments sponsored by the state. After going through the stages of mutual-aid team, small cooperatives, and larger communes, Xiajia villagers found that their land and other major means of production were all collectivized. Xiajia became a production brigade consisting of five teams and included a neighboring hamlet. Later the village was one of the seventeen brigades belonging to the local commune. During the high tide of the Great Leap Forward (1958), Xiajia cadres decided to turn the neighboring hamlet into a livestock farm, and all of the villagers in the hamlet were moved to Xiajia because their houses were needed for the construction of a huge pigpen that was to house 10,000 pigs. When this attempt ended in failure, Xiajia villagers had to pay to reconstruct the neighboring village they had destroyed only a few months earlier. Such social experiments were carried out one after another, the most harmful of which was launched in 1959. To please their superiors and maintain Xiajia as a model village, village leaders forced the villagers to submit their last sack of grain, including the seeds, to the state. As a result, during the winter and spring of 1959–60 and 1960–61, Xiajia residents suffered much more from the famine than villagers in the neighboring communities. According to some informants, village leaders continued to force the villagers to work during the daytime and to study political documents during the evenings, even at the height of the famine. A method of public promotion/humiliation was used to mobilize the villagers. For those who met the requirements of work and study, a red flag was displayed in front of their houses; a yellow flag was prominently displayed in front of the houses of the backward people who failed to accomplish assigned tasks. Former landlords, rich peasants, and other politically disadvantaged people were excluded from such competition, and their houses were marked by white flags, the color of death in Chinese culture.

The 1959–61 famine marked a turning point in the history of Xiajia village, because from that time on most villagers came to realize that to be a model village meant suffering from irrational social experiments dictated from above. Xiajia residents strongly demanded a leadership that could take the villagers' interests into consideration. In 1961, when the previous party secretary was removed from office, a discharged soldier was elected as the new party secretary. Although illiterate, he was a well-known antiauthoritarian character afraid of no one. It is evident that Xiajia villagers wanted a leader who could resist the excessive demands from above. This man stayed in power for only a couple of months, however, and was removed after he made his first serious effort to resist orders from his superiors in the local government. In the following year (1962), the villagers made another bold attempt to protect their interests by stealing the harvest from the collective land. Within a few days, this small-scale theft quickly developed into public robbery, or "free pick-up" as the villagers prefer to call it. The situation was getting out of control, and finally a team of investigators was sent to Xiajia from the local government. The villagers were forced to report the amount of grain they had taken from the collective farms and to return the grain to the collectives. Naturally most people underreported their "income" and thus benefitted from the small rebellion.

After the unusual election of the village party secretary in 1961 and the massive robbery of collective crops in 1962, the subsequent leadership in Xiajia readjusted its behavior. For the next two and a half decades, the cadres in Xiajia were relatively moderate in carrying out their superiors' orders, and Xiajia remained a politically "backward brigade" by CCP standards in the local commune. The most important change was that the new leadership paid much more attention to agricultural production and indeed in this respect achieved great success. The average payment for a day's work in the Xiajia collectives was between 1.10 to 1.30 yuan, from the late 1960's through the 1970's, and this increased to as high as 2.00 yuan on the eve of decollectivization in 1983. This placed Xiajia among the richer villages in north China. With three large tractors and supporting machinery, Xiajia was relatively successful in mechanizing its farming. The village also built the best schoolhouse and most elaborate collective headquarters among the seventeen brigades of the local commune during the early 1980's.

It is not surprising that when rural reforms developed to the stage of decollectivization in 1983, both the cadres and many villagers in Xiajia had difficulty accepting the fact that the collectives were to be dismantled. Much like the political campaign for collectivization during the 1950's, decollectivization was carried out with compelling force from above, regardless of local responses and reservations. At the end of 1983, Xiajia collectives were dismantled overnight, and all property was privatized, including the tractors and other heavy agricultural machines. Farmland, the fundamental means of production, was divided into two categories: subsistence-grain land (kouliang tian) and contract land (chengbao tian). Everyone in the village was entitled to 2 mu of rationed land and every adult male laborer received 10 mu of contract land. Villagers' obligations to provide the state with cheap requisitioned grain only applied to the contract land.

Owing to its poor transportation (with only an unpaved road linked to the major transportation line, which is connected to the county seat), there was no rural industry whatever in Xiajia village during the collective period. Only a few grain-processing factories existed in 1991, all of which were family businesses. In 1994 the major income of most households was derived from farming and family sideline occupations, such as pig raising or traditional handicrafts. Xiajia's heavy reliance on agriculture has been a major obstacle to economic development since decollectivization. According to my 1989 and 1991 surveys, the average per capita income in Xiajia has remained slightly lower than the national average since 1985,[5] indicating that Xiajia has changed from a relatively rich village during the collective period to a marginally unsuccessful farming community in the postreform era. Nevertheless, some households were able to develop family businesses or send extra laborers to work outside the village and thus have become affluent in recent years.

As indicated above, the Shuangcheng area was opened up by both Manchu settlers and Han immigrants. It is true that the early Manchu homesteaders enjoyed various privileges and that the Han immigrants were discriminated against by the Qing. But, after the dramatic social changes in the twentieth century, the two ethnic groups have developed a harmonious relationship with one another, and have been integrated into a local culture that combines both Manchu and Han traditions. Currently, Shuangcheng county has the largest Manchu population in Heilongjiang province. According to the 1982 census, Manchus make up 19 percent of the county's population (128,388 out of 684,380 people). In Xiajia there are 257 self-proclaimed Manchus, making up 16 percent of the total population in 1991. However, the actual percentage of Manchus may be lower than the population data show, because many Han people falsely identify themselves as Manchu in order to take advantage of government population policies, which allow minorities to have more than one child.

The Manchus all speak Mandarin Chinese and share culture and customs with the Han villagers in most aspects of village life, including intermarriage. Unless one checks the household register or, as explained below, looks at rites of ancestor worship, it is almost impossible to distinguish between Manchu and Han villagers simply by observing their daily life. Interestingly, the Han villagers in Xiajia feel that they are closer to the Manchus than to the Han immigrants residing along the Lalin River. The Han villagers in Xiajia argue that although they are not Manchu *qiren* (banner people), they belong to the banners (*zaiqi*). That they prefer to identify themselves as *qiren* might be explained by two factors. First, *qiren* may indicate a broader category than that of Manchu, because in addition to the eight Manchu banners, there are also Mongol and Chinese banners (see Kessler 1976: 11; and Oxnam 1975: 93–101). Second, for a long period, Xiajia remained a subunit affiliated to its original banner village, and the Xiajia land was originally part of the banner land given by the Qing state. These factors distinguish the Han villagers in Xiajia from those in the *minren* villages who arrived later on to cultivate the unclaimed land along the Lalin River.

According to some Manchu informants, the ritual of ancestor worship is the only important determinant that distinguishes the Manchus from the Han in Xiajia. Like villagers in the central plains of north China (see Cohen 1990), the Han villagers write the names of their ancestors on a scroll with painted decorations and worship the scroll during an annual ritual at the beginning of each lunar year. By contrast, Manchu villagers worship a sacred box, which is placed on a small shrine inside their homes; this box is always covered with a yellow cloth. It contains the ancestors' names and a small figure of a naked woman called the Mother Buddha (*fotuo mama*) who, according to a widespread Manchu legend (see Ma 1990), died to save the life of Nurhaci, the founder of the Manchu empire. Manchu informants in Xiajia maintain that the ancestral box can be opened only by the most senior male member in the family during the New Year ritual, and the banquet immediately following must be performed in the dark, without any light, because the Mother Buddha does not wish to expose her naked body. Observing this ritual standard, I found that only 131 Manchu villagers in Xiajia actually participated in the Manchu ritual of ancestor worship—about half the number of villagers officially registered as Manchu.

The Socialist Hierarchy and Its Recent Changes

Although land reform completely altered the previous structure of social status, social equality was not easily attained. The system of class labels, which put people in different ranks, provided varied access to valuable resources and thus inevitably created social inequality (see Parish and Whyte 1978; J. Watson 1984; and Whyte 1981). Moreover, the ruling group—village cadres—obviously enjoyed more privileges, and their misconduct often went unchecked by superiors. It has been well known that, as in other socialist societies, the social hierarchy in China was, until recently, based on bureaucratic "rank order" rather than on a market-based system of "class order" (see, e.g., Walder 1986). So it is appropriate to follow Weber's conventions (1978: 305–7) by identifying the "status groups" in the socialist collectives. In the case of Xiajia, four groups are clearly identifiable according to their prestige, privileges, and ability to gain access to resources and opportunities in the bureaucratic redistributive system of the collectives: (1) cadres; (2) *si shu hu* ("four types of households"); (3) ordinary villagers; and (4) "four bad elements."

The cadres certainly stood at the top level in the system of social stratification within the collectives. By the end of 1982, just before decollectivization, there were thirteen full-time cadres in Xiajia brigade and more than twenty part-time cadres at the lower level of the production team.[6] Because they ran the collectives and controlled the distribution of material goods as well as life opportunities, the cadres enjoyed considerable political power, economic advantage, and social privilege within their little empires, much like their counterparts in other parts of rural China. And as in other places, they also played the role of patron to selected villagers—their clients (see Oi 1989). Additionally, there were more than one dozen former cadres who had fallen or retired from office during the collective period. These former cadres did not enjoy the same privileges as those in power; but they were still regarded with deference and had access to the best jobs in the collectives. Since they were all party members, they had some influence on village politics.

Another group, called *si shu hu*, also ranked at the upper level of the village hierarchy. This category, derived from the household register system and urban-rural inequalities, has received little attention among scholars of Chinese social stratification. These households include the spouses and children of four types of people: state cadres, workers, teachers, and military officers. These people are employed by the government and thus categorized as urban residents according to the official administrative system of classification. Their spouses and children still belong to the category of rural residents, a complicated matter that needs a little more explanation. As Myron Cohen (1993) correctly points out, since the early decades of this century, Chinese urban elites began to refer to the rural population as *nongmin* (usually translated as "peasant"), a term borrowed from the Japanese and having negative connotations, such as being backward and superstitious.[7] In the postrevolution period, however, this ideologically charged notion also had administrative meaning and became an official category. According to the household register system (*hukou zhidu*) established in the late 1950's, the Chinese population was divided into two general categories: *nongmin* and *gongren* (worker) or *chengzhen zhumin* (urban resident), the more inclusive term. To be an urban resident meant to have access to certain commodities at subsidized prices, to enjoy a secured job with retirement and medical benefits, and to be entitled to a wide variety of social welfare programs sponsored by the government. By contrast, a rural resident was disadvantaged in all these aspects. Urban/rural status is inherited through the mother and, until a decade ago, rural-urban migration without official permission was legally banned. Thus, many village women who married urban residents still had to remain "peasants," as did their children (see Cohen 1993; Potter and Potter 1990).

As the result of the social inequalities that existed between rural and urban areas, those in village society who had urban connections were ranked higher than those who did not and, naturally, those who had spouses with urban resident status were higher than anyone else. Hence the emergence of the special group called *si shu hu*. In Xiajia, nineteen households could be considered *si shu hu*. They enjoyed advantages both from the state and from the collective. On the one hand, given that the head of each household was a government employee, the households had a guaranteed cash income from the state; on the other hand, they received their shares of grain and other goods at low prices from the collective distribution system, even though they did not work for the collective. For this reason, they were also called *dui laoshen* (literally, "the gentry of the production teams").[8]

An important indicator of social status in this hierarchy was the privilege of avoiding manual labor, especially farm work. For example, brigade cadres almost never did farm work, and the heads of production teams did so only occasionally. Ordinary villagers in Xiajia accordingly called themselves "black hands" (*hei zhuazi*) because they were continually working the land and thus exposing themselves to the sun. The privileged were called "white hands" (*bai zhuazi*) because they were able to avoid tanning their hands by farm work. Unequal access to opportunities and the discrimination, reflected in the distinction between white hands and black hands, resulted in a serious problem of social inequalities.

While the cadres and the four types of households occupied the upper level of the social hierarchy in Xiajia, the ordinary villagers stood somewhere in the middle. According to Maoist class theory, former poor peasants—that is, those who had been impoverished before the 1949 Revolution—constituted the only reliable revolutionary force in the countryside, and special opportunities (e.g., cadre or teacher positions) should be reserved for them. Because the class label of poor peasant might bring about some advantages even to the ordinary villagers, in making them feel superior to others and granting them bargaining power in job assignments within production teams, it is proper to further classify these villagers separately from those who held the label of middle peasant.

As one might expect, former landlords and rich peasants (in Xiajia no one bore the label of counterrevolutionary or rotten element) were at the bottom of the hierarchy of socialist collectives. They were considered class enemies, and were discriminated against, both politically and socially. They were put under mass control and were always the first targets during political campaigns. In daily life they had to accept the worst job assignments and they received the least remuneration. Within the established system of social stratification, they had no hope of ever improving their status.

To sum up, three basic factors structured the socialist hierarchy in Xiajia village. The first was the control that the collectives held over the villagers' lives, which itself was a reflection of CCP authority. This authority was the central axis of socialist stratification—a hierarchy based on bureaucratic rank, in which cadres enjoyed higher political and social status than their subjects. The second factor was the distinction and consequent inequality between urban and rural status in the household register system, a condition that has been officially endorsed since the late 1950's. This distinction made the four types of households who enjoyed the "iron rice bowl" of state employment superior to ordinary villagers, whose livelihood depended solely on the "clay bowl," a metaphor for farming. The third factor was the "class line," the ideological standard of social mobility established during the Maoist era. The class line saw the four bad elements as virtual untouchables in the socialist hierarchy; it also promised the former poor peasants higher social status and spiritual superiority (see Unger 1984).

The socialist hierarchy, therefore, was based on three sets of binary oppositions, that is, cadres-villagers, city-countryside, and red-black (in class origin).[9] Interestingly enough, these three oppositions were consciously recognized by both the state (represented by local government and grassroots cadres) and by villagers. In official language, people were categorized in terms of the relationships between the leaders and the led, urban and rural, and "we" versus "they." In the eyes of ordinary farmers, the former two were perceived of as the opposition between white hands and black hands and the third between good and bad classes.

This system began to change in the late 1970's under the impact of the economic reforms. First, class labels, together with the emphasis on class struggle, were officially abolished in 1979. As a consequence, the four bad elements regained their social and political rights as citizens. Moreover, although villagers still do not have the right to urban residency, they have been allowed to seek temporary jobs in the cities. Reforms have also reduced privileges of urban residents, so the gap between the rural and urban sectors was diminished to a certain extent. Furthermore, decollectivization has broken the cadres' monopoly over resources and has thus undermined their control over the life of ordinary villagers. As a result, a number of ordinary villagers—including some of the former disadvantaged—have benefitted both economically and socially. In particular, villagers of former middle-peasant origins have done extremely well, challenging the superiority of the cadres and the four types of households. The previous socialist hierarchy is being replaced by a dual system of social stratification characterized by the coexistence of bureaucratic rank with a market-based economic class order. For detailed discussions on these changes in Xiajia and elsewhere, see Yan 1992a, 1994, and 1995.

The Local Kinship Structure

Finally, it is necessary to look at the local kinship system before moving on to the topic of interpersonal relations. As a result of constant immigration throughout its history, the kinship structure in Xiajia displays what Cohen has called "pronounced agnatic heterogeneity" (1990: 511). Present-day Xiajia consists of 38 agnatic groups, comprising 33 surnames. Not surprisingly, the largest group is the Xia, a fact well reflected in the village's name, which literally translates as "Xia's Family." There were 104 Xia households in 1991. Besides the Xia, there are seven groups with more than fifteen households each. The remaining 32 smaller groups are locally called "single-door or small households" (dumen xiaohu), half of which contain three or less families. If we trace the history of these small groups two generations back, many were single doors, namely, one household.

The role of patrilineal organizations in social life appears to be relatively insignificant in Xiajia. Prior to the 1949 Revolution, well-organized lineages could be found only in the larger agnatic groups; among these groups agnatic solidarity was demonstrated and reinforced by annual rituals during the qingming (grave sweeping) festival and the lunar New Year. For instance, the Xia lineage collectively owned trees and a small plot of land near its ancestral tombs. During the qingming festival, Xia males gathered to visit their ancestors' tombs, located six kilometers away from the village. After the visit, a banquet was provided at the home of the lineage master (zuzhang). The local term for these activities is chihui, which means literally "to eat the association." Similar gatherings were held during the lunar New Year, when an ancestral scroll was hung in the main room of the homes of the senior men in each branch. Within the branch all descendants worshipped their ancestors, but, unlike in the qingming gathering, no banquet was provided. Other agnatic groups, such as the Xu and the Liu, had similar practices, but on a smaller scale. For most villagers who belonged to small agnatic groups, agnatic ties existed only in the context of intrahousehold interactions, and there were no elaborate rituals or other social institutions to celebrate patriliny.

After the 1949 Revolution, especially after the high tide of radical collectivization during the late 1950's, the power of patrilineal organizations in Xiajia was further diminished. A public cemetery was established outside the southeastern gate of the village. The Xia, and other groups whose ancestral tombs were far away from Xiajia, began to bury their dead in the public graveyard. The *qingming* visits to the ancestral tombs and the associated banquets (*chihui*) no longer occurred. Ancestor worship during the lunar New Year continued until the Cultural Revolution, and then was resumed during the early 1980's. But it was largely a domestic cult of the dead, and no organized activities among agnates were resumed (see Cohen 1990).

In contrast to the weaker role now played by patrilineal organizations, affinal ties are regarded by villagers as very important. In major family ceremonies, such as weddings, birthday celebrations, and house construction, affines are treated as honored guests and the celebration of affinity often overshadows that of patriliny on these occasions. (It should be noted that funerals are denominated by the notion of patriliny.) Mutual assistance in daily life, long-term cooperation in agricultural production or business, and political alliances are more often based on affines than on agnates.

More important, village endogamy has been practiced for several generations in Xiajia; thus many villagers are bound by affinal ties rather than agnatic relations. The practice of village endogamy can be traced back to the early settlement period. According to an 1819 official report made by General Fu, who was in charge of the settlement project, affinal ties were an important means by which the early Manchu settlers organized their daily life. Fu wrote in his report that in the banner villages, "half of the settlers are affines with each other" (quoted in S. Li 1990: 38). Because intermarriage between Manchu settlers and Han immigrants was strictly prohibited by the Qing court, the Manchu settlers had to find spouses among their fellow banner people. Village endogamy, or endogamy within the five villages of a banner unit, thus became a popular practice among the Manchus. When the legal ban on Manchu-Han intermarriage was lifted and Manchu privileges were abolished after the

1911 Revolution, marriage between new immigrants and native villagers (Manchu and Han alike) became a common pattern.

In the Xiajia case, most of the smaller agnatic groups moved into the village through affinal connections with earlier residents such as the Xia. For those who did not have any kinship ties before settling in Xiajia, the establishment of affinal relationships with native Xiajia villagers was the best way to secure a place in local society. For instance, one informant had settled in Xiajia during the early 1950's when he was discharged from the army. About thirty years later, his three daughters had all married within the village, thereby connecting him to three larger agnatic groups and making him a respectable member of the local community. A more recent example is provided by the Lin family and the Du family, which immigrated to Xiajia in 1974 and 1976 respectively. When I revisited Xiajia in 1991, I found that Lin's son had married a girl from one of the Xia families, and Du's daughter had married a Xu representing another local agnatic group.

The custom of village endogamy was further promoted by collectivization. This was particularly true for young women, who usually worked for five to seven years in the collectives before getting married. During this period, they enjoyed intimate friendships, both at work and during leisure time, and had many opportunities to meet young men. The emphasis on collectivism and the mobilization of female laborers in collective farming encouraged young women to make personal choices in mate selection. The same was true for young men, except that their social interactions with one another continued after marriage. As a result, a new type of courtship and marriage emerged, one characterized by romantic love and conjugal affection. Today, many young people prefer to marry someone from their own village, based on personal choice.[10] According to my 1991 survey, 126 men in Xiajia have chosen wives from within the village (accounting for 35 percent of the household total of 365), of which 102 were married after the 1949 Revolution. These 126 men are connected, by direct affinal ties, to 102 other male household heads, who are either their fathers-in-law or brothers-in-law. Thus, the total number of households connected by affinal ties has reached 228, or 62 percent of the total households in Xiajia. Village endogamy creates a large number of affines within the same community, which in turn has a profound impact on the conduct of interpersonal relations.

Xiajia is by no means unique with respect to the practice of village endogamy. My 1989 survey in Shandong and Hebei provinces shows that in many multi-surname communities, marriage within the village was considered an advantage for the bride and her natal family. As in Xiajia, the number of intravillage marriages increased during the collective era. These findings echo earlier observations in Guangdong province, where not only village endogamy but also intralineage marriage began to emerge after 1949. According to William Parish and Martin Whyte, "Marriage to people of the same village and lineage clearly increased through the mid-1960s, although there may have been a slight reversal of this trend recently" (1978: 171). These changes were due, in their view, to the reduced importance of lineage organizations and the rise in personal selection of mates (1978: 170–72). Sulamith Potter and Jack Potter (1990) report on the breakdown of the taboo against same-surname marriages in single-lineage villages in Guangdong province during the collective era. A similar pattern of "marriage revolution" is discussed by Anita Chan, Richard Madsen, and Jonathan Unger (1984: 188–91) in their village study. They found that "within just a few years, as it became evident that having a daughter close at hand promised an extra measure of security for old age, marriage within Chen Village became the *preferred* match, involving some 70–80 percent of the total" (1984: 191).

In addition to their own close affines (such as one's wife's brother and sister), Xiajia men also pay close attention to their wives' relatives, especially one's wife's sister's husband, who is called *lianqiao* in local usage. Literally, *lianqiao* means "to be connected by a bridge," and the bridge obviously refers to the sororate relationship between one's wife and her sister. It is the local custom that elder sisters often introduce their younger sisters to men who are their husbands' neighbors, in order to maintain closer ties within the communities. As a result, some Xiajia villagers who married women from other villages have found themselves connected by their wives' sororate relationships. In 1991, 86 men in Xiajia were linked by this kind of affinal relationship and, among them, 46 found their wives from other villages. If we add these 46 cases to the previous 228 affines connected by village endogamy, the total number of affines within Xiajia is 274, nearly two-thirds of all households. Furthermore, by local custom, one's brother's affines are regarded as one's own relatives, and mutual assistance can be sought among these second-degree or even more remote affines. If we take the second-degree affines into account, it is clear that virtually every household in Xiajia village is connected by some form of affinal tie. It is no wonder, therefore, that in everyday life affines tend to be more active than agnates in mutual assistance and cooperation, and affinal terms are the most frequently used forms of address. People clearly envision their village as a community of relatives. The prominent place of affines, however, is best illustrated by patterns of gift giving and interpersonal relations, as outlined in the following chapters.

The World of Gifts:
A Preliminary Classification

During a welcoming party two days after I had settled in Xiajia village, I told my village friends that I was going to conduct a systematic investigation of gift exchange in daily life. Many villagers wondered why I was interested in such a simple, commonsensical matter and why I thought it worthy of serious study. As an old friend put it, "Don't you know that gift giving is no more unusual than a hen laying an egg. It happens every day." Some thought I was making a joke and teased me, saying, "You should not read so many books. You were much smarter when you were here fifteen years ago." When I asked my friends to enumerate the types of gifts commonly given in the village and the rules of local gift-giving behavior, however, they appeared puzzled and said, "Look, it's too complicated to be explained in a few words." Then we began to engage in serious discussion; my friends were vying with one another to cite different kinds of gifts, arguing about proper categories. From that moment on, I was convinced that my intellectual journey into this topic needed to begin with a systematic classification of gifts and exchange relations. Though this topic has long been popular in anthropology, there has been little research of this kind in Chinese studies.

Categories of Classification and the Gift Lists

There are many ways to construct a typology of gift exchange or exchange relations in general. In a review article, Befu summarizes five models of exchange relations: (1) perceived dyadic exchange; (2) motivational vs. institutional exchange; (3) generalized vs. balanced exchange; (4) direct vs. indirect exchange; and (5) horizontal vs. vertical exchange (see Befu 1977a: 261–69). While they differ from each other in terms of focus, all these models reduce the complexity of exchange relations to an abstract dichotomy. For social-cultural anthropologists, the key question is how much a model or typology can fit the society they are studying. Or, in other words, how can a local system of social behavior be more accurately classified and presented in academic language? Clifford Geertz once suggested that the best way is "by searching out and analyzing the symbolic forms— words, images, institutions, behaviors—in terms of which, in each place, people actually represented themselves to themselves and to one another" (1976: 225). Following this approach, I will try to construct a classification system in accordance with local conceptions of various gift-giving activities. Nevertheless, in so doing I need to introduce numerous local terms and thus risk alienating my readers to some extent.

The term for gift in Chinese is *liwu*, a word composed of two characters. The first character *li* means rituals, properties, and ceremonial expressions of ethical ideals such as filial loyalty and obedience (see Weber 1968: 156–57). The second character *wu* means material things. It is interesting that, etymologically, the Chinese term indicates that a gift is more than a material present—it carries cultural rules (proprieties) and also involves ritual. So, a *wu* without *li* is just a thing, not a gift. Villagers in Xiajia are fully aware of the complex connotation of this word. In the practice of daily life, they often abbreviate the word by simply using *li*, emphasizing the cultural codes rather than the material aspects of the gift. For instance, those who fail to present gifts properly in the expected ritual situations are criticized by villagers as *queli* or *bu dong li*, which means literally "one who acts without proprieties" or "one who does not understand proprieties." In other words, the material content of the gift cannot be separated from its cultural meaning and ritual context. It follows that a classification of gift exchanges cannot be based solely on the types of material things presented, or solely on the economic principles underlying the exchange of gifts.

Inspired by my informants' repeated emphasis on various rituals of gift giving during our discussions, I found that the best way to construct a classification system was to take the occasions of gift exchange as basic categories and further distinguish them by the different contexts in which these occasions are positioned. By occasion I mean the social events that regularly involve gift-giving activities; exchange behavior on these occasions is culturally codified. By context I mean the social relations existing between the gift giver and the recipient.

Meanwhile I also borrow Befu's dichotomy of expressivity vs. instrumentality to distinguish the motivational features of different types of gift exchanges in Xiajia village. According to Befu, gift exchange serves both expressive and instrumental functions. "The expressive function is that the existing status relationship between the giver and the receiver determines the conditions of gift-exchange (kind and value of gifts to be given), and gift-giving supports the status relationship. This contrasts with the instrumental use of gift-giving, in which the conditions of exchange (nature and value of the gift) determine the status relations; that is, one manipulates the status relations by manipulating gift-giving" (Befu 1966–67: 173–74). In my opinion, expressive gift exchanges are ends in themselves and often reflect a long-term relationship between a giver and a recipient; in contrast, instrumental gifts are means to some utilitarian end and ordinarily indicate a short-term relationship. Nevertheless, in practice, the pure types of expressive and instrumental gifts do not exist; rather, elements of expressivity and instrumentality coexist in almost all activities of gift giving, but in different ratios. Xiajia is a close-knit farming community, and its residents are bound by long-term relations throughout their lives; gift giving that is too obviously concerned with instrumentality as a primary goal is rare within the village.

To classify further situations of gift exchange, another pair of categories needs to be introduced, namely, ritualized vs. nonritualized gifts. In local terms, this distinction is captured as *dashi* and *xiaoqing*, meaning the "great events" and "little events," which require the exchange of gifts. The original meaning of the Chinese word *shiqing* can be translated into English as "affairs," "matters," or "business." However, in local usage this word is also employed to designate rites of life passage and other important ceremonies, such as birthday celebrations. The local expression to ask the date of a wedding is "when will you handle the affair?" Similarly, the expression *daban* means to perform a solemn ceremony, and *bu ban* means to undergo a rite of passage without a proper ceremony (usually for economic reasons). While the term *dashi* includes the ceremonial and thus institutionalized situations of gift giving, *xiaoqing* is used to categorize all events of gift exchanges in daily life that do not require the performance of a ritual or the celebration of a particular festival, such as mutual visits of relatives. Thus, the latter might be called "nonritualized exchange relationships." These relationships have attracted little scholarly attention in Chinese studies. As demonstrated below, nonritualized gifts are not as remarkable as ritualized gifts either in terms of quality or quantity, but they play an equally important role in the creation of life meaning and reinforcement of social networks in village society.

Ritualized gift giving on occasions of great events is characterized by the host's offering of a banquet, formal invitations to selected (important) guests, and the documentation of incoming gifts, all of which are absent in nonritualized gift giving during little events. Banquets, known as *xi* or *jiuxi* (meaning a "feast" or a "liquor feast"), are offered at major family ceremonies, such as betrothal rites, weddings, and house construction. The host invites a small group of assistants including a talented cook to prepare the food. The size of the banquet is usually determined by the number of tables served during the whole ritual event. One table contains four guests; this is half of the size of a table typically found in north rural China, because in northeast China villagers customarily eat their meals on the heated bed (*kang*) and thus use smaller tables. Because a banquet usually involves 25 or more tables, only the most important guests may sit at the tables at the host's house; the others are scattered at neighboring houses. Thus helpers, mostly male teenagers, are needed, and their tasks are to transport the dishes from the kitchen to the tables at the different houses and to serve the guests with food and drink. The quality and quantity of food and drink vary from one family to another, depending on the host's economic capability and personality (either generous or stingy). There is a general standard, however, which reflects the level of affluence in the village as a whole. In the late 1980's and early 1990's, eight dishes with meat or eggs, or both, good rice, white liquor, and cigarettes were "musts" for a banquet. Of course, for expensive items such as meat and liquor, there is always room for the individual host to decide on quality and quantity. The guests at the "high tables," namely, the tables at the host's house, are served better dishes cooked separately by the chief cook.

Only those who have offered gifts are qualified to sit at the banquet; there has never been a case in which someone comes just to eat without making the contribution of a gift. The banquet, thus, can be viewed as an immediate reciprocity made by the host to the guests; for many villagers, attending a wedding banquet is perhaps one of the few chances they will have to enjoy good food and drink. This was particularly true during the period from the 1950's to the early 1970's when most Xiajia villagers, like their counterparts in other regions of China, suffered from prolonged poverty. As Cohen notes: "The excellent food served to guests was in most cases a far cry from their usual fare, and as far as subsistence is concerned, food consumed during ceremonial occasions probably played a very significant nutritional role" (1970: xx). However, the guests usually contribute more to the host than they could possibly take back by eating at the banquet. Owing to lower costs for raw materials and labor in rural areas (the helpers are "paid" only by meals), a village banquet costs much less than one in a restaurant in an urban area. According to several informants, the cost of a banquet is usually one-fifth of the monetary gifts the host receives during a ceremony. For those who have more guests, especially important guests offering larger gifts, the cost of the banquet will be accordingly lower. In any event, the banquet is at best only a small part of the reciprocal return a host can make to his guests immediately after receiving the gifts; the major part of the social debt has to be repaid in the future to individual guests at similar ceremonial occasions.

Like banquets, formal invitations, known as *qingtie*, constitute an important device for major ceremonies; however, unlike the banquet that is provided to all guests who attend the ritual and offer gifts, a formal invitation is sent only to those important guests who are close relatives or best friends and who live outside the village community. Formal invitations are usually written on red paper with a traditional Chinese calligraphy brush, and the wording is polite and elegant, very much like classical Chinese. The invitation is delivered by a messenger or, less formally, passed on by anyone who happens to be visiting the recipient's community. In comparison to villages I visited in Hebei and Shandong provinces in north China, the invitation procedures and the invitation card itself in Xiajia village and the surrounding areas are much less elaborate or formal. It is not unusual for oral messages to replace written invitations for the sake of convenience. More importantly, within the village community there is no invitation issued, and the host merely announces the hosting of a ceremony in advance through informal channels of gossip and chatting.

Several reasons were offered by my informants to explain the absence of formal invitations to guests within the village community. First, villagers feel that there is no practical reason to send a written invitation to someone who resides just across the street or on the other side of the village. Family ceremonies are a central topic of everyday conversation, so everyone knows exactly what is happening or will happen in other families. Moreover, as the rejection of an invitation is tantamount to the ending of the social relationship upon which it is based, an invitation card itself creates a mandatory obligation on the recipient to attend the ritual and offer a gift. Therefore, indiscretions in the sending of invitations are regarded as irresponsible and greedy; namely, they attempt to force others to attend the ceremony in order to accumulate monetary gifts. To avoid such implications, villagers are always careful about sending invitations. As one informant put it, three conditions must be considered: (1) whether a previous gift-giving relationship exists between the host and the targeted person; (2) whether the targeted person would like to receive the invitation; and (3) whether the person lives outside the village and thus needs to be informed of the event in this way.

Furthermore, the basis of the above concerns is that Xiajia villagers believe the proper way of gift giving is to offer actively rather than to give passively—as if they were repaying a debt. In other words, ideal gift giving should be based on the donor's intention to give, rather than on the social pressure created by invitations. This is actually the logic underlying why there is no need to issue invitations within the village community. According to villagers, if one really has the good wish (xinyi, literally the "expression from one's heart") toward the host of a family ceremony, one will go ahead and express it by offering the gift. An informant told me: "It is no good to force an ox's head down to the water if the ox doesn't want to drink. So one should not force a gift out of someone's pocket."

As a result, at most ceremonial occasions, there are unexpected guests who take the initiative to show up and offer gifts; the more such guests like this, the greater the social face of the host. This works very well with guests who live within the village, because they do not expect to receive invitations. Occasionally, too many unexpected attendees may cause embarrassment for the host, if the latter is unable to treat the guests with a proper banquet.

Although Xiajia village is a close-knit community and news about family ceremonies spreads quickly, there is still the possibility that someone may miss a ritual event and thus fail to present a gift. In such a case, one may visit the host afterward and present a delayed gift, locally called buli, meaning "to make up a gift." All my informants agreed that the missing of a ceremony is an embarrassment; thus one should increase the value of the delayed gift in order to make up for the failure to present it at the right time and occasion. In other words, buli is only a better strategy among the worst, so Xiajia villagers always pay attention to the dates of family ceremonies, which reinforces villagers' perceptions that invitations are unnecessary within the community.

Finally, ritualized gift giving is also associated with the custom of making and preserving gift lists. Gift lists (lidan) are homemade books on red paper (funeral gift lists are made on yellow paper) inscribed with a traditional Chinese calligraphy brush. They serve as a formal record of all gifts received by the host of a family ceremony.

At all the major rituals involving the presentation of gifts, such as weddings, funerals, and birthday celebrations, an accounting table is set up in a convenient place near the main setting, for the purpose of recording incoming gifts. The table is called the accounting station (*zhang fang*) and is usually so indicated by a large handwritten sign. All guests visit the accounting station before entering the main hall. There they make prestations and watch as their contributions are recorded. Three men work at the accounting table. One takes the monetary gift (*lijin*) from the gift giver and announces in a loud voice that "so-and-so offers 20 yuan as a gift." The second person (usually an educated man who is a talented calligrapher) writes down the donor's name and the amount of money on a gift list. The third man (who has a close relationship with the host) takes the money from the first man and places it in a box for safekeeping during the ritual events. At the end of the family ceremony, the three accountants report the total amount of the gifts to the host and transfer the money, together with the gift list, to the host.

It should be noted that the compiling of gift records is probably a widespread custom in China and other East Asian societies as well. I observed the custom in villages of Shandong and Hebei provinces, where I conducted my first field research in 1989, and I have been told by several Korean friends that in some regions of their home country, villagers also make written records of incoming gifts. Similar practices were reported by Sidney Gamble from Hebei during the 1930's: "An 'Account Book for the Wedding Gifts' was prepared and a man was asked to serve as secretary and enter in the book all the presents as they were received" (1968: 383). Cohen observed a similar social practice in a village in Taiwan. "When a guest arrives he first goes to a table where a man takes his cash gift and records the amount in a small booklet" (1976: 159).[1] In his *Neighborhood Tokyo* (1989: 200–205), Theodore Bestor describes in detail how the gift lists were made in the context of Japanese funerals. Interestingly enough, this custom of recording gifts is preserved among Japanese Americans in Honolulu as well: "In a precise reckoning, careful records are kept of gifts received so that one can discharge his obligation at the appropriate time in the future" (Johnson 1974: 296).

Checking the gift list is among the first things that a host does after the ceremony. The host wants to know exactly who attended and who did not and the value of the gifts. In other words, any changes in personal relationships will be reflected in the gift list. The host will keep the list in a safe place and treat it as a catalogue of social connections and a record of incoming personal favors. He will also consult the gift list frequently when he needs to determine how much he in turn should give to someone in similar circumstances.

During my survey, most informants were happy to go over their gift lists with me several times and, in many cases, they recalled various stories that occurred at the ceremonies. It became clear to me that gift lists, like photo albums, serve as landmarks, or even monuments, in one's life history. This memorial function also helps to explain the ritual character of the writing of gift lists. For a landmark to be ritually meaningful and worth recalling years later, it must be crafted in an appropriate manner.

From an etic point of view, the writing of a gift list fixes a ritual in recorded time and documents the exchange activities of daily life as a part of local history. Gift lists serve, therefore, as a repository of data on the changing nature of interpersonal relations and as a means to monitor the exchange of personal care, favors, feelings, and material assistance between givers and receivers. In this sense, gift lists can be seen as social maps, which record and display networks of personal connections.

But, emically, a gift is much more than a simple tool of memory and rational calculation for future giving and receiving. In the eyes of the villagers, the documentation achieved by the gift lists endows the gift-giving activities with ritual significance and sacredness. The scene at the accounting station is full of cultural symbolism: an educated and respectable bookkeeper using red paper and a calligraphy brush. These symbols convey the power of writing—a longstanding tradition in Chinese society. It is well known that since the late imperial period China has been a society where written records and documents were of crucial importance in practically all spheres of life. In rural society literacy was considered not only the crucial element of the local elite's power and influence but also the key to successful farm management and commerce (see A. Smith 1970). "Written material was thoroughly incorporated into ceremonial and religious activities; indeed, the written work was in itself often an object of religious veneration" (Cohen 1970: xv). After being entered on the gift list under the category of *lijin*, the cash, which previously had only an economic function, is transformed into a gift that constitutes a social debt between the donor and recipient and thus gains social meanings in the villagers' personal life (see Parry and Bloch 1989: 9–23). In addition, there is always a crowd of people sitting around, smoking, chatting, and sometimes making comments as they witness the gift-giving activities. Under such conditions, one must calculate carefully the appropriateness of one's gift, because social reward or sanction is verbalized right on the spot.

It is not surprising, therefore, that Xiajia residents take the presence or absence of a gift list as a standard by which to distinguish different ranks of gift-giving situations, marking some as *dashi* and others as *xiaoqing*. In everyday conversation, to ask whether an accounting station will be set up is a codified way to inquire about the nature of a given ceremony and to determine one's own gift-giving response to that social event. Thus the act of writing a gift list and the offering of a banquet provide us with an important diagnostic feature in classifying gift-giving activities in Xiajia village.

Expressive Gift Giving on Ceremonial Occasions

In present-day Xiajia, there are ten ritualized occasions of gift exchange. Among these, weddings, birthday celebrations, funerals, and celebrations for house construction are considered major ceremonies, all of which involve both the writing of a gift list and the presentation of a large banquet by the host family. Gift giving at such ceremonies is a public and sacred action, or a rite of exchange in Arnold van Gennep's terms (1960: 30). Ceremonial gift giving provides a special arena for the display of status and connections, visible proof of the relational capital one is able to mobilize. Unlike nonritualized gift-giving occasions where the participants are more intimate and fewer in number, the networks reflected in ceremonial gift exchange actually represent in concrete form the totality of social connections in a given family. According to several key informants, usually more than 80 percent of the gift-giving expenses in a family is used for ritualized occasions, which means ceremonial gift giving is regarded as economically more important than nonritualized gift giving. When

I asked my informants to enumerate occasions of gift giving, many began by reviewing the life cycle from birth through marriage to death. My description below follows this natural order of events.

Childbirth

Celebrations for childbirth are locally called *xianai* (literally meaning "to bring down the mother's milk"). After the birth of a child, at any time during the first month, relatives and friends come to see the newborn baby and to bring gifts to the mother. Gifts presented in this situation normally consist of various kinds of food considered nutritious by the villagers. Among many things, chicken eggs and brown sugar are the most suitable, especially coming from relatives of the mother's natal family, because the relatives want to assure that their presents will be consumed by the woman herself. Additionally, blankets and baby clothes are also preferred. Since the mid 1980's, however, people have begun to give monetary gifts (10 yuan on average in 1991), because increases in the prices of material goods have made it difficult to buy an adequate amount of traditional gifts.

Women are in charge of gift giving at the childbirth celebrations. Local residents believe that if men enter and leave the house of a newborn they may take the mother's milk with them. Young men carrying typically masculine tools, such as horsewhips or carpenter axes, are considered particularly dangerous for both the mother and her baby. According to the villagers, both the mother and her child are extremely vulnerable and are apt to be hurt by the strong essence of men—especially young men. This is related to the Chinese belief about the balance of the *yin* and *yang* elements. As young men (and their tools) possess more *yang* elements, they constitute a particular threat to the mother and the child who are already in the disadvantageous position of having too many *yin* elements. In the words of an old woman, "The mother is very weak at this time so that she could easily be frightened by any unknown force and stop producing milk. This is why people keep saying that men can take the mother's milk away. Actually, men just stop the milk from coming out." As a result of this local taboo, gift exchanges in this context form a large arena of women's subculture. By making gifts at childbirth celebrations women have the opportunity to establish their own social contacts. For instance, my landlord did not even know his wife had a separate gift list for *xianai* gift giving until the day I discussed this matter with the couple. In this sense, childbirth celebrations can be seen as a form of gender specialization in ritual participation.

Abortion and Female Sterilization

Unlike the childbirth celebration, which has existed as long as villagers can remember, gift giving for abortion and female sterilization is a new social phenomenon. In Xiajia, individual acts of gift giving for abortion appeared during the late 1970's and soon became a local custom. Gift giving for female sterilization began immediately following the campaignlike mobilization for birth control in 1982. Both of these appear to be compensatory rituals rather than celebrations. (More will be said about the creation of new rituals in the concluding chapter.) As social practices, they are so new that they have not yet been given local names. Villagers simply call them *liuchan* and *jueyu*, the exact medical terms for abortion and sterilization.

According to my informants, the type of gifts presented at these two situations are the same as those given for childbirth celebrations, except for baby clothes, and the scope of social relations (gift givers) involved in the abortion situation is also similar to that of childbirth. Villagers sometimes call gift giving for abortion "little *xianai*," a term derived from the local phrase *xiaochan* (little birth), meaning miscarriage. In contrast, female sterilization is regarded as a more formal situation for gift exchange, and more people are involved in the gift-giving event. Although women still constitute the majority of gift donors, men have also begun to participate in gift giving for female sterilization. When I was in Xiajia during the spring of 1991, a large-scale mobilization for female sterilization was carried out whereby 21 Xiajia women underwent the operation. Afterward there was an unusual surge of gift giving, with all 21 family ceremonies occurring within the same week. I witnessed many cases where men presented gifts. In one of these an ordinary male villager carried more than ten gifts and presented them to one household after another, as if he were delivering mail. The participation of men in this gift-giving situation may be explained by the fact that sterilization symbolizes the end of a woman's reproductive ability and thus affects not only her health but also the perpetuation of the descent line of the male.

Betrothal Rites

In Xiajia village and the surrounding areas, the betrothal rite is called *kaidan*. Here the Chinese word *dan* is abbreviated for *caili dan*, which means the list of betrothal gifts, and *kai* means to work out or to write down (the gift list). After the two families have reached agreement on a proposed marriage, the prospective bride and the leading members of her natal family participate in a betrothal ritual carried out by the groom's family. The central purpose of the ritual is to reach agreement about the betrothal gifts and to produce a formal list that records all of the betrothal gifts. Following the completion of such a document, the first round of betrothal gifts is passed over to the bride's family from the groom's family, and the close relatives of the groom also present some small gifts to the bride, such as a pair of socks. The ritual serves to announce publicly the marriage agreement. It should be pointed out that what I have summarized above applies to the postrevolution era only. In the past the bride was excluded from the betrothal rite, and it was her parents who received the gifts offered by the groom's family.

Since the early 1980's, however, the betrothal rite has taken on other new features. Now the groom's family also receives monetary gifts from relatives and friends and, consequently, a formal banquet is then prepared for all guests who have come to present gifts. Furthermore, in order to record all incoming gifts, accounting tables to prepare the gift lists have begun to appear at betrothal ceremonies. This change results from the current trend toward conspicuous gift giving and the expansion of personal networks, an interesting phenomenon that will be analyzed later.

Weddings

Xiajia residents consider weddings the most important ritual in life; accordingly gift-giving activities at wedding rituals are both comprehensive and complicated. Four kinds of gifts are presented at weddings: (1) cash gifts given by the guests to the wedding host; (2) various kinds of gifts given to the bride and groom as a property-owning unit; (3) personal presents given to the bride and groom; and (4) gifts in either cash or kind given to the specialists who provide various services and help the ritual host.[2]

Needless to say, an accounting table and the selection of a crew of gift-recording men are among the first things a ritual host has to consider. Two ritual specialists, a male and a female, are invited to direct and manage all procedures during the ritual. They are responsible for arranging the banquet seats for the guests who have presented their gifts at the accounting table and, more importantly, for deciding how and when to present the other categories of gifts to special guests and other ritual specialists, on behalf of the ritual host. The nature of their duties is well reflected in their titles—*dai dong de* (namely, "representatives of the host"). During the wedding, it is the ritual specialists who are in charge of all the gift exchange.

The monetary gifts to the hosts are the most salient prestations, both quantitatively and qualitatively. The value of a gift (or the amount of money) reflects the degree of closeness between giver and recipient. The ceremony performed in the bride's natal family home the day before the one performed by the groom's family is normally less elaborate, and fewer gifts and gifts of lesser value are presented. This may be due to the belief that the real wedding takes place in the groom's family and what occurs in the bride's family is little more than a farewell ceremony.

In addition to the main stream of gifts, which flows to the host family, there are also gifts presented to the bride and groom for their own use. The material gifts given by the groom's parents to the newlywed couple, such as bedding, furniture, and major appliances, and the dowry given by the bride's parents to the bride, are formally and publicly transferred into the conjugal room (*xinfang*) during the wedding. These gifts, plus the monetary gift given by the groom's family to the bride's family at the betrothal rite, constitute the complex of bridewealth and dowry and will be analyzed in detail in Chapter 8.

The bride and the groom also receive personal gifts. During the ceremony in her natal family, the bride receives monetary gifts from her mother's brother and sister (maternal uncle and aunt) as well as from some other close relatives. These gifts are called *yayao qian*, literally the "money to occupy her pocket." At the wedding on the next day, the bride also receives small cash gifts when she serves wine and cigarettes to the senior kinsmen of her husband's family. She is obligated to affix a flower to her mother-in-law's hair and then calls the latter "mother" out loud, ritually announcing her new status as a daughter-in-law. Meanwhile the mother-in-law gives the bride a red envelope containing a substantial cash gift (see Cohen 1976). Much less lucky than the bride, the groom receives personal gifts only when he goes to meet the bride and the team of bride senders midway between the two communities; here he receives a suit of clothing from the bride's family and immediately changes into these new clothes with the help of the bride's brother. This gift becomes his formal wedding garb.

The ritual specialist representing the groom's family immediately gives a cash gift to the bride's brother, in recognition of the latter's service in helping to dress the groom. This countergift, of course, belongs to the fourth category mentioned above, namely, gifts given to those who have provided special ritual services. In addition to the bride's brother, there are other "gift seekers" whom the groom's family must satisfy, such as the preschool-age boy and girl who sit beside the bride during her transfer to her husband's home (thus symbolizing her fertility). Gifts must also be given to the female bride senders who escort the bride and help to arrange the conjugal room. The bride's family also gives gifts to the cooks and musicians who work for the groom's family during the wedding.

House Construction

The ritual for house construction centers around the setting of the main roofbeam in place, known as *shangliang* (raising the beam). A mark of social status is the number of red cloths that are attached to the main beam; each cloth, representing a major gift given on this occasion, is considered symbolically auspicious for the host. In local terms, a gift of red cloth is called simply "the red" (*hong*), and the display of these gifts is called "hanging the red" (*guahong*). A host who receives a large number of cloths is confirmed as a leading member of the community. In addition, monetary gifts are also presented by the guests in a manner similar to that at wedding rituals, which necessitates the preparation of an accounting table and a banquet to thank the guests. The social scope of gift giving for house construction is usually smaller than that for weddings, but it also depends on the extent of the host's social networks. In a case I witnessed in 1991, the host was an influential cadre in the township where Xiajia village is located; he received 4,950 yuan in cash from more than 300 guests—much more than an ordinary villager could expect even for a wedding.

There is, however, another smaller celebration for house construction, performed after the host family has moved into the new house. Xiajia residents call it *wenguo*, literally meaning to "heat the cooking pot," and it appears similar to an American housewarming party. Traditionally, this was a small-scale, domestic celebration and involved only the closest relatives and best friends. The gifts presented in this situation were cooking utensils and food (raw or cooked). And the host provided the guests with tea and cigarettes—no banquet was provided nor was a gift list kept. This was a typical *xiaoqing*, or minor rite of gift exchange. In recent years, however, there have been at least two cases in which the hosts have turned the *wenguo* celebration into formal ritual. On both occasions an accounting table for gift recording was introduced and thousands of yuan in cash gifts were presented by the guests. In 1991 it was still not clear how elaborate this ceremony would become. Some villagers predicted that it could not be transformed into a major situation of gift giving *(dashi)*, because temporally it was so close to that of the *shangliang* ritual.

Birthday Celebrations

Xiajia villagers call birthday celebrations *baishou* (to honor longevity), which vividly depict the ritual moment when all children and grandchildren kowtow to the elder who is celebrating a birthday. Both male and female birthdays are celebrated, and 60 is considered to be the proper age for a first birthday celebration. Subsequently at age 65, 70, 75, and every five years thereafter, birthdays are thought to deserve special congratulations. The scope of gift givers for this ritual is often large and the ceremony also involves the recording of gifts and a banquet. In comparison to the gifts given at other ceremonial occasions, material gifts—especially food suitable for the elderly—are presented at birthday celebrations. It should be noted that one cannot host one's own birthday celebration, because the ritual should be performed by a son as a filial act. Consequently, the guests at this occasion come from the social networks of both generations.

Funerals

Funerals are last-stop rituals for individuals in this world and also the final opportunity to be involved in the networks of social exchange. Since many scholarly efforts have been devoted to the Chinese death ritual (see especially J. Watson and E. Rawski 1988), and the Xiajia case does not display significant differences, it is sufficient to mention only the main features of gift giving in the funeral context. The special gifts given at funerals are ritual offerings, by which the living communicate with the dead and also expect future returns from the dead. As James Watson notes, "Death does not terminate relationships of reciprocity among Chinese, it simply transforms these ties and often makes them stronger" (1988a: 9). Food offerings constitute the most important gifts given to the deceased (see S. Thompson 1988: 71–108). Paper models of horses, maids, servants, and draft animals are usually presented by affines.

The majority of guests present yellow pieces of paper, which are regarded as the currency of the afterlife. A gift-list book is prepared, but, as noted above, it is fashioned out of yellow paper, the same material used in making paper money. A simple meal is provided at the end of the three-day funeral, but no one considers this a banquet because it is small in scale and offered under unhappy circumstances. The social scope of ritual attendance at funerals is larger than that at all other ceremonies. Most households in the village send at least one representative to pay respects to the dead. The agnates and affines of the deceased must make every effort to participate in the ritual. Absence from a funeral without a proper excuse is considered an extremely unfriendly gesture and may lead to a break in the existing interpersonal relationships.

Occasional Celebrations

In addition to the rites of life mentioned above, there are occasional situations of gift giving for the celebration of unusually happy events. The most popular ceremonies of this kind are performed for young villagers who have gained upward mobility opportunities, such as college admission or military recruitment. Given the official distinction between urban and rural sectors, any chance of leaving the village is considered a major achievement. Furthermore, in the Chinese system of social hierarchy, all college graduates are recognized as state cadres, and until recently most discharged soldiers were allocated jobs in urban areas. Having a child enter college or join the army raises the parents' social status in village society. Therefore, a celebration ritual is usually held, and the social scope of guests may be as large as that at an engagement ritual. The host normally receives monetary gifts, which are recorded in a gift list, and a banquet is held.

Although college admission and military recruitment are the most popular occasions for celebrations, other events also warrant attention. The most peculiar case I learned about was that of a ceremony performed by a villager when his cow gave birth to a calf. Although this is an extreme case, it demonstrates that ritualized situations of gift exchange may be created or manipulated by individual villagers for their personal purposes.

The Annual *Yangge* Dance

Finally, gift giving during the local carnival period, called the "*yangge* dance," is also a ritualized event. *Yangge* is a very popular genre of folk dance performed collectively during holiday parades in north China. On the third day of the lunar New Year, a team of young village dancers visits and dances in front of every house in the community. This is regarded as a special form of *bainian*, namely, "to wish everyone a happy New Year." The household heads are supposed to greet the leaders of the team in front of their homes and thank the dancers by presenting them with small gifts—either cigarettes or cash. Villagers believe that the *yangge* can bring good luck to their homes and, thus, everyone is pleased to offer gifts to the dancers. After a day of parading about, the gifts are then distributed among the dancers. Unlike the above-mentioned ceremonies, whereby long-term reciprocity between individuals is emphasized, gift giving in this situation creates a feeling of community, solidarity, and mutual relatedness among the villagers.[3]

Expressive Gift Giving in Nonritualized Situations

By the phrase "nonritualized gift giving," I refer activities of gift exchange that do not involve any formal ceremony but have been routinized into everyday life. In the local dichotomy of great and little events, nonritualized gifts belong to the latter category. Yet, little events are by no means unimportant or less meaningful for the maintenance of social relations.

Mutual Visits Among Relatives

Xiajia residents call mutual visits among relatives *zou qinqi*, which literally means "to walk to your relatives." Recently more people have begun to visit friends as well. The villagers regard visiting relatives or friends as a crucial means of maintaining a good relationship; the best visiting time is during the lunar New Year and during slack periods in the agricultural cycle. With regard to gift giving, lunar New Year visits are particularly noteworthy, because one must not arrive empty handed at this visit. Such visits and gift giving are actually ceremonial as well, because people do not visit each other on the spur of the moment during this period; they know exactly who needs to be visited and what kind of appropriate gifts are to be offered. Gifts presented in this context are mostly in kind rather than in cash, and include bottled drinks (e.g., white liquor), canned foods, cigarettes, Chinese cakes, fresh fruit, and other such items. There is no rank order among these gifts; rather, the rank of a particular offer is judged by how many categories of goods it includes, ranging from a two-in-one offer (e.g., wine and cigarettes) to a combination of eight gifts: wine, cigarettes, canned foods, and cakes, which are given in pairs to accentuate the auspiciousness.

In the villages of Shandong and Hebei provinces (where I conducted field research in 1989), people visit each other in accordance with a fixed schedule. The first day of the first lunar month is reserved for intralineage visits among agnates (see Cohen 1990). The second day is devoted to one's mother's parents and brothers, the closest matrilateral relatives. One's father's sisters and mother's sisters are visited on the third day, and one's wife's parents wait until the fourth day. By contrast, there is no fixed sequence for such visits

in Xiajia village and the surrounding areas, except that the first relative to be visited must be one's wife's parents. Why this difference?
As explained in Chapter 2, for historical reasons, affinal ties play a
leading role in the social life of Xiajia villagers, and the priority status enjoyed by one's wife's parents during lunar New Year visits is
yet more evidence to demonstrate the centrality of affinal ties. Consequently, the gifts presented to one's wife's parents are also the most
generous among those being exchanged in this particular context.

Bai Xinnian and Guaxian

Among the various categories of visitors during the lunar New
Year period, newly married couples are considered special guests. In
local terms, their visit is called bai xinnian (meaning "to greet the first
New Year"), and it is characterized by an immediate return of gifts.
Customarily, the newly married couple must visit all senior relatives
in both the matrilateral and patrilateral lines and present material
gifts (such as food items as described above) to whomever they visit.
The people being visited must give the couple return gifts in cash as
a recognition of their marriage.

Similar to the custom of bai xinnian, guaxian (literally, "to hang
the thread") is another occasion for the newly married couple to receive gifts. After the couple have their first baby, the mother will
carry the baby to visit senior agnates and close relatives. The people
being visited must drape a string composed of five-colored threads
(red, yellow, blue, white, and black, which are related to the five basic elements in Chinese cosmology) around the neck of the baby,
which is believed to prevent the baby's soul from being stolen by
wandering ghosts. In addition, they also need to give gifts in cash
(normally 20 yuan) to the mother to thank her for visiting. It is
worth noting that patrilineal kin also are involved in this situation
of gift giving. The baby symbolizes the continuity of their descent
line, and therefore they are expected to express their gratitude to the
mother of their new agnate.

Xiaojing Gifts and Yasui Money

There are two kinds of special gifts in daily life that are exchanged
between young and old. The first is generally called xiaojing, a classic

term in Chinese, meaning "to give presents to one's seniors"—the latter a category that includes parents, aged relatives, and other authority figures such as teachers. The term is composed of two Chinese characters: filial piety and respect. Etymologically, therefore, the word indicates an upward direction of gift flow in a hierarchical context. No return is expected for *xiaojing* gifts, and the recipient always remains superior to the giver. Such an asymmetrical, upward flow of gifts has gained in social implications and has developed into a special form of hierarchical gift giving outside kinship circles; it is an interesting contrast to the Indian unilateral gift giving known as *dana* (see Yan 1991). Placing the Xiajia case into the context of anthropological studies of the gift in general, I will discuss this issue in detail in Chapter 7.

In village life, *xiaojing* gifts are mainly high-status food, new clothes, and small items such as tobacco pipes presented by adult children to their aged parents or senior agnates. *Xiaojing* gifts are completely embedded in the routine of daily life, but one can still discover the flow of *xiaojing* gifts from careful observation and from villagers' conversations. Quite often aged people enjoy receiving gifts that they themselves do not consume; instead they give these gifts to their grandchildren.

Yasui is the cash given by adults to children on the eve of the lunar New Year. This ancient custom can be traced back to the Han dynasty (Ye and Wu 1990: 32). The word *ya* means "to repress" and the original *sui* means "devils" or "ghosts." The gift (originally copper coins) is thus used to protect children from wandering ghosts. In present-day practice, however, villagers have interpreted the second character *sui* as a homonym meaning "year," and they argue that the cash gift is given to children as a symbol of good luck for the new year. *Yasui* money, like the *xiaojing* gift, is also a one-way, cross-generational gift that does not imply the expectation of a return gift.

Visits to Patients

Visiting someone who falls ill is another situation involving gift giving. According to my informants, the failure to participate in *tanbing* (literally "to visit the sick") is considered one of the most serious breaches of etiquette in the maintenance of both mutual relationships and emotional ties between visitor and visited. In this context, the expressivity of gift giving plays a dominant role, and the villagers emphasize their personal emotions by giving gifts to the patients. Gifts for this situation are usually foods the patient can enjoy, such as fruit, canned items, and Chinese cakes. Monetary gifts are regarded as improper unless one lives so far away that it is impossible to present a gift personally.

Food Exchange in Daily Life

Food plays a central role in social exchanges in Chinese society. Food as gifts can be divided into two subcategories: (1) fine foods, which are given at various ceremonial or routinized situations of gift exchange, as summarized above; and (2) various food items exchanged in daily life among women. The former are limited to traditional food usually purchased at stores and are rather luxurious by village living standards: Chinese cakes, wine, canned food, sugar, and baked meat (also included are chicken eggs, which constitute the major gift for reproductive ceremonies). The value of a gift in this category can easily be determined by its market value, since it is purchased with cash. In contrast, it is difficult to affix a monetary value to food gifts exchanged in daily life. Usually these are homemade gifts, ordinary foods prepared for daily consumption. They embody the ingenuity and personal characteristics of their producers—local housewives—and thus serve as a personalized way to express emotional attachment and friendship.

In a thoughtful analysis, E. N. Anderson identifies the social function of food as one of the key factors contributing to the elaboration of Chinese cuisine and notes that "gourmetship was a part of life, even for the peasants" (1988: 36). Indeed, in everyday conversation, villagers are fond of discussing subjects related to food and endlessly argue among themselves whose wife is the best cook in the village. Growing up in a cultural setting where cooking is so appreciated, many women have developed their own specialties, and they are eager to gain social recognition and respect by displaying their cooking skills. Food exchange, obviously, is the most convenient way to do so.

In daily life, food gifts are exchanged at several levels. First, every married woman has her own circle of close female friends who may be the wives of her husband's agnatic kinsmen or neighbors. Mutual visits among wives are quite frequent. These visits are called *chuan men zi* in local terms, meaning "drop by someone's home." When a woman cooks a special item, she may share it with those in her circle of *chuan men zi*. The varieties of food exchanged in this context are many, and the gift giving is informal—children are often sent to deliver the dishes. Village women also like to present their best culinary specialties to relatives, neighbors, and friends—especially during the slack seasons of agricultural production. Sometimes, food exchanges of this kind go beyond the village boundaries among those who are especially good at cooking. Another way to exchange food in daily life is to share one's garden products, mostly vegetables, with those who are in one's social network. Since the items exchanged are neither purchased nor cooked, these activities are the most common and therefore the least significant in relation to expectations of a proper return.

Food exchanges in daily life are almost exclusively conducted by and among women and are part of informal female networks, which go beyond the more formal, androcentric household networks. Moreover, Xiajia villagers exchange foodstuffs only with their social peers; the relationships cemented by such exchange activities are personalized, emotionalized, and egalitarian in nature. This pattern is an interesting contrast to the patterns of food exchange in the Indian caste system, where food, especially cooked food, is transmitted from a higher caste to a lower one and serves as a means of reinforcing the existing unequal relationship between the superior and inferior caste (see, e.g., Dumont 1980: 141–46; Marriott 1976: 114–23).

Gifts of Love

Although the study of private life is one of the primary concerns of anthropology, the role of sex and love has received little attention in the literature of sinological anthropology (one of the few exceptions is William Jankowiak's 1993 book). Almost all ethnographic accounts of village life in China emphasize only the repression of the individual's emotional life under the domination of the patrilineal ideology and androcentric authority. As a result, Chinese villagers are often portrayed as rational and ascetic pragmatists. This picture is, according to my observations of Chinese village life, incomplete if not distorted. Ethnographic data from Xiajia suggest that romantic love is indeed important in village society; romance can be seen in premarital romances, extramarital affairs, and conjugal relations among villagers. Love songs and love stories are popular all over rural China. The place of love in village life is no doubt a subject worth studying in its own right (see Yan 1992b); here I am concerned only with gifts that express love and personal affection between the two sexes.

In village society most instances of romance are marriage related and, thus, three kinds of love gifts can be identified in accordance with their roles in facilitating marriage. In local usage, the first is called *qingwu*, or "love gift." It is exchanged between unmarried villagers of opposite sexes. As explained in Chapter 2, Xiajia is a multisurname community, and village endogamy has been practiced for many generations. The exchange of little gifts between boys and girls existed long before the communist era, but these exchanges have since developed further. In this connection, collectivization and other political campaigns have doubtless made a positive contribution to the growth of romantic love among unmarried youth. The political movements not only provided more opportunities for young people to intermingle both during work and recreation time but also legitimized romantic love at the ideological level. The gifts exchanged are insignificant in terms of monetary value; in many cases, they are the products of the donor's own labor. A beautifully handmade tool, some bird eggs gathered from the grasslands, or a pocket mirror might be the perfect gifts for boys to give to girls. The return gifts from girls may be handmade tobacco leaf containers or food they have saved from their families' better meals. Since the late 1950's, the exchange of these small items, plus mutual assistance in work and other interactions in daily life, has often helped village young people develop good relationships leading to engagement and marriage.

After engagement, the couples continue to see other (if they are in the same village) or visit each other, and some more-or-less ritualized gifts are exchanged in the name of their respective families.

In addition to these gifts, the young people may present personal gifts to each other. The most common gifts from engaged girls to their prospective husbands are handmade shoes and socks, with beautifully embroidered designs that reflect the girl's ingenuity. The boys usually buy their fiancées such gifts as new clothes or cosmetics. Gifts between engaged people embody much more personal affection than those exchanged in family ceremonies and, more importantly, they are individualized in both the symbolic form of the gifts and the ways in which the gifts are presented.

The third subcategory of love gifts is associated with extramarital sexual relations. Extramarital affairs are unacceptable in village society. However, those who enter into extramarital affairs for purely emotional reasons may be tolerated by fellow villagers. There is no particular term for the gifts exchanged between these illicit lovers, but people often use the word *yisi*, which can be roughly translated as "a token of personal feelings." Interestingly enough, as extramarital affairs are sooner or later exposed to the public, gift giving between illicit lovers often becomes the most interesting topic of gossip and jokes. In a 1990 case, a woman who had been involved in an extramarital affair for several months bought a pack of good cigarettes from the village shop. Her motivation was suspected by the shop clerk and other onlookers, and they made a special mark on the bottom of the cigarette pack. As they expected, it was found in the hands of her lover the next day.

Instrumental Gift Giving in Xiajia Village

Xiajia villagers make a distinction between expressive gift giving and instrumental gift giving by referring to the former as *suili* and to the latter as *songli*. The term *song li* literally means "to present the gift" and is used to refer to the direct exchange of gifts for personal favors. According to villagers, if one suddenly presents a gift to someone with whom one has had no previous interaction, one's motives are suspected; this is called *song li*. By contrast, the term *sui li* means literally "to follow others in offering a gift" and is used to describe obligatory, expressive gift giving in ceremonial or routinized situations. The recipient of the gift, of course, is in the donor's prior personal network. In other words, an initial gift-giving action aimed at changing the pattern of previously existing social relations is likely to be considered instrumental by Xiajia villagers. Customary gift giving, which follows conventional rules and maintains existing social relations, is expressive in nature. If we take the active and initiative feature of *songli* as a local standard for instrumental gift giving, three categories of instrumental gifts are identifiable.

Indirect Payments

Whenever a villager needs help in daily life he or she will first turn to those who are within his or her network of personal connections. However, one may be in the situation of asking a favor from someone who is outside the preexisting networks and thus may fall into debt to the helper after gaining the favor. One way to return the favor is to present a gift of thanks, and this is considered an indirect payment by both sides. But, in wishing to continue the newly emerging relationship, one may choose to wait for a suitable occasion, such as the helper's son's wedding, whereby a wedding gift may be offered without the host's invitation; a new relationship may thus be initiated with the host.

Two points are noteworthy here. First, within the boundaries of village society, it is not appropriate to present a gift with ulterior motives before one asks for an immediate favor—that would be regarded as an insult to the recipient. The best way is to express thanks by later gift giving. Moreover, the timing and occasion of making a return gift are crucial factors that differentiate an expressive gift from an instrumental one. Pierre Bourdieu notices that "the temporal structure of gift exchange, which objectivism ignores, is what makes possible the coexistence of two opposing truths, which defines the full truth of the gift" (1977: 5). The practice of Xiajia villagers substantiates Bourdieu's proposition and reveals the importance of the character of the ritualized situation in determining the nature of a given act of gift exchange. While a shorter interval between an initial gift and a return gift may serve as a strategy to turn a newly established and still ambiguous relationship into one that is balanced, a return gift that is delayed and embedded in a ritualized situation may serve to constitute a long-term and expressive relationship.

Liuxu: Flattery Gifts

The term *liuxu* means "to flatter," and obviously the term signifies judgment rather than an objective category of gift-giving activities. Yet in daily life, villagers often comment that some gifts are flattering in nature and some are not. A possible criterion, according to my observations, is a perceived difference of social status between donor and recipient. If one gives gifts to someone in a position of superior status—such as the village cadre—for the ulterior purpose of seeking protection or other personal interests, the giving is considered an act of flattery. To explain this difference, an informant provided me with an example: a young, ambitious villager presented gifts to the leaders in Xiajia village on various occasions for a period of two and a half years. He was later promoted to a cadre-level position. The informant used the word *songli* to describe the gift-giving behavior, and could not help but express his scorn toward the gift giver.

So, in contrast to gifts as indirect payments, which are exchanged between social peers and thus serve to terminate the instrumental relationship between giver and recipient, gifts of flattery are characterized by vertical transactions between inferiors and superiors. The giver's motive for offering such gifts is to continue the instrumental relationship instead of ending it.

Moreover, a flattery gift does not have to be in the form of material goods or cash; rather, it is often presented in terms of personal services.

Shangyou: Gifts of Lubrication

As many scholars have pointed out, due to prolonged economic shortages and the state monopoly over resources during the past several decades, particularistic ties have become one of the determining factors in the Chinese economy. The strategy of going through the back door (*zou houmen*) has become a normal way for people to gain access to resources that are, otherwise, out of their reach (see, e.g., Walder 1986). Consequently, gift giving has been used as the most important weapon to establish networks of particularistic ties and has resulted in the presence of a gift economy alongside the state redistributive system (see M. Yang 1989). These generalizations can also be applied to Xiajia village. Villagers distinguish gift-giving activities of this kind from other types by calling these *shangyou*, literally meaning "to lubricate" the social machine. If the *liuxu* gift may be regarded as a transaction based on flattery, a *shangyou* gift is probably best seen as an act of bribery, in its broadest sense.

According to my informants, the most salient feature of a lubricating gift is that it is given before a favor is asked. No previous basis of personal interaction is needed. As mentioned above, this ordinarily will not occur within the village boundaries. It follows that lubricating gift giving is usually a businesslike, rational, and calculated act, which can lead only to a temporary and purely instrumental relationship between the giver and the recipient. This transaction is described by Xiajia residents as a "one-hammer deal" (*yi chuizi maimai*). The giver of a lubricating gift never feels inferior to the recipient; on the contrary, it is the recipient who owes a return favor to the giver and thus falls into an inferior position.

Villagers do not generally honor most forms of instrumental gift-giving activities. They believe that certain rewards relating to a person's moral standing and overall capabilities should not be exchanged for material objects. For instance, in the eyes of the villagers, college admission or career promotions should be based on merit, quality, and capabilities, not on the exchange of lubricating gifts. A young man in Xiajia, who gained admission to college by offering instrumental gifts, was despised by many villagers, and his family was considered disgraceful by other villagers. I heard similar comments concerning a cadre who climbed up the bureaucratic ladder by offering a cow as a gift to his superior. In such cases, the recipients are also the target of public criticism. The most common accusation for this type of instrumental gift giving is that "so-and-so has no conscience" (*mei liangxin*). Here, the term "conscience," *liangxin*, refers to the fundamental self-constraint that one should possess.

In contrast, commodity exchange does not involve moral considerations, so it is perfectly understandable, and under some circumstances even admirable, to gain access to scarce goods through instrumental gift giving. It is quite acceptable to go through the back door to buy state-controlled industrial products, such as cement, iron frames (for house construction), and logs. Villagers often gain the right to purchase such items only after offering gifts to the people in charge of distribution. This kind of give-and-take is regarded as trade, and lubricating gifts are seen as the necessary extra fees.

Gifts of lubrication can be found at both the collective and the individual level. Sometimes it is necessary to go through the back door for the public interest of the entire community. Village cadres and appointed individuals with impressive personal connections give gifts from public funds on behalf of the village as a whole. A typical example was the occasion of the installation of electricity in Xiajia during the late 1960's. Owing to economic constraints at that time, the local government assumed responsibility only for installing the main electric cables along the local highways. Villages had to work out special deals in order to receive the electricity. Supplies were extremely limited—even lightbulbs were not available to the villagers because they did not have urban registration cards. Thus a special team of Xiajia residents was organized to explore all possible human resources, namely, the back door. For instance, the village cadres, through two intermediate persons, tried to locate the government official who had been in charge of land reform in Xiajia during the late 1940's. Meanwhile, every villager was mobilized to find urban connections that might be helpful in obtaining electrical supplies, and gifts in various forms were given out in an attempt to build up networks.

As a matter of fact, I myself was one of the gifts exchanged during the battle for electrical installation. In 1971, I went to Heilongjiang from a village in Shandong province in the hope that I could find a place that might provide me with a means to survive during a period of severe food shortages. While I was wandering from one place to another performing various temporary jobs, the Xiajia electricity team was introduced to my cousin, who was a salesman for a state-owned factory in Ha'erbin city. My cousin offered to sell electric wiring and bulbs to Xiajia. As a reciprocal favor, I was allowed to move into the village, which at that time was in a relatively prosperous area.

Apart from village-level, strategic gift giving, lubricating gifts may also be useful when individual villagers leave the community to make purchases, to do business, or to handle personal problems such as hospitalizations. Xiajia villagers usually do not have psychological difficulties in adopting the strategy of instrumental gift giving outside their own community, though it is not acceptable within the village. This different attitude is rooted in the villagers' perceptions of in-group and out-group persons. With the former, one should cultivate and maintain long-term, moral relations through expressive gift-giving activities; while with strangers or outsiders with whom one is unfamiliar, one cannot possibly build any basis for long-term interpersonal relationships. Given the instrumental nature of transactions outside one's community, it is also unnecessary to worry about expressive gift giving. Instrumental gift giving thus serves as the best means for villagers to pursue their own personal interests. All kinds of gifts may be offered to approach targeted resource-controllers. Before the introduction of a market economy, the most common gifts offered by villagers were agricultural products that were under strict state control, such as fine grains, pork, fish, and cooking oil. Because almost everything can now be purchased on the free market, cash has become the universally acceptable gift for instrumental purposes. Villagers must first convert their products into cash and then try to find a way to present the cash gift to the controller of the desired resources.

The interesting feature of instrumental gift exchange in this context is that one cannot simply present the gift to the targeted person—it would be rejected as unacceptable bribery. Instead, the gift must be transmitted through an existing network of personal connections, of acquaintances (see M. Yang 1989; Qiao 1988). For instance, an informant once had trouble purchasing steel frames for house construction. He presented gifts to the state official in charge of the store for construction supplies. To his surprise, the official turned him down and even became angry with him. Later he was informed by some experienced villagers that it was embarrassing for the official to accept a gift from an ordinary villager and that he should have had someone who knew the official transfer the gift for him. Eventually, he achieved his goal of purchasing iron frames, but he never got the chance to see precisely how his gift worked, because it was conveyed through two links of middlemen, both of whom demanded small commissions for their services.

Finding a suitable intermediary for instrumental gift giving is difficult for Xiajia residents, since their lives are normally confined

within the village boundaries. In most cases, they first have to discover a path to the back door through their contacts within the village, or at least from social networks built up by fellow villagers. In
other words, short-term, instrumental gift giving cannot be accom-
plished without the initial support of long-term relations, constructed through years of expressive gift giving (the key to developing social networks). Therefore, in the context of village life, the
periodic need to form instrumental relationships actually reinforces
the cultivation of noninstrumental relations.

In conclusion, gift-giving relations in Xiajia village can be classified into 21 categories, in accordance with emic conceptions. From
an economic perspective, these 21 kinds of gifts include transactions
ranging from what Malinowski calls "pure gifts" to indirect payments (see Malinowski 1984: 177–90). Why are there so many gift-
giving activities? How much do these gifts affect both the economic
as well as the social life of the villagers? More importantly, why do
villagers want to participate in such an elaborate system of gift exchange? Finally, what do the patterns of gift exchange tell us about
the structure of social relations in Xiajia? This effort to establish a
classification system has raised more questions than it has answered;
but I will attempt to respond to them in the chapters that follow.

FOUR

The Gift Economy and
Guanxi Networks

Among those acquainted with Chinese society, few would disagree
that *guanxi* is a complex yet centrally important concept for understanding interpersonal relations in China. In common usage, *guanxi*
can be translated into English as "relations," "relationship," "significance," or "affecting." However, it is also widely regarded as a
social phenomenon, which has been called "personal connections,"
"social networks," or "particularistic ties." As Jian Qiao correctly
points out, none of these translations can fully grasp the rich meaning of *guanxi* (1988: 119).[1] In order to explore the full range of its
meanings in village life, hereafter I will use the term *guanxi* rather
than the translations discussed above.

Difficulties do not derive only from translation; a gap exists between the emic perception and etic interpretations of *guanxi*. Xiajia
residents are morally as well as economically involved with and
bound by exchange networks that reproduce themselves through the
endless process of gift giving. In conversation, villagers refer to their
exchange networks within the indigenous concept of *guanxi*, and

functionally they perceive of their *guanxi* networks as the objective foundation of the society in which they live.

Guanxi in Western scholarly accounts, however, has been mostly treated as the outcome of rational calculation by individuals in the pursuit of personal interests and has been interpreted as "instrumental-personal ties" (Walder 1986: 6–7), "a somewhat casual and nonpermanent alliance" (Oi 1989: 131), or "particularistic ties" (Jacobs 1979: 238). Consequently, gift giving can be seen as the most crucial strategy to establish instrumental *guanxi* networks at the level of personal interactions (M. Yang 1989: 35–36). *Guanxi*, according to these studies, is a process characterized by instrumentality and individual manipulation, and thus the term itself carries a negative meaning (see Gold 1984: 660, n. 18).

Keeping the differences between the emic and etic views in mind, in this chapter I will focus on the process of *guanxi* cultivation expressed in gift-giving dynamics in everyday life, leaving the structural analysis of *guanxi* to the next chapter. I begin with the villagers' expenditures for gift exchange and then describe the moral constraints that obligate villagers to participate in the gift economy and to cultivate *guanxi* networks. I then examine the villagers' reliance on *guanxi* networks during social and economic crises, which will help us to understand better the significance of gift exchange in village life.

Villagers' Expenditures for Gift Giving

In the preceding chapter, I described more than twenty institutionalized situations in Xiajia village where social life is preoccupied with gift-giving activities. Shortly after beginning my systematic investigation in the early spring of 1991, I had an opportunity to observe the impact of gift giving on the economic life of the villagers.

One morning when I visited Mr. Huang, an old friend of mine, I found him in an embarrassing situation—trying to explain to a visiting relative the reason why he had failed to repay him a loan on time. As I have known both Huang and his relative for many years, my visit did not stop their chatting. To emphasize his difficulty and to obtain additional support, Huang told me that he had attended many ceremonies in 1991 requiring the offering of gifts and had borrowed money from his relative when he was short of cash. He recalled that during the first lunar month he had received three invitations for ceremonies on the same day. Realizing that none of the three could be ignored, he had to attend the most important one (the wedding of his sister's son) himself, while delegating his two sons to go to the other two events. Seventy yuan in total were spent on that single day, and that placed Huang in debt when the next invitation arrived.

Huang, age 65 in 1991, is an ordinary farmer with six daughters and two sons. As his sons are younger than his daughters, Huang and his wife have had to struggle with an unbalanced ratio of hands to mouths for many years, and thus, until recently, their economic situation was below average. When I lived in the village during the 1970's, Huang had been known as one of the local "daughter-sellers": he was stingy in providing dowries for his daughters because of his economic difficulties. There were also negative comments about Huang's participation in gift-exchange activities, for he often failed to attend ceremonies in an attempt to avoid the giving of gifts. Consequently, Huang had fewer friends and a much smaller kindred web during that period.

It is very interesting to note, therefore, that Huang gave so many gifts within the first two months of 1991 and did not mind borrowing money to attend the ceremonies. When I asked how much he had spent on gift-giving activities in a year, he told me 400 to 500 yuan. "This was not the first time I borrowed money for gifts. Don't you know the popular saying? *Suili*[2] is as urgent as putting out a fire. It can't wait. A man cannot have a firm position in front of others if he fails to follow the rules of gift giving and escapes his duties."

I was really surprised by Huang's changed behavior, especially his belief about the necessity of gift exchange. In a subsequent survey, I paid special attention to the villagers' accounts of their expenditures for gift exchange and their comments on the behavior of others as well. According to my interviews and a questionnaire survey,[3] expenditures for gift giving constituted a significant portion of Xiajia villagers' annual cash consumption. As shown in Table 1 below, in 1990, 52 percent of Xiajia villagers spent more than 500 yuan on gift-giving activities, and 31 percent spent from 300 to 500 yuan. The

TABLE I

Expenditures for Gift Giving in 1990, Xiajia Village

Amount	No. of households	Percentage of total
< 300 yuan	16	17%
301–500 yuan	29	31
501–700 yuan	29	31
701–900 yuan	9	10
> 900 yuan	10	11
TOTAL	93	100%

most generous gift giver was the village party secretary, who had kept notes of all his expenses and found that he spent 2,650 yuan in one year.[4] Given that the average cash income per household in 1990 was around 2,500 yuan, an expenditure of 500 yuan means that in many families, 20 percent of the household net income was used for gift exchange. The term "gift economy" is indeed not metaphorical when applied to Xiajia village.

Understandably, expenditure on gifts varies according to the economic conditions and demographic structure of each household. The first group in Table 1 comprises mostly young couples and poor families. All the households that spent more than 500 yuan on gifts are above the average economic level. Given income disparities between rich and poor, the actual proportion of money spent on gift giving in poor families tends to be greater than that in rich families. Among the ten households that spent more than 900 yuan on gifts, six are the richest households in Xiajia, and the remaining four are much wealthier than average. In a survey conducted in 1989, I discovered that the net per capita income for the top ten households in 1988 was more than 700 yuan, and the poorest households earned less than 300 yuan (see Yan 1992a: 9, n. 17). In 1990, these two figures increased to 850 and 400 yuan respectively, based on my follow-up survey on changes in economic conditions. The 1990 census shows that the average household in Xiajia village consists of four to five (4.28) people. In the richest households, 10 to 15 percent of the annual family income was used for gift-giving activities; for those who spent from 700 to 900 yuan, the proportion of gift-giving expenses was even greater (20 percent), since their annual income was much less than that of the top ten households. In other words, the burden of gift giving appears to be greater for the poor than for the rich. According to my informants, expenditures on gifts have increased rapidly during the last decade, especially since decollectivization in 1984. This is due to several factors. First, new rituals emerged in the 1980's, such as the compensatory ritual for female sterilization and abortion (discussed in Chapter 3), which presented new demands for gifts. Second, gifts tend to cost more. Gift lists from the early 1970's reveal the average gift value to be 2 to 5 yuan, with the lowest 0.5 yuan. These figures have doubled, sometimes tripled, during the 1980's, and the average gift in 1990 was 10 yuan. Third, inflation is a contributing factor; 5 yuan could hardly buy anything valuable in the late 1980's, and thus people had to spend more for gifts for important rituals, such as weddings. Finally, the recent increase in rural income is also related to increased gift-giving expenses, because people tend to be more generous as their own standard of living has improved.

Mr. Wang's personal accounting book provides an invaluable, concrete example of the relation between gift expenditures and domestic economic management among the villagers. At the age of 39, Wang is widely regarded as one of the most organized and hardworking men in the village. When he and his wife established their conjugal family in 1976, their total income was 259.37 yuan. After paying 127.32 yuan to the production team for grain and other subsistence items such as cooking fuel, they were left with only 132.05 yuan for all other expenses for the year. By 1991, after fifteen years of hard work and thrift, their economic situation had improved to above the village average. The most intriguing part of Wang's story is that, since 1976, Wang had kept notes on all his income and expenses in an effort to plan his family budget well. Wang generously allowed me to transcribe the whole accounting book. Table 2 summarizes the economic transactions in the family over seven years.

It should be pointed out that the costs for daily subsistence items such as food and cooking fuel are not included in Wang's accounting book, because he, like most Chinese villagers, regards only commodities bought with cash as expenses. Since decollectivization,

TABLE 2

Records of Economic Transactions in Wang's Family, 1984–90

(RMB yuan)

Year	Annual cash income	Expenses for consumer goods	Investments for agricultural production	Medical costs & education fees	Gift-giving expenses	Annual surplus
1984	1,250.00	290.65	193.77	12.53	48.00	705.05
1985	1,535.10	410.83	101.70	11.86	69.00	941.71
1986	1,605.25	378.07	147.40	129.85	216.00	733.93
1987	1,930.50	597.52	247.70	47.08	223.00	815.20
1988	2,383.02	725.33	334.60	56.50	250.00	1,016.59
1989	2,820.35	894.52	296.25	70.10	270.00	1,289.48
1990	3,067.00	625.79	389.00	72.30	344.00	1,635.91

grain and cooking fuel have been produced by the villagers themselves, and so they are not included in a review of consumption
costs. By the same token, consumed grain and other subsistence
items are also not considered income. Thus the living expenses in
Table 2 refer only to such commodities as clothes. Education fees are
for his two children. It should also be noted that, unlike workers,
farmers usually receive most of their cash income after they sell their
surplus grain at the end of the year. The amount that appears in the
last column in Table 2 must be saved for expenses in the coming year.

I selected only the records since 1984 because Wang did not actively participate in gift giving until 1986, ten years after he and his
wife established their own household. Wang told me that when he
started his own household in 1976, he was poor and unable to participate in many gift-giving activities. Moreover, as the head of a
new household, he did not have many social connections, except for
a few friends and his in-laws and he did not need to host any family
ceremonies. When his children were growing up, however, he and
his wife felt it was necessary to participate more actively; they
needed a larger network of both economic and social support as their
children approached marriage age and for the hosting of such family
ceremonies as betrothal, wedding, and house construction. Wang's
case is typical for young couples just establishing their own households: they usually have the smallest exchange networks and avoid

involvement in the endless process of gift exchange until their children are teenagers. In other words, patterns of gift giving are related to the developmental cycle of family organization. Older couples tend to withdraw from gift exchange after all their children have established their own families, which means that they have fulfilled most of their obligations in gift giving and family ceremonies.

Since 1986 Wang's expenditures for gifts have consistently been at least 10 percent of his annual income and more than 20 percent of his family consumption expenses. As income has increased, the Wang family has had to spend more on gifts. By comparing column 4 with column 6 in Table 2, we can see that the Wang family spent almost the same amount on gift giving as it did on agricultural production, which included the costs for purchasing crop seeds, chemical fertilizer, pesticide, and so on.

As indicated above, Wang and his wife are well known for their exceptional ability to control the family budget and to plan their expenses. Wang has actually tried hard to minimize the costs of gift giving, because he personally does not like the custom. In local terms, young couples just entering into the game of gift exchange are called *xiaohu*, meaning small households, while those who have children of or close to marriage age, and thus are at the peak of performing various rituals, are called *dahu*, namely, large families. When we consider that small families like Wang's have to spend so much on gift giving, the central importance of gift transactions in everyday life for the majority of Xiajia families, and especially for large families, is apparent.

Obligatory Gift Giving and the Cultivation of Guanxi

Even though I learned all these facts and collected the statistical data in the early stage of my fieldwork, I was still puzzled over the rationale of the villagers who spent 10 to 20 percent of their income on gift giving. After attending a number of ceremonies and actually participating in gift exchange on several occasions, however, I began to understand the social and moral forces that drove the villagers to compete as generous gift givers. A birthday celebration in Mr. Liu's family was a ritualized situation from which I learned about the obligations of giving and receiving—a classic theme in anthropological analyses of gift exchange.

While I was chatting with several village friends in the village office, a boy brought in the news that Liu was going to host a celebration for his father's seventy-first birthday. The boy said that he saw Liu's wife purchasing food in the village shop and that Liu was preparing an accounting table for the recording of the gifts. The first thought that occurred to me was to observe the reaction of my friends, because ever since I came to the village I had heard many negative comments about Liu's previous celebrations for his father's birthday.

According to some informants, Liu had hosted a birthday ritual every year since 1986, and many suspected that Liu's motivation was to claim return gifts. Some people even suggested that Liu was utilizing the birthday of his aged father to make money. Interestingly, the Liu family always complained that they were forced by the villagers' good wishes to perform the rite. According to their version of the story, after the ceremony for their father's sixty-sixth birthday, they did not want to host the ritual anymore. Yet the presence of the guests and their gifts forced them against their own will to hold ceremonies in the following years.

As I expected, the news produced criticism immediately. Nevertheless, all the villagers in the room began to plan to attend the ceremony. My question was: Why did they have to participate in this ceremony since they did not want to offer gifts? One of my key informants explained it to me this way:

If I had not heard the news, I could probably have let it pass and save some money. But since I already know it, I have no choice but to go there and offer my gift to the Liu family. I will feel uncomfortable if I deliberately escape this ceremony just for the sake of saving money. Living in the same village, we run into each other almost every day. How shall I face Liu tomorrow if I miss the ceremony today? How could I maintain a good image in my *guanxi*? Red flowers need the support of green leaves. If you want to be somebody, you need friends, need to be involved in situations like this one. That is how *guanxi* works.

I asked him about how uncomfortable he would feel if he escaped the ceremony. He thought for a while and then said simply, "I would feel shamed." Another villager added that nonparticipation "feels like you are caught on the spot while you are stealing something from someone you know very well." A third man in the room told me that from childhood he had learned that one could repudiate a gambling debt but could never forsake responsibility for gift giving. With a reputation for refusing the obligation to give gifts, one would lose the trust of the village community and become isolated without a proper *guanxi* network.

The interesting point here is that although these villagers did not receive any invitations (written or oral) from the Liu family, all of them felt social pressure to attend the ceremony and offer gifts. Why didn't they simply pretend not to hear anything about the event and thus avoid the obligatory gift giving that they complained about? Here it is important to note that, as I discussed in Chapter 3, one's intentionality is considered very important for expressive gift giving within the village community. By definition, expressive gifts are meant to express one's moral or emotional concerns, and the best way to do so is to offer the gift without waiting for the invitation from the host. From the host's point of view, the news of a family ritual performance spreads quickly within the community, so there is no need to send invitations. As in the present case, the boy's stopping by in the village office brought the news to everyone in the room, and this was as good as a formal invitation from the host himself. Of course, it is totally up to the individual whether or not to offer a gift; but not to attend will signal the person's intention of not keeping (or creating, if for the first time) a good relationship with the host. As indicated in Chapter 3, the local custom of presenting make-up gifts precludes the excuse that one simply has not heard any news of the event—if one has the intention to offer the gift he or she can do it later.

Therefore, despite all the complaints, everyone in the room that morning eventually went to Liu's house without waiting for any kind of invitation. Each presented either a ten-yuan monetary gift or a material gift of equivalent value, and naturally they were warmly received by the Liu family and joined the others at the banquet. A total of 129 guests attended the ritual, and according to the gift-list record, Liu received 1,470 yuan in cash, plus some material gifts of wine, canned food, fruits, and cookies.

Afterward both Liu and his wife came to me to explain that they had not intended to hold the ritual until so many people stopped by with gifts. They felt they actually had been forced to hold the ritual. Some of Liu's close relatives and friends testified to me that Liu was telling the truth. They admitted that, at the beginning, they had convinced Liu to have a small ceremony for his father's birthday, which would provide them an opportunity to get together and increase good feelings amongst them. However, many unexpected guests stopped by to celebrate the birthday without waiting for Liu's invitation, and an accounting table had to be set up for the recording of the gifts. Upon checking further with different sources, I also found what Liu said to be true. The original small birthday party organized by Liu's friends indeed was upgraded to a large public ceremony by unexpected guests, who appeared to be driven by a compelling yet invisible force—to voluntarily fulfill their obligations in gift giving within their exchange networks.

Recognizing my strong interest in his case, Liu showed me both his personal record of gift-giving expenditures and the gift list for his father's birthday celebration and generously allowed me to transcribe the two documents. To highlight the obligatory aspects of gift giving, I have put Liu's personal record of outgoing gifts in Table 3. According to this written record, he spent more than 520 yuan in the first half of the year, and the busy season for gift giving was yet to come, since engagement rituals and weddings are mostly performed after the autumn harvest. Moreover, gift expenses for visiting relatives during the lunar New Year period (more than 200 yuan) were not included in the record. Liu told me, "Actually, some of the guests came because I had given them gifts before this ritual. You can see it from my record. We just exchange things."

The document in Table 3 reveals several interesting points. First, 23 out of the 28 people in this record attended Liu's father's birthday party and gave return gifts. The remaining people had specific reasons for not attending. For instance, No. 6 lived in the county seat far from Xiajia village and obviously did not hear about the unexpected performance of the ritual. No. 19 was a local cadre in the township government who, because of his special status, was not expected to show up.[5] Both No. 27 and 28 received Liu's gifts after Liu's father's birthday. The only person who failed to make a return

TABLE 3

Liu's Record of Outgoing Gifts, Jan.–June 1991

Recipient's relationship to Liu	Gift-giving occasion	Value (RMB yuan)
1. Sister's husband	daughter's wedding	100
2. Wife's mother's cousin	son's wedding	10
3. Wife's patrilineal cousin	son's wedding	10
4. Sister's husband's brother	daughter's wedding	10
5. Wife's cousin's husband	wife's sterilization	20
6. Brother's wife's brother[a]	mother's funeral	20
7. Mother's sister's son[a]	daughter's wedding	20
8. Father's sister's son	father's funeral	10
9. Mother's sister's husband	son's wedding	20
10. Mother's fictive sister's son	son's engagement	30
11. Mother's fictive sister's son	son's engagement	10
12. Close friend	son's wedding	40
13. Friend	daughter's wedding	20
14. Friend	son's engagement	10
15. Fellow villager	house construction	10
16. Friend	house construction	20
17. Fellow villager	house construction	10
18. Fellow villager	father's funeral	10
19. Friend[a]	house construction	20
20. Friend	wife's sterilization	20
21. Friend and neighbor	wife's sterilization	20
22. Fellow villager	wife's sterilization	10
23. Friend	wife's sterilization	20
24. Fellow villager	wife's sterilization	10
25. Fellow villager	wife's sterilization	10
26. Fellow villager	wife's sterilization	10
27. Fellow villager[a]	wife's sterilization	10
28. Fellow villager[a]	wife's sterilization	10
TOTAL		520

[a] Those who did not attend Liu's father's birthday celebration to give a return gift.

gift for no obvious reason was Liu's matrilateral cousin (No. 7, his mother's sister's son), which made Liu wonder whether something was wrong with their mutual relationship. According to Liu, it was still too early to predict anything. However, if Liu's cousin does not make any positive gesture, such as an explanation or a make-up gift, or if Liu decides to respond in a negative way by not offering a gift to his cousin in a ritual context, then it is very likely that the relationship between them will be terminated. Obviously, Liu's record of outgoing gifts serves as a credit list for incoming gifts, while his list of incoming gifts (*lidan*) from the birthday celebration will become the debits catalog for which he will have to compensate.

It is also noteworthy that return gifts are somewhat larger than the previously received gifts. For example, Liu offered a gift of 30 yuan to his fictive matrilateral cousin (No. 10) in March when the latter's son became engaged. Three months later, the cousin gave 40 yuan as the return gift for Liu's father's birthday celebration. A similar case is found with Liu's close friend, No. 12. He received 40 yuan from Liu in early February for his son's wedding; at the birthday celebration he presented Liu with 50 yuan.

The list of gift recipients in Table 3 also shows that kinship ties, especially agnatic ties, are not as important as friendship ties in Liu's network of personal connections. This is a common feature of the network structure in Xiajia village, and I will return to this point in the next chapter.

When interpersonal relations go awry, the existing pattern of gift exchange may be affected; however, there are many ways to adjust one's gift-giving obligations in response to changed personal relationships. Retreating from the exchange network is the simplest strategy but definitely not the most appropriate. More commonly villagers continue gift giving, while finding a way to show their discontent, as in the case below.

During an evening in mid-July 1991, a wedding invitation from the vice chairman of the local government, Mr. Gao, was brought to Mr. Li, one of my best friends in Xiajia. The unexpected invitation immediately became the central topic of conversation and led to an evening-long discussion among Li, his wife, and myself. According to my past experience, a discussion of this kind usually focused on the proper value of the gift and who would present it. Then the conversation would change to recalling memorable things that occurred during previous interactions between the two parties. To my surprise, that evening the first question raised was whether the family should in fact attend the wedding, and Li suggested not. Because I knew Li and Gao were friends when I was living in Xiajia fifteen years ago, this struck me as odd, so I inquired about the relationship between the two families. Li's wife told me that although there were no longer good feelings between the families, the gift-giving relationship continued. The last transaction occurred in 1983, when Gao attended the Lis' first son's wedding and gave a ten-yuan gift. So their return gift should have been about twenty yuan.

Li explained that because Gao had hurt him emotionally, he wanted to send Gao a message by not making a return gift. According to Li, in early spring 1988, Li had been forced to resign from village office after a direct confrontation with a villager. He thereafter suffered from emotional depression. A few months later when he hosted a solemn wedding for his second son, many people, including the cadres of the local government, attended the ceremony to show their sympathy and respect for Li. But Gao did not come during the wedding, nor did he appear in the following days. Li said Gao's absence was a snobbish reaction to Li's recent fall from power, something he felt definitely should not occur between friends. Li stressed that Gao's absence grieved him for a long time, because he previously had regarded Gao as one of his few trustworthy friends in the local government. "I am not trying to get even," said Li, "because there is a huge gap in social status between Gao and me now. I just hate to continue having a gift relationship with him and I want him to know it."

Li's wife agreed with Li's views, but disagreed with his plan. She argued that Gao had acted so disgracefully because he was not a good person. "But we are not that kind of people and we will never do that kind of thing. I will feel extremely uncomfortable if I fail to return the gift. Besides, not everyone in Xiajia knows of Gao's wrongdoing, and not everyone understands your feelings either. They might think you are just too stingy to give a gift, or they may see us as people who do not know how to maintain *guanxi* with friends."

Finally, the case was resolved in a sophisticated way. Li did not attend the wedding, and his wife, on his behalf, asked someone to take ten yuan as a gift to Gao. During the day of the ceremony, Li's wife went to the natal family of Gao's daughter-in-law and presented twenty yuan as a gift for their daughter's wedding. Interestingly enough, the family she visited lived just in front of Gao's house, so she was making a symbolic protest by passing the setting of Gao's ritual in front of many eyes. Because of her action, everyone understood that social distance and an emotional dispute prevented her from personally presenting the ten-yuan gift to Gao. Li's wife both observed the rule of gift giving, meeting her obligation to return a gift, and expressed her discontent and anger to the recipient.

This story shows us that a long-term relationship must be maintained carefully through expressive gift giving by both parties involved, and when the mutual relationship is interrupted or damaged, one has to remedy it by making an extra effort. Gao's absence at Li's second son's wedding damaged the friendship between Gao and Li, and his failure to appear in the following days further broke the relationship. Although Gao sent a formal invitation to Li, years later, in the hope of reviving the relationship, he did not make any extra effort. Gao's act, of course, may have had something to do with his higher status in comparison with Li, because a superior's invitation itself would be regarded by many people as a valuable resource in network building. Contrary to Gao's expectations, however, the Li couple did not give special weight to Gao's status and they thought a perfunctory invitation was not good enough for a broken relationship. Clearly, what bothered Li and his wife was the lack of proper behavior in gift giving as well as *guanxi* cultivation. Although they recognized Gao's higher social status and power, they did not put utilitarian considerations ahead of moral and emotional concerns. From a purely instrumental point of view, their decision was not rational, because by protesting, they forfeited both their money and their personal relationship with Gao. Viewed from the perspective of a moral economy, however, their conduct is perfectly reasonable, because they ended an undesirable relationship while fulfilling their obligations in terms of a balanced return gift. They remained at a moral advantage and set Gao at a disadvantage. Of course, they did not act only by instinct or by moral norms; instead, they took into consideration possible public reactions and carefully planned their battle. Clearly, rational calculation also played a role in their decision, albeit in a complementary form.

We can draw two inferences from the above-mentioned cases. First, at the behavioral level, the obligations to give and receive overrule individual opinions and attitudes toward a given situation of gift exchange. We can see that gift transactions constitute a system of moral economy, where moral principles often surpass economic considerations, as when Huang borrowed money to present gifts. A custom such as gift exchange may exert an independent influence after it enters into one's social life. This was the case for Liu, where both the host and guests were involuntarily involved in gift exchange.

Second, on a functional level, the obligatory giving and receiving provide villagers with a fundamental means of cultivating, maintaining, and expanding their *guanxi* networks. According to James Scott, "The narrowness of the peasant's economic margin leads him to choose techniques that are safe even if they give away something in average yield. Socially as well, the peasant in principle seeks to transfer as much of his economic risk as possible to other institutions—to give income as ransom for safety" (1976: 35). The costly participation in gift exchange we find in Xiajia can be understood as the villagers' efforts to transfer economic risk to and to seek social support from an accessible institution: *guanxi* networks.

Gift Giving and Guanxi Networks in Action

As I indicated in the beginning of this chapter, early scholarly accounts of *guanxi* networks in Chinese society focused primarily on the individual actor's strategies to manipulate interpersonal relations in the pursuit of personal interest (e.g., Jacobs 1979). The cultivation of *guanxi* is interpreted as a power game (Hwang 1987), or as an art of making personal connections (M. Yang 1989, 1994). The question arises here: Is it appropriate to conceive of gift giving and network building as merely a power game played out by individuals and families for desired resources? Even if the pursuit of personal interest does dominate the motives, it is still worth determining how the gift economy plays this role and how people exchange resources through the mechanism of personal networks. The Xiajia case, however, demonstrates that the cultivation of personal networks in village society is both a power game and a life-style; *guanxi* involves not only instrumentality and rational calculation, but also sociability, morality, intentionality, and personal affection. The rich meaning of *guanxi* for Xiajia villagers is best manifested by its economic, political, and social functions.

Economic Function

Economically, Xiajia residents rely heavily on their *guanxi* networks for agricultural production and for personal financing and, since decollectivization, for mutual assistance and cooperation in various forms. Unlike in the collectives, where all the villagers had to cooperate with one another in a highly organized way under the guidance of the cadres, in Xiajia now villagers must deal independently with all kinds of problems of agricultural production, from purchasing seeds before the spring plowing to selling grain after the autumn harvest. According to my informants, mutual assistance is particularly important at six crucial, labor-intensive periods during the agricultural busy seasons: spring plowing, planting, fertilizing during the summer, cutting the maize (the main local crop), removing corncobs by hand during the harvest, and threshing. All these jobs demand a division of labor and efficiency, because they must be completed in a limited time period. There are two forms of mutual assistance. An immediate exchange of labor between two families locally is called *huangong*, literally "to exchange laborers." Those who lack capable hands for farming must seek favors from their relatives and friends, later looking for an appropriate opportunity to repay the helpers. This is called *qiu banggong* (literally "to ask for help").

In addition to these regular occasions for mutual assistance, which apply to almost everyone, larger-scale cooperation is needed if one wants to engage in business or change from farming maize to cash crops. For instance, growing watermelon requires many extra hands during the planting and harvesting seasons. When making such plans, one must determine how many people can be depended on to help during these critical periods. House construction also requires the contribution of free labor: at least 100 man-days are commonly needed from volunteer helpers. This sometimes presents great difficulties for those who do not have many personal connections. Recently, contracting work to professional construction teams has become a good solution to the problem of house building, but it applies only to the main frame of the house; there is still a lot of other work to be completed.

From an economic point of view, mutual assistance is by no

means cost free for the host family. It actually costs no less than hiring paid laborers. The host family must provide good food, alcohol, and cigarettes, and the host has no control over the quality of the work or the length of time for completion, since the assistance is from friends rather than from employees. Moreover, the quality of the meals and drinks must be constantly upgraded, because host families want to treat their helpers better each time in an attempt to show gratitude. This, in turn, increases the cost of mutual assistance.

Despite the considerable costs of *qiu banggong*, it remains the socially acceptable way to get things done. My informants insisted that it would be improper and unthinkable to hire outsiders to work when they could seek help from relatives and friends. Some people told me that in the village, money alone could not do everything, and "this distinguishes us from urban people who count on nothing but money." However, there are some villagers who prefer the commercialized way of seeking assistance, but who must follow the community rules because they live in the village. As one young man explained to me, it would be embarrassing if a person had to hire workers to do traditionally unpaid tasks, because it would tell the world that he had no face in the village and his *guanxi* was near to zero. Furthermore, most people would not work merely for the payment of several yuan. They preferred to work for free and claim credit for personal favors later when they needed help in similar situations. In a close-knit village society, personal networks are, in many cases, more valuable than goods or money, and the demand for mutual assistance reinforces the custom of gift giving and *guanxi* network cultivation.

The second type of economic activities dependent on *guanxi* networks is personal financing. Until recently no private banks existed in socialist China, and all banking resources were under the tight control of the government. Yet financial aid is very important to villagers, especially when they must host an important ceremony or expand investment in production. Since few villagers can acquire state loans from the local state bank or credit union, they must depend on the traditional system of credits and loans—that is, getting financial aid through networks of personal connections. The Xiajia residents distinguish between two types of private loans. Borrowing money is called *jieqian*, and no interest is charged no matter the length of the loan. If interest is charged, it is called *taiqian*, and the annual interest rate varies from 10 percent to 50 percent. The close relationship between the lender and the borrower provides a moral basis for the financial transaction. For loans with interest, personal connections also are needed. All transactions depend on the existing mutual trust between lenders and borrowers; otherwise, a middle-man is responsible for bridging the distance between the two sides and for establishing mutual trust and moral obligation between them. The *guanxi* network and its moral values serve as the basis for this local unofficial banking system.

Social Support Function: The Famine Case

Gift giving and *guanxi* networks also serve as a system of social support, which may help individual villagers survive life crises in two ways: (1) by providing basic needs such as food and shelter in case of personal emergencies; and (2) by providing social support during critical periods. A good example of the former is the Xiajia villagers' experience of the famine from 1959 to 1961.

Rural populations in China have suffered from periodic famines for many centuries (see, e.g., Mallory 1926), and the associated suffering is so much a part of social life that institutions, such as public and lineage granaries, have been established traditionally to cope with such periodic crises (see Wong and Will 1991). Family and kinship organizations also have long served as important institutions for coping with famine and other social stresses (see Freedman 1966; Skinner 1971). In the past, social exchange both within and between communities has always been critical for survival during famine periods (see Li 1982). By the late 1950's, these traditional institutions had been destroyed by the radical efforts of socialist reconstruction, especially the Great Leap Forward. As a consequence, during the famine of 1959–61, millions died of starvation (Ashton et al. 1984: 614–30; Bernstein 1984: 350–69; Ding 1989: 109–16; Jowett 1987; and MacFarquhar 1983).[6]

Like rural residents all over China, Xiajia villagers experienced the most radical social changes in their life from 1958 to 1960. Xiajia was hit by the famine more severely than other neighboring communities because, unfortunately, it had been designated a model village during the Great Leap campaign as a result of the radicalism of the village party secretary. This man followed every radical policy to revolutionize the village and forced the villagers to contribute almost all their grain products to the state in order to fulfill the high procurement quota. His work was so much appreciated by his superiors that he was selected in 1959 to attend the National Day ceremony in Beijing as one of the delegates from the grassroots level. His personal glory meant disaster for the Xiajia villagers—they suffered from hunger even while their leader was boasting in Beijing.

According to my informants, Xiajia was the first village in the area to run out of grain in early winter of 1959. Moreover, because all privately owned grain, together with other property, had been collectivized during the communization campaign, the Xiajia residents immediately began to experience hunger when the collectives ran out of grain, and this continued for several weeks until state relief arrived. It was at this crucial period that the networks of personal connections manifested their most significant role of social support. Villagers who had good relations with relatives or friends in other communities benefitted from their *guanxi* networks, while those who did not have such human resources suffered much more hunger and even starvation.

Mr. Guo recalled that his younger sister fainted several times owing to food deprivation and he too fell seriously ill during the famine. However, his family did not suffer as much as many others, because his elder sister, who had married into a village four miles north of Xiajia, gave them a great deal of help. Despite a similar threat of famine, his sister's family lent Guo's family 180 *jin* of grain. Guo said: "I still remember clearly the evening my sister's husband came to our house and carried a sack of maize on his bicycle. That saved our whole family." In another case, a villager hid some grain in his home before the famine year, and when the village militia searched for grain from home to home, he was able to protect his grain stock because of his friendship with the head of the militia. That saved his family from hunger for half a year. In my survey in 1991, I collected more than twenty cases where informants suffered less by being able to resort to help via their *guanxi* networks outside Xiajia village and four cases in which grain was hidden successfully thanks to personal connections between grain owners and the village cadres or militia. There is no doubt that *guanxi* networks served a crucial role in helping the families cope with the famine.

In sharp contrast, those who did not have *guanxi* networks outside the village suffered more from hunger, and a 59-year-old woman died of starvation for this reason.[7] Many of these villagers were ordinary political activists in the sense that they actively followed the CCP's every call during land reform and the subsequent political campaigns, but they were neither cadres nor close to the resources controlled by cadres. They were poor, less competent, landless laborers, formerly marginal elements in village society; thus they were easily mobilized by the cadres during land reform. Prior to the 1949 Revolution, their *guanxi* networks were smaller than average, because their economic difficulties prevented them from cultivating networks. After the revolution, they were among the first groups that willingly accepted the new pattern of interpersonal relations promoted by the CCP, which criticized traditional personal networks and promoted a new pattern of comradeship featuring loyalty to the party-state (see Vogel 1965). Although these villagers formed a group of political activists centered around the party branch in the village, their personal networks were even smaller than before. Moreover, because of their political activities and loyalty to the CCP, they had previously offended many people in their personal networks, which further isolated them in village society. When the famine hit, most found themselves in a helpless situation: their networks based on comradeship did not provide them any actual help in terms of grain or money and they had fewer personal relations to which to resort. As a result, they had no choice but to wait for relief grain from the state. It is not accidental that all three deaths due directly to starvation in the village occurred in the families of these political activists.

The function of family and kinship webs in coping with famine has been recognized in scholarly inquiries about social stress (e.g., Dirks 1980; Jelliffe and Jelliffe 1971; Prindle 1979: 54; and Torry 1979: 520). Empirical research on the Dutch famine of 1944–45 demonstrates the important role kinship and friendship networks can play in acquiring food during the most difficult times (see Stein et al. 1975).

The Xiajia case provides more empirical evidence to show the active role of kinship and friendship in coping with social crises. This is particularly true in a moral economy. As Scott points out, "There is an entire range of networks and institutions outside the immediate family which may, and often do, act as shock absorbers during economic crises in peasant life" (1976: 27). It is not surprising that all reported examples of mutual assistance during the famine period, such as Guo's case, are found among those who previously had intensive interactions with others in their *guanxi* networks. The moral obligation, together with the mutual indebtedness resulting from previous social exchanges, created a highly reliable mechanism for emergency aid. In Guo's case, his sister's family risked their own hunger to help Guo's family because they were morally and socially obligated to do so.

Both S. Epstein (1967) and Peter Prindle (1979) show that the threat of famine in rural India increases local people's reciprocal ties; hence, the Jajmani system is reinforced by demands for communal aid during periods of crisis. Similarly, the experience of the 1959–61 famine taught the Xiajia villagers an unforgettable lesson: *guanxi* networks are vitally important to survive difficult times. As an informant said, "No matter the dynasty [political regime], we ordinary people are always the victims and have no one to rely on except our own relatives and close friends [*shizai qinyou*]. I lost my mind once and devoted myself completely to the collectives, but after the three difficult years [the famine period], no more!"

It is not by accident that after the famine, traditional patterns of social exchange and performance of rituals were revived, for example, in the elaboration of betrothal gifts (discussed in Chapter 8). Even during the radical attack on traditional culture and customs during the Cultural Revolution, gift giving and the cultivation of *guanxi* networks remained alive in village life. It is, therefore, impossible to overemphasize the link between the persistence of social exchange activities and the famine experience among Xiajia residents.

Social Support Function: Life-Cycle Rituals

Life-cycle rituals such as weddings and funerals constitute another arena where *guanxi* networks function as a social support system. One's social status and position in village society are displayed
vividly by the attendance of guests, as well as by the financial and
spiritual support showed by these guests during the rituals. According to local custom, the more guests who attend and the longer they
stay, the more the host gains social prestige and "face." Onlookers
are also welcomed, because they help to make the ritual more elaborate. Ideally, after they present their gifts to the host, the guests
should participate in the ritual performance as much as possible, and
they may also chat with one another in the ritual setting or help the
host family in some way. At the very least, they should remain long
enough to show their spiritual support for the host family. This is
particularly important at funerals, when there is no elaborate banquet held for the mourners.

During my 1991 fieldwork, I was able to observe three funerals
in Xiajia village. Two were considered normal and successful by local standards, for the ritual settings were filled with guests, mourners, and onlookers at every important moment during the three-day
ritual. The third funeral was considered a failure by the villagers.
The host was known for his poor treatment of the deceased—his
mother-in-law—and was regarded as a nonsocial person by the
other villagers. He was aware that fewer mourners would come to
his house and thus simplified the funeral by shortening the three-day
ritual to two days, in an attempt to avoid the humiliating situation
of being ignored by his fellow villagers. Even so, it was considered
disastrous when only a few guests came to mourn and no one except
the family members showed up to accompany the deceased to the
graveyard. Villagers typically express their dissatisfaction with a
person's behavior by deliberately isolating that person during critical
situations.

I was told of another less dramatic case that occurred in 1990, involving a man who did not respect his aged mother and even mis-
treated her by limiting her supply of food. When his mother died at
the age of eighty-four, many villagers staged a protest: they went

briefly to mourn the deceased and immediately left the ritual setting without even greeting the host. According to the host's best friend, for several hours on the mourning day of the funeral, only two guests (including himself) stayed on the scene. Although the record of incoming gifts finally showed that more than 150 guests came to mourn the deceased and offer gifts, less than two dozen of them attended the burial rite, which was considered very embarrassing for the host. The guests' boycott of the funeral also made the host lose face in village society.

In a village in Hebei province where I conducted a short-term survey, similar social sanctions were imposed on one of the most capable entrepreneurs in the community. This man was a successful contractor for construction work and a leading reformer in the sense that he tried to organize his construction team based on impersonalized rules and discipline. While his workers were able to earn a considerable amount of money, he did not win any praise from fellow villagers because he treated his workers in a cold-blooded way and did not hesitate to fire incompetent workers, regardless of personal relations. As a result, he offended many people and destroyed his *guanxi* in the village. When the entrepreneur's father died, no one attended the funeral or helped him in the ritual. Even though he had money and was willing to pay, he could not even find enough people to carry the coffin to the graveyard. Finally, he had to visit the village elders and beg forgiveness before he was able to complete the funeral. Thereafter this man left to work for an urban construction team and gave up his ambitions to establish himself in the village.

Political Function

Finally, gift giving and *guanxi* networks are also important in local politics and during village disputes on various subjects. To cultivate good relations with superiors is vitally important for village cadres. The construction of horizontal networks helps cadres exercise their power and remain in office, because, like politicians everywhere, village cadres need supporters and allies. Even though gifts are not involved in collecting votes (see Jacobs 1979), political alliances are created and destroyed by *guanxi*. Chapter 7, which deals with the relationship between gift exchange and social domination, will address this issue in more detail. Here I will explore the other side of the issue—that is, the political implications of *guanxi* networks for ordinary villagers.

A large network of personal relations can act as a defense mechanism for villagers when they have conflicts with village cadres and other agents of the local government. Those who achieve extensive and intensive *guanxi* networks enjoy higher status in the village. They are respected by the village cadres and are capable of influencing local affairs. One tailor has remained independent and successfully self-employed since the 1949 Revolution. Even during the most radical periods, he was exempt from collective labor and political meetings. The secret to his independence is simple: he has cultivated one of the largest exchange networks in the village, such that all cadres and other influential persons in the village are nodes in his network. His independent status as a professional tailor provides him with a strong economic basis to maintain and expand this network, and the network in turn has protected him from political criticism, thus securing his lucrative occupation.

There have been several cases in which villagers have had conflicts with local cadres, but have won their battles by mobilizing their personal networks. In one interesting case I witnessed, a widow was suspected of stealing public trees. When two local policemen tried to confiscate a motorcycle from her family as a fine, a physical confrontation occurred between the two parties. The widow accused the policemen of beating her and declared that she was going to use her personal connections in the county police department to punish the offenders. Although no one knew whether she had relatives in power or not, the local policemen decided not to risk offending the higher authorities and encouraged the village office to give the widow 50 yuan as compensation. Nevertheless, the policemen did not want to lose face in the village; two weeks later they detained the widow's son in jail on a four-month-old charge of gambling and asked the widow to pay a fine of 300 yuan to free him. The widow appeared to be defeated but, to the surprise of all, she went to the county seat and came back with a note from an official in the county government requesting that the local police department return her money. This case demonstrates that the most important means for self-protection is cultivating a large *guanxi* network.

The Structure of *Guanxi* in Village Society

Anthropological studies of gift exchange have been primarily concerned with the relationship between modes of exchange and social structure.[1] The exchange theory inspired by Mauss views gift giving as a cultural mechanism that creates, maintains, and reinforces various social bonds—be they cooperative, competitive, or antagonistic (Mauss 1967). Gift transactions and interpersonal relations are thus closely related in a dialectical process of social integration. As Sahlins generalizes, "The connection between material flow and social relations is reciprocal. A specific social relation may constrain a given movement of goods, but a specific transaction—'by the same token'—suggests a particular social relation. If friends make gifts, gifts make friends" (1972: 186).

Following this theoretical tradition, I begin with Xiajia villagers' conception of *guanxi* as the dynamic structure of the local world, which is best illustrated by the endless process of gift exchange. Next I examine the structural features of *guanxi* networks by analyzing patterns of interpersonal relations as documented by the gift lists. Finally I conclude with a discussion of the significant role played by affinal ties and community relations in the *guanxi* networks of Xiajia villagers. My findings seriously challenge the applicability of the lineage paradigm to rural communities in north China.

The Local Conception of Guanxi As a Small Social Universe

Throughout my field research, I was intrigued by the way Xiajia villagers perceived their *guanxi* networks. Whenever I discussed the subject of gift giving and other forms of social exchange, the term "society" (*shehui*) was always referred to in one way or another. An informant explained the expansion of the *guanxi* network in his family as a sign of "taking a better place in the society." Personal connections are referred to as "social relations" (*shehui guanxi*), and people who are active in situations of social exchange, such as weddings or community ceremonies, are called "people in the society" (*shehui shang de ren*).[2] It should be pointed out that for villagers the concept of society does not have clear boundaries. In a broader sense, society may refer to the whole country in a discussion about something taking place in Beijing or somewhere else outside their village. Or the term may be used to refer to their village when they are discussing community matters. However, in many cases, society may mean *guanxi* networks of personal relations that encircle a given individual. It is this common usage that is understood by villagers in the local world.

There are three local categories that define the nature of various personal relations in a given *guanxi* network: (1) *shizai qinqi*, which means literally "real and close relatives"; (2) *kao de zhu de*, referring to people who can always be counted on for help; and (3) *yiban qinyou*, meaning relatives and friends in a broader sense. Using the local definitions, I translate these terms as "personal core," "reliable zone," and "effective zone," respectively. Personal core consists of one's family members—the close agnates and affines—such as siblings, first cousins, and one's wife's siblings. This group is also the core of one's kindred web, and all people within this central circle are related by consanguinity as well as by mutual duties and rights. Reliable zone consists of one's good friends. The distinctions between the core and reliable zone are not that clear, because best friends may be regarded as closer than relatives and may thus enter the core of one's personal connections. Unlike the first two categories, effective zone embraces more people and is more open in recruitment. All relatives, friends, colleagues, and some fellow villagers are included in the effective zone. In theory, the effective zone may be expanded to the scope of the village community, because co-residence and membership in the village community also provide the necessary channels for mutual assistance and other interactions. In practice, however, few people are capable of turning the entire village into their personal network, and thus villagers usually regard their village community as an outer circle of personal relations.

Using my own interviews and analysis of gift lists, I present the structural configuration of *guanxi* networks in Fig. 1. It should be noted that in practice, the distinctiveness of these relational zones exists only in the dynamic process of social interactions, especially that of gift exchange.

Fig. 1 actually represents a symbolic space, which is divided into several zones by the various degrees of reliability of personal relations. An individual villager's local world consists of the personal core, reliable zone, effective zone, and the village community. Beyond these areas, the person will enter the outside world where primary connections are almost useless and he or she has to invoke short-term, instrumental gift-giving activities. In such cases, *guanxi* is converted into a means of getting things done, which is unnecessary within the village boundary.

This symbolic space based on reliability embraces not only kinship relations, but other kinds of personal relations and thus differs from Sahlins's famous model of primitive exchange. Sahlins (1972: 199) takes kinship distance as the major social variable that determines the three types of reciprocity: generalized, balanced, and negative. The main problem with his model is that kinship proximity does not always necessarily result in generosity; and under certain circumstances extraordinary hospitality is displayed to guests, strangers, or potential enemies. Lebra criticizes Sahlins, saying, "He treats three variables—kinship distance, sociability, and generosity—as completely overlapping, as if they by necessity converge with one another; the three should have been regarded as only partially overlapping" (Lebra 1975: 552).

Gift-giving occasion[a]	Core zone	Reliable zone	Effective zone	Village society	Beyond village
Childbirth	●———————————▶				
Abortion	●———————————▶				
Female sterilization	●———————————————————————▶				
Engagement	●———————————————————————▶				
Wedding	●———▶				
House construction	●———————————————————————▶				
Birthday celebration	●———————————————————————▶				
Funeral	●———▶				
Ancestor worship	●———————▶				
Occasional celebration	●———————————————————————▶				
Yangge dance[b]	●———————————————————————————————————▶				
Mutual visit	●———————————▶				
Bai xinnian[c]	●———▶				
Guaxian[d]	●———▶				
Xiaojing[e]	●———▶				
Yasui money[f]	●———▶				
Visits to patients	●———————————▶				
Food exchange	●———————————▶				
Love gifts	●——▶				
Indirect payment				●———————————▶	
Flattery gifts			●———————————————————————▶		
Lubricating gifts			●—————————————————————————————▶		

NOTE: Arrows indicate the span of personal relationships involved in each gift-giving occasion. Relationships are grouped by degree of reliability, from most reliable (core zone) to least (beyond village).

[a]These gift-giving occasions and their contextual situations, except for ancestor worship, are discussed in detail in Chapter 3.

[b]The annual parade, during which Xiajia villagers offer gifts to the parade participants.

[c]A local custom requiring newly married couples to visit their close relatives during the lunar New Year period.

[d]A local custom requiring newly married couples to visit their close relatives after the birth of their first child.

[e]Gifts offered by junior people to their parents or elder kinsmen.

[f]Gifts given by elders to their children or junior kin.

FIG. 1. *Gift-giving relations and* guanxi *structure*

Several interesting points emerge from Fig. 1. First, the de facto boundaries of the relational zones are maintained in the dynamic relations of gift exchange. The closer to the center in a given *guanxi* network, the more gift-giving relations are involved. The personal core, the primary and most important part of one's *guanxi* networks, involves all kinds of gift-giving activities except instrumental ones; instrumental gifts are used mainly beyond the community boundary. An elastic area lies somewhere between the reliable zone and the effective zone, where people may adjust their mutual relations. The size of the *guanxi* networks varies mostly depending on an individual's effort to expand his or her reliable and effective zones.

Second, there are clearly defined boundaries in some situations, which are reflected by the plain bars in Fig. 1. Gift giving for ancestor worship (No. 9) is strictly confined to close agnates—or within the circle of the five-grade mourning system as explained by the villagers—while the *yangge* dance as an annual parade involves all villagers and thus stands for the village community. Gifts of love, discussed in Chapter 3, are mostly associated with marriage and thus indicate the boundary of the conjugal family. In other words, these gift-giving relations respectively define conjugality, patriliny, and community, and thus represent one's fundamental social relations: affinity, agnation, and coresidence.

Third, a clear line can be drawn between the village community and the outside world, paralleling the distinction between expressive and instrumental gift-giving activities. As shown in Fig. 1, all except the last three categories of gift exchange belong to the expressive type of gifts, and all instrumental gift-giving relations go beyond the village boundary. Thus far, scholarly attention has focused primarily on the latter three categories, especially gifts of lubrication (No. 22). It is obvious that lubricant gift giving is just one of many kinds of gift-giving relations. Earlier studies based solely or even mostly on an analysis of lubricating gifts therefore hardly grasp the totality of *guanxi* networks in social life.

Fourth, there are many gift-giving relations that are open-ended (symbolized by the arrows in Figure 1), especially those in wedding and funeral contexts. Indirect payments and lubricating gifts provide the most typical opportunities to link the villagers with people outside the village. In many cases of outside-village gift giving, market transactions are mingled with gift exchanges and monetary gifts are offered both as payment and as tokens of gratitude, such as for the hiring of a band of folk musicians or to see a doctor who practices traditional Chinese medicine. Through these exchanges, and with other market transactions, the village links itself to the outside world. On the other hand, the most important part of one's *guanxi* network still exists within the village boundaries. Hence, for most villagers' lifetimes, *guanxi* networks are one's local world, or, as they refer to it, *shehui*. This way of perceiving *guanxi* networks may be better illustrated by examining attitudes toward those who fail to construct *guanxi* networks.

Given the vital importance of *guanxi* networks for Xiajia residents to establish themselves in village society, it is no wonder that those who do not cultivate such networks are relegated to socially disadvantaged positions. The local term for these people is *si menzi*, which means literally "dead (closed) doors," with door meaning personal connections or *guanxi*, as in the well-known expression "going through the back door" (*zou houmen*). Such people are generally considered "not to have any *guanxi*," or "so-and-so does not know how to be a human being" (*buhui zuoren*). The second charge sounds more serious, but the implication is the same, i.e., the person has failed to establish a respectable place for himself or herself in the society, thus showing a lack of knowledge of what it means to be a human being. The term *si menzi*, therefore, symbolizes both the incapability and inflexibility of these persons and thus at a deeper level their social death in the domain of social exchange and network construction.

Interestingly enough, I found similar emic terms in other regions as well. In the northern part of Hebei province, people who are extremely introverted and incapable of maintaining personal networks are called *sipi*, meaning literally "dead skin," while their counterparts in rural areas of Shandong province are called *sixing*, "dead tempers" or "dead characters." It should be noted that in all cases the word *si* is used as a modifier, meaning either inflexible or dead. Given the widespread belief in death pollution and the related fear of the dead among the Chinese (see, e.g., J. Watson 1988b), the negative connotations of these terms are obvious. In sharp contrast, those who are active and capable in network building are widely described as *huo*, which means literally flexible, alive, and vigorous. For instance, it is a common expression in Mandarin Chinese to say so-and-so "*luzi hen huo*" (literally, "has vigorous and wide networks"), which means to have many personal connections and thus to be very capable, flexible, and vital. In this connection, the Chinese words *si* and *huo* constitute an interesting binary opposition between inflexibility and flexibility, incapability and capability, and finally between (social) death and life. The social significance of *guanxi* networks is fully captured in these descriptive terms.

The disadvantages of failing in social exchange and network building are not limited to verbal expressions—there are also social sanctions. Most commonly, those who cannot fulfill the obligations of gift giving and other forms of social exchange are isolated by the majority in the village, and during personal crises this isolation becomes a serious social sanction. In a case I witnessed a young couple was extremely embarrassed when the wife underwent a sterilization operation and no one came to visit her. According to some informants, the couple could blame no one but themselves. Because of their higher education (high school) and perhaps also because the husband had worked in an urban area, they disliked the village life style, especially the endless process of gift exchange. They deliberately avoided attending village ceremonies and gradually isolated themselves until their time of crisis. As described in Chapter 3, female sterilization has inspired a new ritual whereby the family of the woman who has undergone the operation is visited and presented with gifts in money or in kind. The ritual serves to compensate for the woman's loss in both physical and spiritual terms (strength and *qi*). It also provides an effective means of emotional consolation; to receive no guests or gifts on this occasion implies that no one really cares about their crisis. This is particularly distressing for the wife, because she is the one in need of support.

Similar cases can be found among older villagers. Mr. Lu, in his fifties, is known as one of Xiajia's "dead doors." He does not talk much and isolates himself from the villagers. Some villagers attribute his strange behavior to his family's class label of landlord, which caused a lot of trouble for him during the period of collectivization. When I arrived at Xiajia in the spring of 1991, Lu was preparing his son's wedding. Two months later he still could not raise enough money for the ritual; he was also worried about how many people would attend. The ceremony was, however, finally performed after he took out a usurious loan from someone in another village. Lu's fellow villagers regarded this situation as a serious loss of face; Lu had to resort to the most despicable means of raising money because of his lack of social connections. Generally, few villagers need to rely on usurious loans to hold a wedding: Since marriage is the most important event in one's life, one's relatives and friends are usually obligated to help; and since a considerable amount of money will be received as gifts during a wedding, a wedding loan should be considered secure because of the probability of immediate repayment.

In Lu's case, fewer than 80 guests attended the wedding, which is less than half the average number on such occasions. To avoid this loss of face, Lu did not reveal the total amount of gift money. Most villagers believed that the gift money could not have been more than 600 yuan, because the gifts were exceptionally small—ranging from 4 to 10 yuan. This story was discussed in the village for a rather long period, demonstrating the significance of *guanxi* networks in the public arena.

The Configuration of Guanxi *Networks*

How are the villagers' *guanxi* networks structured? Fortunately, the local custom of preserving gift lists provides documentary evidence to help answer this question. Based on a stratified selection of households, I collected 43 gift lists and put them into a computer database containing a total of 5,286 individual gift transactions. To understand the social relations reflected in these lists, I interviewed the owners of all the lists and asked them to describe the nature of their relationship with the donors. I thus obtained 43 social maps, vividly displaying the content and configuration of interpersonal relations in Xiajia village. More importantly, the maps are based solely on the villagers' own definition of their personal relations, which, as shall be seen, sheds new light on our understanding of social relations in village society.

I have chosen to focus my analysis on the gift list for Xu's second son's wedding in May 1988, because it is one of the most complex gift lists in terms of the variety of social relations involved. Forty-nine years old in 1991, Xu is recognized as one of the most knowledgeable, capable, and respected men in Xiajia. He came from one of the smaller surname groups in Xiajia, and even worse, his father was falsely assigned the class label of rich peasant during the land reform. Although the label was corrected to upper middle peasant one year later—which was better but still not as good as that of middle peasant or poor peasant—for a long period his family was isolated from his kinsmen and discriminated against by other villagers. In addition, his father's introverted, nonsocial personality resulted in an unusually small network of personal connections, which isolated the family even more. In 1963, when his father started to build a house and asked for help from the collectives, his request was refused by the team leaders; a further appeal did not produce a sympathetic reaction from the team members. This was understood as punishment for his father's unsociable and eccentric behavior.

The social pressure against the family turned out to be a strong motivation for Xu to establish himself in village society. He worked hard at school and later in the collectives, in the hope of "climbing up to take a better place in society," as he explained it to me. Gradually, he was recognized as a promising young man and was appointed a cadre, which secured his political status and opened the door for him to expand his *guanxi* network. He finally arrived at the pinnacle of the village power structure by working as the village party secretary for nine years, retiring from office in 1988. His wife has been a teacher at the village school since the mid-1960's and is considered a genius at diplomacy. She has taken on full responsibility for all gift giving and other interhousehold activities and has made great progress in network building. Another sign of Xu's achievement is that his first son got a job at the local department store and his second son entered the army. Thus, by the time of his second son's wedding in 1988, Xu had good reason to be proud of himself; he had completely changed his family's social status in village society. The gift list from the wedding, shown in Table 4, is evidence of his status.

It should be noted that Table 4 and all other tables below focus on the family head as the host with whom interpersonal connections are defined, unless otherwise noted. And, as my informants explained it to me, all gifts are registered in the name of families represented by the male family heads, such as sister's husband (*jiefu*) or niece's husband (*waisheng guye*), even though women as gift presenters attended gift-giving rituals no less than their husbands.

In exchange theory, gifts can be regarded as markers of interpersonal relations, or "tie-signs" as Erving Goffman calls them

TABLE 4

Xu's Gift List, 1988

Donor's relationship to Xu[a]	No. of guests by value of gift						Total no. of guests
	4–5 yuan	10 yuan	20 yuan	30–40 yuan	50–60 yuan	100 yuan	
1. *Shuzhang*		3					3
2. *Qinjia*		1	3	1			5
3. *Jiefu*		6	6	1		2	15
4. *Neidi*		6	2		2		10
5. *Lianqiao*		3	5				8
6. *Waisheng guye*		1	3	1			5
7. First son's *neidi*	1	1	3	1			6
8. First son's other affines	3	2	3				8
9. *Qisheng*		8	1				9
10. Uncle				2			2
11. Patrilineal cousin		4					4
12. *Gubiaodi*		1	3	2			6
13. *Jiubiaodi*			3				3
14. Sister's son		6	4				10
15. Fictive kin		3	3		1		7
16. Fellow villagers (*tunqin*)	92	37					129
17. Friend in village		4	7				11
18. Friend beyond village		16	10	4	4	1	35
19. Colleague		8	3	1			12
20. Wife's colleague		6	1	1			8
21. First son's colleague		11	4				15
22. Second son's friend		6	3				9
TOTAL	96	133	69	12	7	3	320

[a]Kinship terms: *shuzhang*: wife's father's brother; *qinjia*: children's parents-in-law; *jiefu*: sister's or cousin's husband; *neidi*: wife's brother or cousin; *lianqiao*: wife's sister's husband; *waisheng guye*: sister's daughter's husband; *qisheng*: wife's sister's son; *gubiaodi*: father's sister's son; *jiubiaodi*: mother's sibling's son.

(1971: 194), because gift transactions contain evidence about the nature of the relationship between donor and recipient. The primary question I am concerned with here is how the detailed gift list informs us about the configuration of Xu's social network. First, let us examine the gift list to determine the kinds of relations involved. There are 320 donors, who fall into 22 different relational categories. These categories can be classified as two basic types of personal ties: inherited relations and created relations. The former consists of kinship connections represented in the first fourteen categories—the primary social relations inherited from one's own family or one's spouse's family.

Unlike preexisting kin relationships, the latter seven personal connections are created by individual efforts—what I would call non-kin relationships. In Xu's gift list, *tunqin* in category 16 means literally "relatives of coresidence"; the word *tun* is the local term for "village" and *qin* means "kin" as well as "close" or "intimate." Not every fellow villager can be counted as a *tunqin*—only those who are regarded more or less as social intimates. This limitation differs from pure community relations in the sense that *tunqin* is still a kind of personal relationship created through individual cultivation rather than a preexisting membership for anyone born into the community. The local term for such a pure community relationship is *tong-tun* (living in the same village) in the past and *sheyuan* (commune member) or *duiyou* (production teammate) during the collective era. I have translated *tunqin* as "intimate fellow villagers," but part of the original meaning is lost in translation, i.e., the similarity between coresidence and kinship ties. Categories 17 to 22 refer to friendship created through channels. In anthropological literature, friendship in a village community has often been considered secondary in comparison to kinship. However, as we will see later, in contemporary Xiajia community friendship is secondary only in the sense that it is created by personal efforts and thus cannot be passed on from one generation to another. Functionally, voluntarily constructed friendship and the *tunqin* relationship play a decisive role as important as the preordained kinship.

Category 15 "fictive kin" (*ganqin*) lies somewhere between the above two basic types of personal relations. Considering that fictive kin are created on the basis of previous friendships between families or persons, I prefer to classify it in the general category of friendship, or non-kin relationships. In the socialist period the custom of making fictive kin (*bai ganqin*) gradually died out in this region. Since the late 1950's, however, making best friends has emerged and become a widely accepted social practice among the younger generations, especially after the Cultural Revolution. As one might expect, friends also address each other in kinship terms. When asked about the local practice of fictive kinship, some older villagers reported that "*ganqin* is the same as a good friend in today's terms."

The composition of Xu's gift list reveals an unbalanced ratio between the two basic types of personal relations. As shown in Table 4, 94 people are connected to Xu through a variety of kinship ties, which constitutes only 29 percent of the total 320 guests. Moreover, 69 are affines, thus constituting an absolute majority; meanwhile agnates are relatively insignificant (6 in total). Unlike agnates who are considered family members in a broader sense and are closely bound by natural and moral ties, affines can easily adjust and manipulate their mutual relationships. Thus affinal relations require more effort to maintain and develop. The larger number of affines on Xu's gift list indicates the close connectedness between Xu and his affinal relatives.

In sharp contrast, 226 guests are connected with Xu's family through non-kin relations. Even if we take the conservative position of not including fictive kin in the category of friendship, non-kin guests still number 219, almost 2.5 times more than those with kinship ties. Furthermore, there are 129 *tunqin*. The large number of non-kin guests confirms Xu's account that they built their exchange network from a very low starting point, and their success resulted mostly from their own efforts rather than from their parents' legacy. In Xu's case, we may assume that his achievement in developing a network of social relations can be judged from the gift list in three areas: the size of the exchange network, the proportion of affines, and the ratio between kinship and friendship ties. These hypotheses will be tested by more cases below.

Let us turn to another related feature reflected in Xu's gift list— that is, the emergence of several unconventional types of personal ties. In addition to *tunqin*, 90 guests are identified by Xu and his wife as friends or colleagues—almost as many as their kinsmen. As shown in Table 4, Xu identifies eleven friends within Xiajia village and distinguishes them from the rather ambiguous term fellow villagers. Actually, when Xu and I discussed his gift list, Xu was very careful about labeling his friends. In two cases, he hesitated for a while, changing their status from friend to fellow villager and then back to friend. In answering my question regarding the difference between the two, Xu said that a friend was much closer and more trustworthy than a *tunqin*, because one was connected to friends not only by obligations but also by mutual understanding and emotional attachment.

It is also interesting to note that Xu had 35 friends who lived in other villages or urban areas. Two were Xu's middle-school class-mates when he was the chairman of the student union, and they have remained good friends. Of course the majority of Xu's friends out-side the village boundary are those who became acquainted with Xu through collegial relationships, a natural by-product of Xu's twenty-year career as a village cadre. For instance, the man who pre-sented a 100-yuan gift was formerly the party secretary in the local township government and currently a major official in the county government. Despite the huge gap in social status between them, they maintained their friendship for more than ten years. The gift list also shows that six urban friends attended the wedding. Because of increased inequalities between urban and rural areas, and the legal ban on peasant migration to the cities until the mid-1980's,[3] it has been considered not only a necessity but an honor among villagers to maintain a good relationship with urban relatives. An urban friend is considered accumulated social capital.

Colleagues constitute another unconventional category in village society. I have observed that part of the cultural legacy of collectiv-ization in Xiajia village, as in most other places, has been the deval-uation of physical labor, especially the farming of fields (Yan 1992a: 6). As a result, ordinary villagers do not consider their coworkers as colleagues, while village cadres refer to one another as colleagues (*tongshi*). To claim a colleague per se, therefore, indicates a higher social status, such as in the case of Xu. Among the twelve colleagues he identified from the gift list, ten are cadres either from neighboring villages or from the local township government. The remaining two are folk musicians with whom he worked in his youth. It should be noted, however, that as a result of the diversification of the rural economy since the reforms, a number of villagers have participated in a great variety of nonagricultural occupations, and the notion of colleague is beginning to spread. For instance, an informant referred to several of his friends as colleagues because they all owned small tractors and were engaged in the transportation business.

Since Xu's wife and sons have their own nonagricultural jobs, they have their own social connections, and in many cases, these connections are not related to formal household interactions. For in-stance, 24 donors, categories 21 and 22, came to the wedding solely because of their good relationships with Xu's two sons. Thus I refer to their gifts as individualized gifts. In this respect Xu's case differs from the traditional type of village networks, which normally centers around the male head of the household, because all family members are engaged in the same enterprise: farming within the village. Yet Xu's case is by no means unique in present-day Xiajia, and in my sample gift lists I found 69 individualized gift transactions. Along with the economic development and industrialization of the rural regions, more surplus rural laborers will be engaged in nonagricultural enterprises, thus establishing networks outside the family boundaries. It can be expected that more individualized gifts will emerge, and the networks in village households are likely to become multi-stranded and pluralized, as in the case of urban families.

Now I would like to discuss another feature conveyed by Xu's gift list—that is, the degree of closeness between Xu and each donor, as reflected by the gift value. It has been noted that generally the closer the relationship between donor and recipient, the more valuable the gift (see Cohen 1976: 159). Xu's gift list provides us with concrete data to test this observation. We see that although gift values vary from five yuan to 100 yuan, most cluster in the first three values, namely, 5, 10, and 20 yuan. The bottom row in Table 4 shows that 96 guests presented gifts of four or five yuan, and 133 people offered gifts of ten yuan. A total of 91 people gave twenty yuan or more. It seems that in 1988, 10 yuan was the average wedding gift, five yuan was considered a small gift, and twenty yuan was a generous one. Of the 129 *tunqin*, 92 gave small gifts and the remaining 37 gave average-size gifts; in contrast, only four out of the 94 kinsmen presented small gifts, and many of them gave gifts of twenty yuan or more. It is safe to say that relationships with fellow villagers lie in the outer circle of Xu's personal network and kinship relations lie in the inner circle.

Who, then, are the most generous donors? According to Xiajia villagers, one can expect to receive the most generous gifts from one's sister's husband (*jiefu*), one's wife's brother (*neidi*), one's wife's sister's husband (*lianqiao*), and one's best friend. Acknowledgment of the significance of one's best friend represents a new development in the villagers' perception of personal networks. These accounts are well demonstrated in Xu's case. The three donors who presented the largest gifts (100 yuan) are Xu's two sisters' husbands and his best

TABLE 5

Composition of Personal Networks, Xiajia Village

Donor's relationship to recipient[a]	Xu's gift list		Other gift lists	
	No. of guests	Percentage	No. of guests	Percentage
1. Affines	69	22%	1,043	21%
2. Agnates	6	2	497	10
3. Patrilateral kin	16	5	199	4
4. Matrilateral kin	3	1	149	3
5. Fictive kin	7	2	49	1
6. Fellow villagers	129	40	2,384	48
7. Friends	46	14	447	9
8. Colleagues	44	14	198	4
TOTAL	320	100%	4,966	100%

[a]Kinship or other social relationship between donor and recipient, viewed from the latter's perspective. "Patrilateral kin" refers to the recipient's father's sisters and their children; "matrilateral kin" refers to the recipient's mother's siblings and their children. These categories are used in the same way in Tables 6 and 7.

friend (the county cadre mentioned above). We find that seven guests presented gifts valued from 50 to 60 yuan. Again, four of the seven men are Xu's friends, two are Xu's wife's brothers, and the last is his fictive sister's husband.[4] Within the same category of kin relationships, people may offer different gifts, resulting from actual differences in degrees of kinship proximity. For instance, among the fifteen people who fall into the classification of *jiefu*, only three are Xu's full sisters' husbands who offered "super gifts"—100 yuan and 40 yuan. The remaining thirteen are Xu's female cousins' husbands, who followed the majority in presenting average gifts. Finally, it should also be mentioned that agnates usually do not present the largest gifts. In Xu's case, his first cousins presented average value gifts (ten yuan) and his two uncles each gave twenty yuan.

The above observations are further supported by my survey of 42 other gift lists. These results are summarized and compared to Xu's case in Table 5. Looking at donors in the two columns, we see that kinship ties in relationship categories 1 to 4 make up 30 percent of the donors in Xu's case and 38 percent in the other 42 cases; friendship ties in categories 6 to 8 constitute 68 percent of the donors in Xu's case and 61 percent for the other lists. Within the system of kinship ties, affines occupy 22 percent in Xu's case, exceeding the ag-

TABLE 6

Comparison of Personal Networks Between Xia and Non-Xia Families

Relationship[a]	Xia family gift lists		Non-Xia family gift lists	
	No. of guests	Percentage	No. of guests	Percentage
Affines	124	19%	422	19%
Agnates	138	21	211	9
Patrilateral kin	32	5	98	4
Matrilateral kin	15	2	59	2
Fictive kin	3		25	1
Fellow villagers	260	41	1,157	51
Friends	49	8	175	8
Colleagues	24	4	127	6
TOTAL	645	100%	2,274	100%

[a] See note to Table 5.

nates (2 percent) by more than ten times. Certainly one may argue that such a sharp contrast results from the fact that Xu belongs to a small agnatic group. But the pattern is similar in the other 42 cases, where affines (21 percent) outnumber agnates (10 percent) by more than two times. The largest donor group is that of *tunqin* in all cases, and the relatively smaller percentage of fellow villagers in Xu's case can be explained by the involvement of more friends and colleagues.

Considering that Xu and other individuals in my survey sample belong to small surname groups that have small numbers of agnates, I compare the largest lineage—the Xias—with the other groups listed in Table 6. Because one's social network is best illustrated by the guests attending the wedding ritual, the seventeen gift lists in this comparison are exclusively from weddings. It is not surprising, then, that for the four Xia gift lists, agnates slightly outnumber affines (21 percent vs. 19 percent), since there more than 100 Xia households in Xiajia. For the non-Xias, the ratio between affines and agnates (19 percent vs. 9 percent) remains the same as in Table 5. However, it is indeed surprising that among the Xias, the overall number of kin gift donors (categories 1 to 4) is less than that of friend donors (categories 6 to 8). This fact indicates that in building personal networks, even the Xias must rely heavily upon non-kinship ties created by individual effort. Actually, in each of the four Xia family gift lists, the number of agnates is less than 40, which means that at least 60 percent of the agnates did not attend the wedding. In a comparison of Xias with non-Xias, the only noticeable difference lies in the proportion of fellow villagers to agnates. Since the non-Xias have fewer agnates, it is not surprising that the number of their personal connections with fellow villagers exceeds the number of their connections with agnates.

In short, considering all factors, the overall structures of the personal networks in Tables 5 and 6 are very close, though not identical, indicating that the above analysis of Xu's case is fairly representative of the general situation. The structure of social networks in Xiajia village is characterized by a heavy reliance on friendship ties as opposed to kinship relations, the involvement of a large number of fellow villagers, and an active role of affines. Obviously it is the interplay of kinship and non-kinship principles, expressed by the mechanism of *guanxi* networks, which serves to organize Xiajia villagers' everyday social interactions. Such a relational perspective leads my inquiry to the complex of kinship, community, and personal networks in village society.

Practical Kinship and Personal Networks: Further Implications

It has been traditional in anthropology, especially among the British structural-functionalists, to consider kinship as the structural basis upon which social relations are built. As A. R. Radcliffe-Brown asserts, "A system of kinship and marriage can be looked at as an arrangement which enables persons to live together and co-operate with one another in an orderly social life" (1987: 3). This special interest in kinship systems is developed by Maurice Freedman as a lineage paradigm of Chinese society (1958, 1966), in the sense that "it assumes a fundamental model of Chinese society in which the ideology of patrilineal descent takes precedence over all other principles of social organization" (J. Watson 1986: 274). Since the 1960's, this paradigm has been applied to all major studies of powerful patrilineal organizations in south China (see, e.g., Baker 1966, 1968; Potter 1968, 1970; J. Watson 1975; and R. Watson 1981a, 1981b). As a result of the prolonged influence of Freedman's approach in the field of sinological anthropology (see B. Gallin and R. Gallin 1985), patri-lineage and descent principles have become what Arjun Appadurai calls the "gatekeeping concepts," in that they "define the quintes-sential and dominant questions of interest in the region" (Appadurai 1986b: 357).

The limitations of the lineage paradigm have been recognized by those who worked in regions outside the patrilineal belt of south China, notably in Taiwan. Norma Diamond (1969) challenges the universality of the lineage model in Chinese societies by demon-strating that kinship is not the only working system that binds people together (see also Sangren 1984). Bernard Gallin (1960, 1966) shows that matrilateral and affinal relationships are as important as agnatic ties for villagers in Taiwan. Burton Pasternak compares two Taiwanese villages, one of which displays strong agnatic organiza-tion while the other manifests equally strong interlineage coopera-tion. He shows that the differences between these two communities are determined mainly by three important factors: the initial settle-ment pattern, the distribution of wealth, and the need for coopera-tion across agnatic lines for economic or defense purposes (1972: 149). Taking the networks of connections between families as a so-cial system in its own right, Stevan Harrell argues: "In Ploughshare, villagers have ties with practically all other villagers, and the net-work of dyadic links is much thicker within the village than outside of it" (1982: 132). Judith Strauch's case study (1983) of a multilineage village in Hong Kong's New Territories, a region known for its powerful patrilineages (see Baker 1966), reveals that villagers from different lineage groups make various efforts to extend their kinship ties to and seek interlineage cooperation for the sake of survival. As she notes: "Lineage solidarity in the small multilineage village can successfully coexist, as demonstrated in the Fung Yuen case, with a more inclusive sense of community which supersedes but does not replace it. Kinship as an idiom, rather than as a rigid template, pro-vides a coherent force, in variant forms, throughout all levels of Chinese society" (1983: 48).

My findings from Xiajia village in northeast China echo these studies of small and shallow agnatic groups in rural Taiwan and Hong Kong, where community solidarity and intrafamily cooper-ation are maintained through both kinship ties and non-kin relationships. Two important implications emerge from the above analysis of the *guanxi* networks among Xiajia residents.

First, there is a tendency for both community and kinship relations to be incorporated into personal networks and thus become what Pierre Bourdieu calls "practical kinship." According to Bourdieu's distinction of official and practical kinship, the uses of kinship based purely on genealogical relations are reserved for official situations in which they serve the function of ordering the social world. By contrast, there are also practical uses of kinship that are situational and flexible and that represent "a particular case of the utilization of *connections*" (1977: 34, italics original). In Xiajia village, most relationships in *guanxi* networks, such as affines, friends, and colleagues, are made or cultivated by villagers themselves instead of inherited from their parents or ancestors, and villagers want to do something with these connections for their practical concerns. In this sense *guanxi* networks can be seen as expressions of practical kinship.

An important feature of this kind of kinship is flexibility in alliance making. The Xiajia case shows that when people are allowed to choose with whom to make an alliance, affines, as apposed to agnates, tend to be more desirable. As reflected by the gift lists, except for the Xia families, there are twice the number of affines involved in gift exchange as there are agnates, and in addition, affines present the more valuable gifts. Even for families of Xia lineage, the dominating patrilineal group in the village, affines still constitute the main body of donors within the kinship relations. Moreover, the concept of affinity as perceived by Xiajia villagers appears to have wider connotations, including relationships such as one's wife's sister's husband (*lianqiao*) and one's children's parents-in-law (*qinjia*).

The closeness of one's wife's sister's husband is reflected in its local term, *lianqiao*, which means literally men who are linked by a bridge, namely, the bridge of the sororal relationship between their wives. Unlike brothers, people linked by their wives' sororal relationship have no inherited conflict of interests among themselves; thus mutual assistance and cooperation can be easily supported and facilitated by their wives (see Judd 1989). We have seen from analysis of the gift lists that the most generous gifts can be expected from one's wife's sisters' husbands, and in daily life these individuals are also among the first to offer help. For instance, the most lucrative crop in the area is watermelon, but it requires larger capital investments and depends on unpredictable market demands. Therefore, the villagers prefer to plant watermelon together with one or two partners, in an attempt to share the risks. In 1991, seven out of the nine watermelon farmers in the village cooperated with their wives' sisters' husbands in various ways, while no one worked with one's brothers. I was told that it was easier to work with the former, because they were more reasonable and trustworthy.

It should also be pointed out that, while emphasizing the importance of affines, Xiajia villagers seem to have a narrower definition of patrilineal kinsmen. When asked to identify the donors on their gift lists, they were reluctant to include all lineage men in their inner cycle of *guanxi* networks, which was quite different from their positive attitude toward affines. According to Mr. Xia, a knowledgeable informant who has taken care of the ancestor scroll in his sublineage for many years, his significant agnates include only those who are still within the five mourning grades system. Those beyond the boundary of the five mourning grades are similar to *tunqin*, even though they share the same surname Xia. When I pointed out that they were the descendants of his remote ancestors, he laughed and said: "Close neighbors are better than remote relatives" (*yuanqin bu ru jinlin*).

Furthermore Xiajia villagers have gone beyond the boundary of the kinship system to build networks through all kinds of interpersonal relations based on friendship: friends, colleagues, and *tunqin*. The nature and function of these non-kinship relations deserve further research. For example, the category of friends among ordinary villagers may provide a new direction for our understanding of village life. As the above analysis of gift lists demonstrates, close friends are among the most important gift donors, and this may indicate the construction of voluntary social relationships in rural communities. Most previous studies of gift exchange in anthropology have overwhelmingly emphasized the obligatory nature of gift giving, but the Xiajia case shows that voluntarism exists at least among friends. The workplace and common interests usually provide the most convenient channels for villagers to make close friends. Gift lists reveal that those engaged in some nonagricultural occupations, such as carpenters or folk musicians, have more close friends than ordinary farmers.

As shown in Tables 5 and 6, *tunqin* constitute a considerable proportion (40 to 51 percent) of gift donors in the *guanxi* networks. The large proportion of intimate fellow villagers in all cases demonstrates that preexisting community ties are increasingly absorbed into family-centered gift exchange relationships. In the precommunist period, ordinary villagers' personal networks were limited to close agnates, affines, and a few neighbors. Beyond these primary connections, there was a general category of *tongtun* (coresidents in the village) that separated community ties from personal networks. Collectivization helped to incorporate the previously remote community ties into personal networks, because the collective ownership of land and other important means of production tied all members of a collective together and created a new sense of connectedness among them. This extended connectedness was reflected in new terms—*sheyuan* (commune member) and *duiyou* (production teammate)—as well as in the intensification of gift-giving activities among villagers. After decollectivization, while community activities declined remarkably, the necessity of maintaining a large personal network became more and more obvious. The increase in family income, which leads to a new wave of elaborate gift giving in ritual life, also contributes to the current trend of expansion of personal networks by involving more and more fellow villagers in family-centered networks. Given the vital importance of personal networks in postreform China, this trend will likely continue for the near future.

It seems to me that most previous studies of Chinese villages tend to examine village life from a collective or organizational perspective, and accordingly, villagers' social actions are interpreted as contributions to either patrilineal principles or community solidarity. By contrast my analysis of *guanxi* networks in Xiajia is aimed at understanding village life at the individual level and thus emphasizes villagers as active agents. From this perspective both formal kinsmen (agnates and affines alike) and non-kin relationships can be seen as practical kinship absorbed into *guanxi* networks by which individual villagers mobilize their human resources and achieve various social benefits. A common feature shared by affines, friends, colleagues, and fellow villagers in these *guanxi* networks is that they are all lateral (or horizontal) connections between families rather than vertical filiations within families, such as agnatic ties. These relations represent alliances created by individual villagers and maintained through mutual indebtedness in social exchange. They are practical because they must be continuously maintained and cultivated (see Bourdieu 1977: 35); hence the endless process of gift giving.

The second implication of my study is that in both the collective and post-collective periods, rural cadres can absorb more non-kin ties into their personal networks and build larger networks, thus reinforcing their dominant social position. (For a detailed analysis of gift giving in hierarchical contexts, see Chapter 7.) As indicated earlier, there is an apparent relationship between Xu's historical prominence in Xiajia village and the greater number of outside friends and colleagues on his gift list. The changing composition of the *guanxi* networks in the Yang and Han families provides another good example.

Yang is an ordinary farmer in his early forties. Because of his father's early death, he has been household head since his marriage. Economically, his family stands slightly above average, but he has made little improvement in the last decade, for he works only in farming. The first gift list shows the guests attending his wedding in 1974, which means that the personal network reflected on this list belongs mainly to his father. The second list, fifteen years later, records the guests for his youngest sister's marriage and reveals how much he has improved his family's social position in terms of network building.

Han is the current party secretary in the village. He was born to one of the poorest families in Xiajia, but has now become one of the richest and most powerful members of the community. He had worked as a production team leader for more than ten years before he was promoted to village head in 1981, between his eldest son's wedding (1979) and his second son's wedding (1986). Han's two gift lists tell us about the changes that occurred after he climbed to the top of the village power structure. In Table 7 below the first two gift lists belong to Yang, and the last two are Han's.

A comparison of these two cases reveals several interesting features. First, the size of the networks highlights differences in prestige

TABLE 7
Comparison of Personal Networks

	Yang's guests				Han's guests			
Relationship[a]	No. in 1974	Percent-age	No. in 1989	Percent-age	No. in 1979	Percent-age	No. in 1986	Percent-age
Affines	10	12%	14	15%	41	19%	60	17%
Agnates	11	14	13	14	4	2	2	1
Patrilateral kin	5	6	11	12	10	5	8	2
Matrilateral kin	5	6	8	8	5	2	11	3
Fictive kin	1	1	1	1	0		0	
Fellow villagers	50	61	46	49	132	62	189	53
Friends	0		1	1	12	6	43	12
Colleagues	0		0		9	4	45	12
TOTAL	82	100%	94	100%	213	100%	358	100%

[a]See note to Table 5.

between an ordinary farmer and a cadre. As shown in the bottom row in Table 7, Han's guests increased from 213 in 1979 to 358 in 1986, which means he managed to expand his *guanxi* network by 67 percent over seven years. In contrast, Yang's records show that there was little improvement (from 82 to 94 guests), even though the time interval was much larger (fifteen years). Actually, most guests who attended the second ritual were present at the first, except for those in the first category—affines. This fact indicates that Yang simply inherited his father's network of personal connections and acquired only a few affinal ties of his own.

Second, the ratio between kin and non-kin ties shows the difference in social status between Yang and Han. For 1974, in Yang's network (or more precisely that of Yang's late father) 39 percent of guests represented kinship ties and 61 percent represented non-kin ties, including fellow villagers. Fifteen years later, the figures were 50 percent and 50 percent, respectively. The drop in the number of non-kin ties in Yang's second gift list can be explained by the impact of decollectivization, because several people who had been working with Yang in the same production team cut off their gift-exchange relations with him after the collective was dismantled. In Han's gift lists, just the opposite occurred. He had successfully increased his friendship ties (from 72 percent to 77 percent), and his kinship ties, especially affinal ties, also increased in absolute terms even though they appear to have decreased in terms of percentage (from 28 percent to 23 percent). Given that kinship ties are mostly inherited from one's family or one's wife's family, and that friendship ties are created by one's own efforts, the ratio between these two types of relations is the best indicator of the status differences between Yang and Han.

Finally, in his last two types of relationships—friends and colleagues—Han is distinguished from other villagers such as Yang. As we saw in the preceding section, farmers generally do not have colleagues, because farming is not considered a special occupation. Therefore, it is unlikely that Yang has colleagues in his network, while Han has many, some of whom are cadres in other villages or local governments. It should be noted that Han's most impressive progress has been the expansion of his network of friends and colleagues. This development, of course, is closely related to his political promotion in 1981. As one of the two top leaders in Xiajia village, he gained many new opportunities to meet people outside the village and attracted new friends who wished to cultivate good relations with him. As a result, the number of guests in these two categories increased from 12 to 43 and from 9 to 45, respectively. More important, as the figures indicate, because Han has the kind of personal connections that few other villagers have, he obviously enjoys a much higher social position than his fellow villagers in Xiajia community.

In short, the most impressive development indicated by the Xiajia case is that during the past four decades, especially during the 1980's, the villagers' personal networks have generally expanded, mainly due to the absorption of more preexisting community ties into one's personal network. As the power of lineage organization was undermined considerably after the 1949 Revolution, Xiajia residents gained more freedom to choose how to construct their personal networks. Voluntarily constructed non-kin ties thus became a new frontier for individual pursuit in network expansion, and friendship and colleagueship constituted a new type of privileged connection. Under the political economy of socialism, however, it was the cadres who could get ahead quickly, just as they did in other aspects of social life. Their larger personal networks, important connections beyond village boundaries, and more elaborate gift-giving ceremonies distinguished them from their subordinates and thus helped to maintain their superior position in village society.

SIX

The Principle of Reciprocity
and *Renqing* Ethics

Renqing constitutes another centrally important concept in the Chinese system of social exchange. As does *guanxi*, the term *renqing* connotes a wide range of meanings and can hardly be translated into a single English word. In common usage *renqing* embraces four different yet related meanings. First, it means human feelings—the basic emotional responses of an individual in confrontation with various daily life situations. In this first meaning, *renqing* is social in nature and requires that one have an understanding of others' emotional responses in accordance with his or her own. Second, *renqing* indicates a set of social norms and moral obligations. These norms and obligations require keeping in contact with those of one's *guanxi* network and participating in the exchange of gifts, greetings, visits, and assistance. Third, in its extended usage *renqing* can be regarded as a kind of resource, such as a favor or a gift, and can be used as a medium of social exchange. Finally, in certain contexts, *renqing* is used as a synonym for *guanxi*. People may talk about how much *renqing* they possess when in fact they are referring to the size of their *guanxi* networks.[1] In order to avoid distorting its rich meanings, I will hereafter use the word *renqing* in the hope that, along with the term *guanxi*, it will be accepted eventually as a conceptual instrument in social analyses of China.

I begin this chapter with a discussion of the rules of gift giving and the various forms of reciprocity in Xiajia village. I then analyze both the moral and emotional aspects of the *renqing* complex. In the concluding section, I try to interpret *renqing* as a system of ethics based on commonsense knowledge in village society.

Rules of Gift Giving and Variations of Reciprocity

Before my fieldwork, I read a great many anthropological, sociological, and social psychology works on gift giving and social exchange. On the one hand I was deeply impressed by the central role of reciprocity in particular systems of social exchange; at the same time I was puzzled by the universality of the principle of reciprocity. More specifically, I was intrigued by the question of whether people always act in accordance with the same principles of reciprocity.

Inspiration finally came from reading Alvin Gouldner's essay on the norms of reciprocity. Gouldner emphasizes the universality of reciprocity, but he also notes its variations. "A norm of reciprocity is, I suspect, no less universal and important an element of culture than the incest taboo, although, similarly, its concrete formulations may vary with time and place" (1960: 171). Indeed, even though reciprocity as an abstract principle may exist in every society, how it actually regulates behavior in specific contexts of social life is still unclear. I began to survey the concrete activities of giving, receiving, and returning gifts, and gradually I discovered four operating rules of gift exchange among Xiajia residents, each of which reflects the principle of reciprocity in a different way.

The first rule is that a good person always interacts with others in a reciprocal way. This reciprocity is characterized by the obligation of giving, receiving, and returning gifts in the long run, as captured in the proverb *li shang wanglai*. Here, the *li* means propriety, ritual, norm, and, as indicated earlier, gift. *Shang* as a verb means to uphold or to advocate something, and *wanglai* is a noun literally meaning coming and going, or interactions. Thus "the system of propriety upholds the reciprocal interactions among people."

The origin of this saying in written form can be traced back two thousand years. The Confucian classic *Li Ji* (*Book of Rites*) explains its meaning in the following famous passage:

> In the highest antiquity they prized (simply conferring) good; in the time next to this, giving and repaying was the thing attended to. And what the rules of propriety value is reciprocity. If I give a gift and nothing comes in return, that is contrary to propriety; if the thing comes to me, and I give nothing in return, that also is contrary to propriety. (Legge [trans.] 1885:65)

While the purpose of this statement was to emphasize the necessity of social interactions in maintaining a harmonious social order, its most intriguing point is that it directly links gift-giving activities to the notion of propriety. The notion of propriety (*li*) is widely known to have played a central role in traditional Chinese culture, for it constituted "the basic concept of Confucianism" (Weber 1968: 156) and provided a set of norms governing people's behavior in daily life. Ideally one is expected to control every act of his or her life conduct according to the requirements of propriety. In highlighting the proper form of gift exchange as an example of reciprocity, the *Li Ji* embodies the practice of propriety as the conduct of giving and receiving and confers on gift giving the highest value. Actually, this passage has been quoted so many times it has become a proverb in Chinese popular culture. Nowadays, it is quite common for ordinary Chinese to explain their motivations for making gifts by referring to "propriety upholds reciprocal interactions."

The most important concern of my research, however, is not knowing what the ancient text says per se, but understanding to what extent these ideas can be seen in people's lives. During the early stage of my investigation, the ancient text seemed to be entirely reflected in villagers' behavior. Many informants referred to the proverb *li shang wanglai* in an attempt to explain their gift-giving activities. Nevertheless, when I asked them to write down the saying, after hearing them quote it repeatedly, what they wrote was different from the original.

The villagers' version differed from the ancient text in the second character. Without exception, my informants replaced the second word, *shang* as a verb (to uphold, to advocate), with its homonym as an adverb designating "above" or "upper." While the pronunciation remains the same, the meaning of the phrase changes considerably. Idiomatically, the first character *li* followed by *shang* as an adverb should be understood as "gift" rather than "propriety." Therefore, the villagers' version of *li shang wanglai* states that "people interact with each other in terms of gift exchange."

As indicated above, the original passage in the *Li Ji* highlights the significance of gift giving by considering it an example of the principle of reciprocity. Xiajia villagers, however, obviously have gone further to convert it into a concrete rule of gift exchange, while deemphasizing its original concern with social order. Nevertheless, although Xiajia villagers have altered the emphasis of the classic version of *li shang wanglai*, its essence—the principle of reciprocity—is maintained and continues to function as a primary rule in daily-life transactions.

The second rule of gift giving is that the offer of a gift should not break the existing hierarchical system of social status in either kinship or social terms. In the language of my informants, one must know what kinds of gifts are suitable for which categories of relatives or friends (*dui shenme ren, sui shenme li*). I discovered this rule first by transcribing the gift lists, for I noticed that relatives in the same category usually present similar gifts in a ritualized situation. Moreover, their names often appear together on the gift lists—an indication that they may come to present their gifts at the same time.

My assumption was proved correct by the villagers. They told me there were indeed standards for gift giving and that everyone knows the code. For instance, in 1990–91, the standard gift to attend one's wife's younger brother's wedding was 50 yuan, while that for a fellow villager (*tunqin*) was a maximum of 10 yuan. Except under special circumstances these amounts are generally observed, and a gift which is either less or more indicates the donor's lack of knowledge. More importantly, an unsuitable gift may offend the recipient as well as the other donors. One such case occurred during the early 1960's, when a young villager who had moved to a city wanted to show his generosity during a visit for a wedding in Xiajia. Although knowing the standard at that time, he offered a gift three times higher in value than the average. This was interpreted by both the host and the villagers as boasting of his success, which was a distasteful personality shortcoming. The gifts of others in the same kinship rank paled next to this young man's unusually large offering. In the end, the young man's parents apologized for their son's improper conduct; interestingly enough, they attributed his misconduct to the fact that he was still too young to understand *li*.

In order to observe the rules and to avoid any embarrassment resulting from lack of information (as in the case above), many villagers prefer to attend the ritual setting together with kin of equivalent rank, especially when they attend ceremonies outside their village. Hence their names appear together on the gift list.

My informants also warned me not to rely completely on fixed standards of gift giving because there is a third rule, locally called *li cong wanglai*, or "making gifts in accordance with previous interactions." Here the second Chinese character *cong* means "following," "in accordance with," or "based on." *Wanglai* means not only the previous gift exchanges but also other daily-life interactions between the two parties. If A has offered help to B, then B may wish to create a new type of gift-giving relationship with A by increasing the value of her or his gift or by presenting a gift for a situation in which B is not necessarily required to do so. So the *li* needs to follow previous *wanglai*. Under this rule, the villagers can adjust their gift-giving relations with each other, and some unusual social exchanges can be explained in terms of changing patterns of interaction.

The fourth rule concerns the proper manner of returning gifts. Villagers agree that a respectable man should avoid the appearance of gift exchanges as payoffs. The most common way is to increase somewhat the value of the returned gift. Concrete examples can be seen in Table 3 in Chapter 4, where several two-way transactions between the host Liu and his relatives and friends are recorded. For instance, Liu offered a gift of 30 yuan to his fictive matrilateral cousin in March 1991. Three months later, the latter returned 40 yuan as a gift for Liu's father's birthday celebration. Another person, who is both Liu's friend and neighbor, presented a gift of 20 yuan for the birthday celebration of Liu's father. Five days later, this man's wife underwent sterilization. Liu considered it was not right simply to return a monetary gift after such a short time interval, no matter whether he increased the amount of the gift or not. After discussing it with his wife, Liu bought 29 chicken eggs (a number symbolizing health and longevity), four tins of canned food, and a blanket—which cost him 25 yuan in total—and presented them to his friend.

It is worth noting that the Lius were particularly uncomfortable about the short time interval between the two transactions, because it might give the impression of repaying a debt if not handled in a proper way. From an etic point of view, we may say that Xiajia residents avoid clarifying the balance of gift exchange between them so that they can retain positive interactions with each other. As Bourdieu notes, "In every society it may be observed that, if it is not to constitute an insult, the counter-gift must be *deferred* and *different*, because the immediate return of an exactly identical object clearly amounts to a refusal (i.e., the return of the same object)" (1977: 5).

When making a different countergift by increasing its value, one should not increase it too much, lest it create unusual pressures on the recipient. In local terms, this is captured by the saying *li da ya si ren*, which means "an unusually large gift could crush a person to death." As an older villager said: "If you return too big a gift, you are making trouble for the recipient, because he has to increase the value of the gift and return it to you the next time. If this person happens to be in difficulty and cannot afford to return a bigger gift, he will hate your gift."[2]

It is clear that while the norm of reciprocity serves as the fundamental principle of gift exchange among Xiajia residents, the realization of this principle varies depending on many dynamic factors. The four rules of gift giving appear to conflict with each other under certain circumstances, as when making a proper return gift. To generalize these rules only creates confusion. Whenever I discussed the subject with my informants, they provided me with some cases that did not fit the rules and warned me not to be trapped by the rules. With their help I gradually gained the insight that most rules of social exchange in Xiajia (and perhaps in rural China in general) could be, and frequently were, modified to some extent by specific contexts and under the influence of numerous factors. Discovery of these contexts and factors, no doubt, is the key to understanding the nature of social exchange in Chinese culture.

In this regard, Weng, a knowledgeable and intelligent 72-year-old man, offered very valuable advice. Weng lived in a village several miles north of Xiajia and was widely recognized as one of the best ritual specialists in the area, a respectable role he played for more than 40 years. Before I visited him I had heard many stories about his passion for and knowledge of ritual procedures, folk beliefs, and etiquette in daily life. He always kept a small notebook in his pocket in order to take notes on the different customs, ritual details, and good ritual speeches he encountered on various occasions. Weng even had a personal file containing basic information about the village youth, such as birthdays, personal characteristics, and family background, which made him ready at all times to serve as manager of marriage ceremonies. He gave me the following advice during one of my visits:

Gift giving is something both complicated and simple. To say it is complicated, I mean that there are so many rules, manners, and details of etiquette. I have worked on these things my whole life, but I still can't answer all your questions. If you don't know all the rules, don't worry. Remember one thing: gift giving is a way to express *renqing*, and *renqing* is just human feelings. Everyone knows something about *renqing*. All rules of gift giving must conform to *renqing*. *Renqing* is the basic rule. Following the demands of *renqing*, you will do nothing wrong. It's just as simple as a hen laying eggs.

Renqing *and the Morality of Gift Exchange*

In my opinion, *renqing* can be regarded as a system of ethics, based on common sense, which consists of a set of norms and values. The best way to disentangle the *renqing* complex is to examine the basic norms and values embodied in the process of gift exchange. Having discussed reciprocity—one of the most important norms of *renqing*—in the above section, I will now focus on two indigenous notions that underlie the moral domain of *renqing* ethics, namely, sharing (*zhanguang*) and face (*mianzi*).

Sharing as the Moral Basis of *Renqing*

The literal meaning of the Chinese word *zhanguang* is "to share the light." In daily life it is commonly used to indicate one's intention or action to benefit from some particularistic connections. Yet, it also means that one is obligated to let others within the network share his or her privileges or social resources. Sharing might be the closest English translation of *zhanguang*, even though in many cases this kind of sharing is characterized by involuntary and obligatory acts.

There is a famous folk story in China that may help us understand the Chinese notion of sharing. It is said that after years of Taoist self-cultivation a man finally understood the universal way (*dao*) and thus made himself immortal. When he ascended to the immortal world in heaven, people found that his dog and chickens also flew up with him. Because of their association with him, these animals shared the man's merit and also became immortal. This popular story is expressed in the proverb "*yiren de dao, jiquan shengtian,*" meaning one man's achievement benefits all his associates. Here, the expectation of sharing is quite obvious.

In Xiajia, *zhanguang* plays an important role in the construction of *renqing* culture. First, it serves as a strong moral force for mutual assistance among relatives and friends. A good example of this from Xiajia appears in the case of Mr. Du, a local legend who migrated to the United States in the late 1980's and is currently living in San Francisco. In the late 1940's, Du joined the communist army to fight the nationalist party (KMT) in southern China. After the civil war, he left the army and became a cadre in a local government in Guangdong province. By the late 1970's, he was promoted to an important position in a commercial bureau in Guangzhou city. When several government leaders from Songjiang district, where Xiajia village is located, visited Guangzhou, Du entertained them warmly and helped them solve many problems, even though he had never met them before. The leaders felt they owed him a huge favor, so they asked him if they could do something for him back in his home village. Du thanked the leaders and asked for nothing specific, merely mentioning that he had a niece and a nephew living in Xiajia and he missed them very much. A few weeks later, two of the leaders visited Du's niece and nephew in Xiajia and found out that Du's niece hoped to change her peasant (*nongmin*) status into that of an urban worker (*gongren*). Within about three months, Du's niece was offered a job in a department store in a nearby town and gained urban status.

This incident occurred while I was living in the village. At the time, I knew none of the background information; what I knew was that my neighbors talked about it over and over again as a case of *zhanguang*. Everyone agreed that Du was a respectable man who cared about his relatives and admired Du's niece's good luck in sharing in her uncle's power. After I investigated the case in 1991, however, I realized that the first to share in Du's resources were the district government leaders, whom Du helped as fellow provincials from Heilongjiang. I also learned that more than ten Xiajia villagers had gained help from Du in various forms, and that many of them had no personal connections with Du except that of being fellow villagers (*tunqin*).[3]

Another interesting case occurred during the lunar New Year period in 1991, when the county government sent out teams to Beijing, Shanghai, and Guangzhou in an attempt to establish associations of fellow townsmen (*tongxiang hui*). In Beijing, more than 80 people were invited to join the association, and the county government promised to help them in their home villages. The county government's purpose was, of course, to "share" in these people's various powers of position in Beijing. According to a county cadre, this county was among the last to organize such an association. Since that time, two joint-venture projects have been established with the help of the association. It is clear that the concept of sharing has gained legitimacy at higher levels in the communist system.

The concept of sharing functions as a moral constraint for both the helper and the helped. For the helper, *zhanguang* means the obligation to share with others, indicating others' right to share in the helper's resources. The influence of this notion became clear to me when I had a discussion with several village friends about my own behavior. After a few months of observing my behavior (just as I was observing theirs), they concluded that I still acted like a student and did not know how to enjoy such privileges as attending free banquets with local cadres or using the government car. I argued that I enjoyed life but would rather spend my own money doing it. They all laughed, and one criticized me in a joking manner: "See, this is exactly the response of a silly student. You have become a big guy now, so you should take advantage of public resources as much as possible. If you have money, you can save the money to help your relatives, friends, and fellow villagers like us. Come on, why not let us share some light [*zhanguang*] with you? We are your good friends, like brothers, aren't we?" My friends were not serious about sharing my light, yet they were seriously worried about my "stupid ideas" and they did believe in the notion of *zhanguang*.

In addition to the obligation of mutual assistance, the concept of sharing also governs people's behavior in daily life and in ritual performances. For instance, wedding candy is widely distributed in order to allow many people to share in the happiness and good luck of the host family.

The most popular, yet perhaps least noticed, practice based on the notion of sharing is smoking behavior. Villagers in northeast China are known for smoking strong tobacco. According to my 1991 survey, more than 70 percent of the male adults in Xiajia were smokers, and many women also smoked. It is safe to say that tobacco is the most popular medium of gift exchange. Offering cigarettes to visitors is both a routine local custom and a sign of hospitality similar to the offer of a drink in Western societies. In Xiajia and the surrounding areas, until recently it was traditional for the hostess to fill a pipe or make a handrolled cigarette for the guests. Failure to do so would be considered evidence of not knowing about propriety (*bu dongli*) and was a face-losing matter for the whole family, especially for the family head. Therefore, many parents encouraged their female children to smoke, because they believed that a girl who did not smoke might be unable to learn proper etiquette, especially in offering tobacco-filled pipes to guests. This custom was quite popular when I was in the village during the 1970's, but has gradually died out, since most villagers now smoke cigarettes instead of pipes. However, inviting guests to smoke is still the best way to express hospitality.

One cannot host a ritual without offering a lot of cigarettes (and alcohol too, if a banquet is prepared). The offering of cigarettes constitutes an important ritual procedure in ceremonies such as engagement rites and weddings. As in the case of distributing candy at weddings, cigarettes offered by the new couple are called "happy cigarettes" and are believed to bring good luck to the recipients.

Finally, the notion of sharing governs villagers' smoking behavior on public occasions in an explicit way. If a villager wants to smoke in a public place, he or she must have brought enough tobacco or cigarettes for all the people in the area. It is an unwritten rule that one must share one's cigarettes or tobacco with others; the local term is *sanyan*, which means literally "to distribute cigarettes." An individual who refuses to share cigarettes with others in this context usually is considered selfish and unsocial. Those who always enjoy others' cigarettes at public gatherings but who never make their own contributions are regarded as discourteous or low class.

I discussed my findings with some friends in Ha'erbin and in Beijing, and learned of similar phenomena in these urban settings. I was told that one must take a quick decision when facing a group about whether to share one's cigarettes with the group. As the obligatory distribution of cigarettes may cost too much for low-income Chinese, some people may choose not to smoke in public in order to save both money and face. If one is offered a cigarette by someone, one also needs to decide whether to accept the offer, because accepting a cigarette initiates an obligation to return the gift, thus entailing an eventual cost. A decision not to accept requires good excuses. Often, if one's cigarettes are of inferior quality, that person may decide not to smoke in public. A cigarette brand symbolizes one's social and economic status, so smoking cheap cigarettes can be embarrassing.

As in the case of mutual aid between relatives and friends, the pattern of smoking behavior is based on the notion of sharing. Again, what deeply impressed me was the strong feeling of moral obligation: one side was obligated to offer and the other had a claim or the right to receive. For instance, I noticed that my stay in my landlord's house greatly increased his expenditures on cigarettes, because many of the villagers who came to visit me felt free to smoke my landlord's cigarettes, which he left on the table. Usually, my landlord warmly and sincerely invited my visitors to smoke, but even without invitation they would help themselves or ask the landlady to offer them one. To avoid causing this extra cost to my host family, I once bought some cigarettes for my guests. To my surprise, this was not appreciated by my landlord and his wife; on the contrary, they criticized me for not considering them "family members" (*zijiaren*).

They insisted it was their responsibility to offer cigarettes to guests in their home, no matter whom the guests came to visit. They said: "Because you read too many books, sometimes you forget the common sense of *renqing*."

Their friendly criticism made me ponder the significance of this cigarette incident to them, to the other villagers, and to myself. I was finally convinced that sharing was a concept that underlay the ethics of *renqing* culture and gave meaning to the villagers' everyday social exchange activities. My act of buying cigarettes to compensate my host family could, according to the logic of *renqing*, be interpreted as a distancing gesture on my part, a sign of refusing to share with them. That, of course, was definitely not what I had intended. They knew this, so they thought that I had merely lost my common sense.

Face As a Moral Constraint in Social Interaction

Another important concept in *renqing* ethics is *mianzi*, called "face" in English. The significant meanings of this term in Chinese society have long been recognized by Western observers. One hundred years ago, Arthur Smith began his description of the Chinese character with a discussion of face (1894). Since there have already been a number of theoretical discussions on the concept (Chen 1988; Ho 1975; Hu 1944; Hwang 1987; King 1988b; and Zhu 1988), I will begin with a specific case of "face struggle," and then test the applicability of the theories to social practice in Xiajia village.

An incident of face struggle occurred between a cook and a cadre in the town government under which Xiajia village is administrated, and it had a dramatic conclusion. Mr. Zhao had worked as a cook in the town government for many years. Partly because of his occupation and partly because of his careless and muddleheaded character, he earned the nickname of "big bread Zhao." He has managed to maintain good personal relations, however, with most of the cadres in the local government by offering his cooking skills for rituals hosted by the cadres. In addition to his services, he always gives gifts to the host families and is quite proud of having built a *guanxi* network, which, he believes, demonstrates that he is much smarter than a "big bread."

In late spring 1991, Zhao hosted a wedding for his youngest son, an elaborate ceremony for which he had prepared a long time. He sent invitations to all the government cadres to whom he had given gifts in the past. Some cadres came to the wedding and some did not, but all made return gifts—except Mr. Lin, the deputy party secretary in the town government. Zhao was disappointed and angry with secretary Lin because Zhao had cooked twice before for Lin in similar ritual situations and had also given gifts on various occasions. Zhao tried to rationalize that Lin might have merely forgotten to attend the wedding, thus missing the opportunity to return a gift. However, local custom does allow the presentation of make-up gifts when a ritual is missed. So Zhao waited several days, while complaining of his dissatisfaction through gossip channels. To his surprise, Lin did not respond at all.

Zhao thought he had been treated unfairly and thus felt insulted. Without consulting anyone, he decided to get even on his own. One day he ran into the conference room of the town government where many cadres, including Lin, were meeting and asked Lin directly to explain why he had not returned a gift. Zhao noted all the gifts he had given Lin in the past and accused Lin of lacking a basic knowledge of *renqing*. He said: "Even though I am an ordinary cook, I know *li shang wanglai* very well. But you don't, secretary Lin!"

All the cadres were shocked into silence, and the accused could find not a single word with which to defend himself. Then some cadres began to talk with Zhao and tried to calm him down. Finally, Zhao left the room, and party secretary Lin also left the meeting. In the evening, Zhao received a return gift from Lin via a middleman.

Understandably, the case soon became well known in the surrounding area. By the time I investigated it two months later, several versions were circulating with different details and a variety of reactions from the public. All my informants, except for one of Lin's colleagues, commented that Lin was morally wrong, and many said they could not believe a person in Lin's position could behave like that. About Zhao's behavior, however, opinions were diverse. From the numerous comments, I found public attention focused generally on three particular aspects: (1) Zhao's unusual action to claim a return gift; (2) Zhao's complaints about Lin, which initiated gossip;

and (3) Zhao's inviting of cadres to his son's wedding, which was regarded as his attempt to gain face.

About the first point, most informants agreed that even though Lin had broken the rule of gift exchange and had really acted in an immoral way, Zhao should not have demanded a return gift at a public occasion. They insisted that gift giving was not a loan—it could not be claimed like a debt. Zhao's act merely proved he was a "big bread," a muddleheaded person. Some informants suggested that Zhao was morally wrong too, because his act violated the common sense of *renqing*, which required people to save face for one another. This criticism was so severe that Zhao became ashamed of his victory and did not want to talk about it at all when I tried to get his explanation of the event.

Others maintained that the conflict would have been solved at an earlier stage if Zhao had not publicized Lin's failure to return a gift in the first place. According to these people, Lin would have made every effort to save his own face, even to the extent of secretly presenting a make-up gift to Zhao, because Lin was one of the top leaders in the town government and needed to be careful about his face. But it was unacceptable for Lin to offer a make-up gift after being publicly humiliated, for that showed the world he had bowed down before a cook who worked in his office. In other words, it was unreasonable to expect someone in Lin's position to apologize in words or deeds to a low-status villager. Therefore, Zhao made a strategic mistake, perhaps resulting from his lack of cleverness. This kind of criticism of Zhao, however, was rejected by a number of younger informants. They argued that Lin's disgraceful initial act demonstrated that Lin was a person whose face was extremely thick skinned (*lianpi hou*).[4] *Li shang wanglai* was something that even children knew very well; how was it possible that Lin did not think about returning a gift?

The most interesting comments implied that Zhao's invitation to the cadres was an ill-conceived effort to gain face because he did not take the huge status gap between himself and the cadres into consideration. As these informants explained, the cadres who received Zhao's invitations were confronted with a dilemma. They felt obligated to attend the wedding and offer gifts, according to the rules of gift exchange, but to be so close to an ordinary cook, and especially one who had a reputation for stupidity, was an embarrassment. This was why only a few cadres actually attended the wedding, while many others had their gifts delivered by an intermediary. According to these informants, it would have been better for Zhao not to have invited the cadres, thus leaving them the option of whether they wanted to attend. They could have easily found out about the wedding, since they all lived in the same small town. If they did not want to attend, they could have pretended not to know about the ritual, thus saving face. Given their difference in social status, Zhao should have been satisfied with his good relations with these cadres, which already added a great deal to his face, rather than expecting the intimacy of an equal exchange of gifts.

This gift-giving dispute and the related reactions of the public reveal the tension between reciprocity and social hierarchy, an important issue I will discuss in detail in Chapter 7. Here I would like to examine further, using this empirical evidence of face struggle, how the concept of face works in real life and whether the previous theoretical interpretations of face fit everyday practice in Xiajia village.

Among the earlier studies, Hsien-chin Hu's well-known essay (1944) is perhaps the first systematic analysis of the Chinese concept of *mianzi*. Hu maintains that the word *mianzi* connotes a much wider range of meanings than can possibly be indicated by the English term "face," and he further distinguishes between two kinds of face, reflected in two different terms in northern Chinese dialect. The first kind indicates social prestige and is called *mianzi*. "This is prestige that is accumulated by means of personal effort or clever maneuvering. For this kind of recognition ego is dependent at all times on its external environment" (Hu 1944: 45). The second category is *lian*, which means "the respect of the group for a man with a good moral reputation: the man who will fulfill his obligations regardless of the hardships involved, who under all circumstances shows himself a decent human being" (Hu 1944: 45). Unlike the former, which completely depends on others' evaluation, the latter "is not only an external sanction for behavior that violates moral standards, but constitutes an internal sanction as well" (1944: 61).

While Hu's elaborate distinction between *mianzi* and *lian* has provoked further conceptual inquiries (see, e.g., Ho 1975), most studies still emphasize face as being an aspect of social prestige (*mianzi*) and as having the function of regulating people's behavior externally. John Fairbank's generalization represents the latter. " 'Face' has been a social matter. Personal dignity has been derived from right conduct and the social approval it has secured. 'Loss of face' came from failure to observe the rules of conduct so that others saw one at a disadvantage" (Fairbank 1979: 135). King has criticized this tendency to overlook the second kind of face (*lian*) and has rephrased the double meaning of face as a distinction between social face and moral face (King 1988b: 325). According to King, the moral face (or Hu's *lian*) does not resort to an external environment or an audience in regulating a person's behavior. On the contrary, moral face is based on a person's feelings of shame (*chi*), a Chinese notion close to the Western concept of guilt, and thus serves as an internal moral constraint (1988b: 335–38).

My findings from Xiajia sustain the theory that there are two kinds of face, social (*mianzi*) and moral (*lian*). As the villagers' comments reflect, what Lin lost was his moral face because he violated the basic moral principle of gift exchange. When one villager said: "Secretary Lin will have no face to be seen by the people," he used precisely the Chinese word *lian* (*meilian jianren*). Moreover, while Lin exposed his moral failings to the public and was caught acting inappropriately to one of a much lower status, he also completely lost his social face. Actually, it was the pursuit of social face that caused the dispute—Zhao wanted to gain face by receiving gifts from cadres, and Lin refused to offer a make-up gift in an attempt to save his own face.

Zhao's victory in this dispute shows that in a public conflict concerned with the loss of moral face, it is usually the person in a superior social position who is more vulnerable to sanction by public opinion. This case supports Hu's argument that "the higher the social standing of a person the more dignity he has to maintain, and the more vulnerable this *lien* [*lian*] becomes" (1944: 47). It does not mean, however, that the moral mechanism of face is designed to favor those in inferior positions, because the ethics of *renqing* requires those of lower rank to help protect the social face of those of higher rank. So although people of higher social standing can easily lose a battle concerned with moral face, as in this case of Lin, Zhao did not gain anything in terms of social prestige because he did not follow the ethics of *renqing*.

This dispute challenges previous models in one important aspect. Both Hu and King, among others, assert explicitly that social face is achieved and possessed mainly by people in the upper classes and that ordinary people do not care much about their social face. According to Hu, "To be able to count on the confidence of his fellow-men even the poorest peasant or laborer will be anxious to preserve his *lian*. He cannot achieve *mien-tzu* [*mianzi*], the reward for success in life, but he can conduct his life so that no blemish can be cast on his character" (Hu 1944: 63). King also maintains that "the people in the lowest rank of a society have no social face" (1988b: 329). These views are negated when we consider Zhao's struggle to gain social face. It is interesting that even for those who criticized Zhao's sending of invitations to the cadres in the first place, Zhao's pursuit of social face was beyond criticism. In the eyes of the villagers, Zhao might have chosen a stupid strategy, but he did do the right thing by pursuing and fighting for social face.

The most important thing we learn from this case is that the concept of face plays a decisive role as a moral constraint in social interactions among Xiajia villagers. While the pursuit of social face motivates villagers to participate actively in the game of gift exchange, the constraint of moral face regulates all the participants' behavior. The concern with face, especially moral face, provides an internal moral constraint that directs individuals' actions. In Chapter 4, I discussed a case where a villager said that if he did not attend a birthday celebration and fulfill his obligation of gift giving, he would feel uncomfortable and shamed, just like a thief caught in the act of stealing. The phrase "feeling uncomfortable" was frequently used by my informants when they spoke about the pressure to make gifts. Another common expression was "face isn't bright," and the term for face used in this context was *lian* (*lianshang bu guangcai*). Nevertheless, my analysis also indicates that in real life one's concern with moral face can hardly be separated from the fear of external social sanctions. As reflected in the cases of gift exchange, the two kinds of face are often entangled.

Emotional Aspects of Renqing *and the Meaning of Gift Exchange*

As explained at the beginning of this chapter, the word *renqing* also means human feelings. This definition can also be traced back at least two thousand years. According to the *Li Ji*, "What are the feelings of men [*renqing*]? They are joy, anger, sadness, fear, love, disliking, and liking." By definition, it follows that *renqing* contains an emotional aspect, which is expressed in daily life by the term *ganqing*, another important indigenous concept.

Like the concepts of *renqing* and *guanxi*, the Chinese notion of *ganqing* is also troublesome to translate or interpret. *Ganqing* can be roughly translated into English as "sentiment," "emotional attachment," and "good feelings." Because of its flexible usage dependent on specific contexts, Jacobs, among others, maintains that it cannot be translated adequately (1979: 259). Although Jacobs's point is well taken, to avoid introducing too many Chinese words in my text, I still prefer to use "good feelings" or "sentiment." But I will provide additional explanations as needed.

The word *ganqing* is composed of two Chinese characters: *gan* and *qing*. The second character alone connotes all three meanings of *ganqing*. However, the first character is not a meaningless syllable. As a single-syllable word, *gan* means to feel, to experience, and to be moved emotionally. The combination of these two characters implies that *ganqing* exists only when sentiment, emotional attachment, and good feelings are felt by people involved in social interactions.

The term *renqing* shares the second character *qing* with *ganqing*; this obviously signifies the emotional aspect of *renqing*. My attention to the composition of these two words was originally inspired by an educated villager. During one of our talks, he gave me his explanation of *renqing*: "You see, *ren* stands for personal relations here, like the relationship between you and me. And *qing* is an abbreviation for *ganqing*. So, the term *renqing* should be understood as personal relations based on good feelings."

Morton Fried was perhaps the first to notice the role of sentiment in personal relations in China. He defines *ganqing* as "the quality of the relationship between the parties"—the relationship generally being between people of different social classes who do not share kinship ties. Fried continues, saying that *ganqing* functions as "the primary institutionalized technique by which class differences are reduced between non-related persons" (1953: 103). Basically agreeing with Fried's definition, Gallin suggests that *ganqing* also exists in agnatic and affinal relations, but that it must be hierarchical in nature (1966: 171). The limited role of sentiment was challenged by Donald De Glopper, who finds that *ganqing* can refer both to non-kin and equal relations, and is actually "the affective component of all human relations" (De Glopper 1978: 312). Moreover, as Jacobs points out, the connective nature of *ganqing* can tie groups as well as dyads (1979: 260).

Indeed, sentimentality plays an important role in the daily life of Xiajia residents. Emotional responses constitute one of the measures by which villagers make judgments on personal character. It is quite common to hear remarks such as "so-and-so can be easily emotionally charged" (*dong ganqing*) or "so-and-so lacks sentiment" (*mei ganqing*). The latter comment is an exaggeration that actually means "being indifferent to many emotional issues." Moreover, the quality of sentiment is used to describe the most intimate relationship, that of husband and wife, as well as other personal relations. To say that a couple has good feelings toward each other (*ganqing hao*) is equivalent to saying "they love each other" in English. It is interesting that in a recent divorce case in Xiajia, one of the reasons for divorce given by the wife (who demanded the divorce) was "having no good feelings" (*meiyou ganqing*) toward her husband.[5] Although elements of sentiment affect the villagers' lives in a variety of ways, I am concerned here with the role of sentiment in gift giving and in the *renqing* complex only.

Villagers evaluate the affective component (*ganqing*) of personal relations and express their emotional preferences in many ways during daily-life interactions. The expression *ganqing hao* is not limited to intimate relationships between a man and a woman; instead, it is frequently applied to almost all kinds of close relations. Hospitality is considered a way to express one's good feelings toward guests; therefore, the offering of cigarettes and alcohol is extremely common. Greetings are another important way to express one's good feelings. In a close-knit community, people may run into each other every day, but they never neglect to give a warm greeting to each other, unless they want to deliver an unfriendly message. An informant told me that he was once very angry with his nephew because the nephew had called him by his official title instead of by a kinship term. After receiving this strange greeting a few times, he could not stand it anymore and asked his nephew to explain what was wrong with the good feelings between them. With the help of a kinsman, the man had dinner with his nephew in the kinsman's home, drank a lot of alcohol, exchanged ideas, and clarified the misunderstanding caused by gossip, finally reviving the good feelings they once had toward each other.

Gift giving is perhaps the most common channel for expressing one's emotional responses. Although many gifts are exchanged because of rational concerns or moral obligations, all my informants maintained that gift giving always involves personal feelings, good or bad. A man explained to me that "there are two kinds of gift giving: one is joy and another is suffering. For those with whom I have good feelings, I am very happy to present gifts when they host ceremonies, because the gifts come from my heart. But, I often have to attend rituals and offer gifts to people with whom I have no good feelings, and that is really awful." As indicated in Chapter 4, the gifts exchanged between friends are usually more valuable than those exchanged between kinsmen (except the closest relatives) and fellow villagers. This was identified by my informants as the result of strong emotional ties between friends.

During my fieldwork I heard many stories that emphasized the emotional attachment between friends. For instance, a key informant's mother had two women friends in her natal village about ten miles south of Xiajia. After she married into Xiajia, she tried to convince her friends to look for husbands in the village. In the end, one was successful and became a lifelong good friend of the informant's mother. Over a period of 50 years, the two women frequently visited each other's houses, spent spare time together, assisted each other during life crises, and also kept a close relationship by gift exchange. As a result of their friendship, good feelings also tied the two families together, and the gift exchange relationship still exists today, although the two women have passed away. During our talk, the informant recalled many details about the warm, intimate relationship between his mother and her friend. He concluded with the same phrase: that "they had really good feelings toward each other." This case is by no means the exception. Most men and women in Xiajia are emotionally attached to some good friends or close relatives for a very long time, and they describe these attachments as *ganqing hao*. Usually, people who share good feelings spend their spare time together: chatting, playing cards, gambling (mainly men), sewing (women), and, recently, watching TV.

It is interesting to note that villagers make an implicit distinction between personal relations with good feelings and personal relations without good feelings. They maintain that interactions in daily life (*wanglai*) do not necessarily imply the existence of good feelings between two parties, because in many cases people are obligated to interact with kinsmen they do not like. This is particularly true in cases of gift exchange at ritual situations such as weddings or funerals. For those who do have good feelings toward each other, however, their interactions are greatly intensified. In addition to routinized gift exchange, people with good feelings visit each other quite often, spend time together, and emotionally depend on each other. In local terms, this type of intimate interaction is called *zoudong*, meaning literally "walking and moving," a metaphor for mutual visiting.

The local distinction between *wanglai* and *zoudong* reveals two interlocking dimensions of social exchange. On the one hand, the morality of gift giving requires the maintenance of certain kinds of formal relations and the completion of the institutionalized and prescribed task of gift exchange (*wanglai*). On the other hand, one can also find room to develop emotional ties with select people in terms of more intimate, informal, and nonritualized interactions in daily life (*zoudong*). Therefore, two villagers who maintain a formal relationship of ritualized gift giving are not necessarily emotionally attached to each other and may no longer have emotionally charged interactions. For instance, one informant told me that he had stopped visiting his father's youngest sister more than ten years earlier, even though she had married a Xiajia man and lived in the same village. The reason, according to him, was mostly a personality conflict; he could not stand his father's sister's bad temper, and she did not treat him well when he was a little boy. "We did not have good feelings toward each other from the very beginning," the informant concluded. Nevertheless, he had to fulfill his obligations of ritualized gift giving and prescribed visits during the lunar New Year, which could not be affected by emotional concerns. As a compromise, he sent his wife to represent him on these occasions and increased the value of his gifts in an effort to show his respect. This informant's strategy was a common method of solving the conflict between moral obligations and emotions. Men who dislike each other try to avoid interactions of all kinds, including seeing each other, and therefore may choose to send their wives, or adult children, to represent them in ritualized gift-giving situations.

While the existence of *ganqing* normally reinforces a given interpersonal relationship, sometimes it may cause unexpected problems for the two parties. In one case, higher expectations due to good feelings destroyed a friendship. When a villager had business trouble, he turned to his good friend for financial aid. With a lot of effort the friend found a relative to lend some money to the first villager so that he could solve his problem quickly. Things began to sour, however, when the first villager learned that he would need to pay interest on the loan. As explained in Chapter 4, in local financial dealings, a loan with interest is called "raising money" (*taiqian*), and applies only to loans between people without good personal relations. Because of the interest, the first villager felt that his good friend was treating him as an unrelated stranger. He believed that his friend had betrayed him and was taking the side of his relative, even though the friend made every effort to explain that he could not convince his kinsman to lend the money without charging interest. The first villager was so outraged that he went to his friend's home and accused him in public of not knowing the duty of a good friend, thus not qualifying to be a man. When I interviewed this villager, he insisted that it was not a matter of money, or even a matter of friendship; instead, it was a matter of sentiment. "I was emotionally hurt," he stated.

This case shows that emotional attachments are entangled with moral obligations, and good feelings can be expressed in terms of the commitment one feels toward one's duties in personal relations. The overlapping roles of morality and sentiment in motivating social exchange may best be illustrated by the highest kind of *renqing—enqing*.

The term *enqing* refers to the more significant favors or the help one receives that influences one's life in the long run. The most common type of *enqing* is that from parents, who give life to their children and raise them (*yangyu zhi en*). If we regard *renqing* as various kinds of favors, *enqing* stands at the pinnacle as the greatest favor, and thus the recipient is indebted to the grantor for a lifetime. More importantly, ordinary favors generally can be exchanged, but the highest kind of favor (*enqing*) cannot. While ordinary favors may or may not add to *ganqing* between the two parties, *enqing* requires that the recipient feel gratitude forever.[6]

In Xiajia, although the classical meaning of *enqing*, such as that of parents to children, is understood by villagers, the term is more often employed to indicate the important favors that save or change the recipient's life in economic, political, or social terms. For instance, during the Cultural Revolution, the then village head of Xiajia was falsely accused of murdering an old villager who had been beaten up during a struggle session and had died shortly thereafter. The investigators were friends of the dead man's son, who had been promoted to high rank in the county government. They were biased against the village head and used improper methods to collect false testimonies against him. The village head was thus in great danger. When the investigators questioned the last witness, the notetaker of the struggle meeting, he provided a completely different testimony, which convincingly proved that the village head was not present at the struggle session. The case was dismissed because of this testimony: what he did was no doubt *enqing* to the village head. During the following twelve years, the village head kept a close relationship with this honest witness and tried to help the latter whenever possible. He was so deeply indebted to the witness that he still recalled the incident several times when he was dying in 1979.

According to my informants, making an effort to return the greatest favor (*enqing*) was not the key issue; the most important thing was never to forget it and always feel gratitude. A villager told me that he owed much to two men in Xiajia who saved his family more than 40 years before. His family was mistakenly classified as rich peasants during land reform, and the family property was thus subject to confiscation. When the village militia searched the property, the leader ordered the militiamen to leave some basic supplies for the family. A few months later, another village cadre found out about the mistake and made a great effort to correct it, which saved this family in a more important sense. The villager's mother told the villager these stories and asked him never to forget the *enqing* from these two men. When the man grew up and became a cadre in the village, he took every opportunity to show his gratitude to the two men and even helped their children. Yet he told me that what really mattered was the feeling of gratitude, because a favor that saved a whole family could not possibly be repaid.[7]

It is clear that in the social life of Xiajia village, sentiment affects villagers' behavior just as significantly as do moral obligations. The spiritual substances embedded in gifts are both morally and emotionally charged. Villagers exchange gifts to increase *ganqing* with each other, as well as to reinforce *guanxi*. In other words, it is the combination of developing emotional attachments and cultivating personal relations that gives meaning to the practice of gift exchange.

A Tentative Generalization Regarding Renqing

Thus far I have purposely focused on the moral and emotional aspects of *renqing*, because they (especially the latter) by and large have been overlooked in earlier studies (see, e.g., Hwang 1987; Jacobs 1979; and M. M. Yang 1989). This neglect has been due to the previous emphasis on *renqing* as an exchangeable resource or as an outcome of rational calculation. Nevertheless, I do not mean to imply that rational calculation is less important than moral obligation or emotional attachment. On the contrary, I am convinced that Xiajia residents do take personal interest into consideration in each of their *renqing* actions, and they make rational choices based on their judgment of possible gain or loss. What I am trying to emphasize in this chapter is that villagers do not interact with each other only for utilitarian purposes, and the *renqing* complex is much more than a win-or-lose power game (see, e.g., Hwang 1987).

To sum up, *renqing*, as perceived and practiced by Xiajia villagers, is a system of ethics that guides and regulates one's behavior when dealing with others within one's *guanxi* network. At the normative level, *renqing* relies on the basic concepts of reciprocity (*bao*), sharing (*zhanguang*), and face (*mianzi*). In practice, *renqing* represents socially accepted, correct interpersonal behavior, and the violation of *renqing* is regarded as serious misconduct. As King notes, "From a sociological point of view, the word *renqing* refers to interpersonal relations, namely, the ways of living with others" (1988a: 78). *Renqing* ethics can be applied only to those within one's *guanxi* network. The boundary of *guanxi* and the effective scope of *renqing* are defined and proved by various forms of ongoing social exchange, especially gift exchange. Nevertheless, an interesting social phenomenon frequently observed in Chinese society is that one tends to pull as many people as possible into one's *guanxi* network and thus has to apply the *renqing* ethics to a wider and wider range of people.

The system of *renqing* ethics has three structural dimensions: rational calculation, moral obligation, and emotional attachment. The complexity and flexibility of *renqing* in action results from the changing composition of its three structural elements. Although all three dimensions coexist in all social interactions concerned with *renqing*, actual emphasis can be placed on any one of them in a given situation. In other words, one individual can be extremely rational and thus calculate carefully any act of social exchange in order to pursue personal interests; while another person may be just the opposite, paying attention primarily to moral obligations or acting primarily in accordance with good feelings in interpersonal relations. Moreover, it is not uncommon that an individual acts in different ways in different situations, and may change his or her emphasis according to the particular needs of the specific circumstances.

It follows that *renqing* may appear in different forms, resulting from changes in the configuration of its three structural elements. Given that people may choose to emphasize any of the three elements in concrete actions, observations of village life in Xiajia have led me to the conclusion that, at least in the domain of gift giving and social exchange, moral obligations are more likely to dominate behavior. After all, it is a moral economy in which Xiajia residents live.

Power and Prestige in Gift-Exchange Relations

Although expressivity and reciprocity take a prominent place in the creation of *renqing* culture, gift exchange among Xiajia residents is not always balanced. An asymmetrical flow of gifts is quite common, especially in the context of hierarchical social relations. In many cases, unbalanced gift giving involves other forms of social exchange and thus begets power and prestige in interpersonal relations. With a focus on gift exchange in hierarchical contexts, my inquiry in this chapter is primarily concerned with two issues. First, who gains prestige and power generated by the gift exchange—the donor or the recipient? And second, in which direction do asymmetrical gifts flow in the system of social hierarchy—toward social superiors or toward subordinates?

These two questions early on attracted the attention of anthropologists (see, e.g., Malinowski 1984; Mauss 1967) and have remained important. Most previous studies arrived at the conclusion that it was the donor who gains prestige and power by transforming the recipient into a debtor, and thus in the case of unbalanced transactions, the gifts usually pass downward in the social hierarchy (see, e.g., Befu 1966–67; Raheja 1988; Sahlins 1972; A. Strathern 1971; and Vatuk and Vatuk 1971). Gregory goes further in asserting that the superiority of the gift giver is "a feature that is common to gift exchange systems all over the world" (1982: 47).

The system of gift exchange in Xiajia, however, presents a sharp contrast to these earlier generalizations: Gift receiving rather than gift giving is regarded as a symbol of prestige. In some contexts, gifts are unilaterally directed up the ladder of social status, with the recipient remaining superior to the giver. After outlining the asymmetrical flow of gifts in Xiajia village, I describe two types of unbalanced reciprocity: One results from the developmental cycle of the family, and the other from a gap in social status. My analysis then focuses on the latter, that is, the one-way movement of gifts from lower to upper social strata within the socialist hierarchy. I discuss the social-cultural mechanisms that sustain this unilateral gift giving and attempt to explain why the Xiajia case reveals features that differ strikingly from those in earlier studies. Finally, I address the simple yet central issue for all studies of gift exchange: Why do people want to participate in gift giving? Patterns of gift behavior found in Xiajia suggest that it is the prestige of receiving that motivates villagers to give.

Imbalance in Gift Exchange

During my fieldwork, many villagers complained that they had to offer so many gifts that gift giving had become unaffordable. While complaining about the huge expense, they tried to convince me that they were not stingy. On the contrary, they understood *renqing* ethics very well and wanted to be generous in gift exchange. As a result, more than half the Xiajia households needed 500 yuan or more for a year's expenditures on gifts (see survey results in Chapter 4). When discussing the economic burdens of gift exchange, most villagers maintained that they had given more gifts than they had received.

If so many villagers gave more gifts than they received, where did these gifts end up? In other words, were there some people who received more than they gave? According to ordinary villagers, the answer is "Yes, the cadres." They attributed the recent increase of gift-giving activities to the cadres' ulterior motives. As a schoolteacher in Xiajia put it: "These days people make every effort to host ceremonies and receive gifts. The more criticism there is of the 'gift-giving wind' in newspapers, the stronger it blows. Why? Because the wind comes from above. All the new customs [of gift giving] are created by cadres and other people above, because they can receive gifts but they don't worry about returning them." However, when I posed the same question to the village cadres, they all denied that they had ever failed to return gifts. A cadre maintained: "That would make me a shameless person, a person who is ignorant of human feelings and morality [budong renqing]. Nobody wants to do such a stupid thing to hurt one's own reputation." Yet some of these local cadres went on to complain about their superiors for the same reason: They offered gifts to state officials in the township or the county government, but the latter did not return the gifts.

Inspired by my informants' ambiguous and often contradictory answers, I conducted a special survey on the balance of gift exchange. I discerned that the asymmetrical flow of gifts was determined by two factors: the cycle of family development and the social status hierarchy. The former is a universal process within every family; it was not given much attention, nor did it generate complaints from Xiajia villagers. The latter causes asymmetrical gift giving only when a disparity in social status exists between the donor and the recipient, and, in this context, some people (mostly cadres) indeed received gifts without fulfilling the obligation to return them.

Let me first explain why the development cycle of the family may cause an unbalanced flow of gifts among social equals. After family division, young couples need to build up their conjugal families both economically and socially, and they also have to decide with whom they should begin a long-term relationship of gift exchange. As they will have few opportunities to host a ceremony before their children are grown, they can expect to be engaged in unilateral giving for at least a decade. During this period, the young couples are designated givers, and some of their gifts may not be reciprocated owing to changes in interpersonal relations over long periods of time. Every conjugal family goes through this period, but some may take more risks than others. If a man wants to be an important person in village society, he needs the largest possible social network. Therefore he must take the risk of giving gifts to those with whom he has never had gift-exchange relations before and perhaps never will again.

The same thing occurs in the final stage of family development. If an old couple lives alone after family partition, they must pay back the gift debts inherited from the earlier stages of family development, but they have few opportunities to host other ceremonies for themselves, except birthday celebrations hosted by their children. (According to many informants, claiming "credit" in gift giving is precisely why birthdays have become so important in recent years.) Consequently, gifts unilaterally flow out again from these senior conjugal families to other families in the network, although senior couples have gained the prestige to receive the *xiaojing* (filial piety and respect) gifts from their own children.

Since these are natural stages every family must pass through, this one-way flow of gifts does not have a significant impact on the social relations of these villagers. To minimize the cost of unilateral giving, until their children become teenagers many young couples delay entrance into the mainstream of gift exchange and limit their gift-giving relations to only the closest relatives and best friends. Elders may adopt the same strategy, but because they were previously involved deeply in the process of gifts, it is not easy to limit exchange relations.

Because gift giving is closely related to family ceremonies, single people and childless couples also find themselves in the position of being obligated gift givers. By singles I mean the unmarried male villagers who are over 30 and live in independent households. In 1991, there were nine singles and three childless couples in Xiajia. In addition, there were three single women over age 30 who were unlikely to be married in the future. But they all live with either their parents or brothers and so do not act as independent households in social life, including gift exchange. While obligated to participate in gift-exchange rituals for their relatives and friends, the nine male singles do not have any chance of hosting a family ceremony unless they get married, which will terminate their status as singles. A 62-

year-old bachelor told me that in the past 30 years he had participated in gift-giving rituals more than 100 times (three or four times each year), but he never had received a return gift. He explained that he had tried to keep the number of rituals to a minimum, but he still was obligated to attend some of them, such as his nephew's wedding or his neighbor's childbirth celebration. The same is true for childless couples, for they too have no reason to host any family ceremonies, but are still obligated to offer gifts to some close relatives. The only way for these people to achieve balanced reciprocity is to retreat from the cycle of gift exchange, which in turn worsens their already low status in village society. In addition to the obligatory aspect of making gifts to one's kinsmen, material needs for assistance in daily life and psychological needs to belong drive singles and childless couples to become permanent givers in the game of gift exchange.

Status differences constitute another social force that may break the equilibrium of gift flow under certain circumstances. In Chapter 3 I discussed the gift called *xiaojing*, given by the younger generations to the senior generations with no expectation of a return gift. In fact, the reverse order is considered improper in intergenerational gift giving.[1] Such gift giving symbolizes the junior person's gratitude and respect to the elder, and thereby the more gifts one receives, the more prestigious one becomes. It is common for an older villager to make a show of a gift recently given by his son (daughter, nephew, or other junior kinsmen) and to enjoy hearing the public's appreciative comments. In this connection, the one-way flow of gifts serves to restate the kinship rank between the two generations in symbolic terms.

Unilateral, upward gift giving is also found in public life between subordinates and social superiors. According to older informants, before 1949 gift exchange beyond the web of kinship was rare and few villagers had connections with important figures in the outside world. The most common interstrata interactions were between landlords and tenants. All informants agreed that tenants had to show respect to their landlords by giving gifts during ceremonial occasions or during the lunar New Year. The landlord, however, usually did not make return gifts directly; instead, he might offer benefits to the tenants in daily life, such as allowing the tenants' children to pick up the remaining grain in the field after the harvest or giving a banquet at the end of the year. When the tenants hosted ceremonies, the landlord might send a representative and offer a gift, but he did not come unless a special relationship had developed between the two parties.[2] To explain the absence of the landlord at the ceremonies, my informants referred to the difference in "face." They told me that the landlord's face was bigger than that of the tenants, so a gift presented by a representative of the landlord was already considered an honor. In addition to the landlord-tenant relationship, there was another kind of interrank interaction in daily life—between villagers and local officials, such as police officers or tax collectors. But local officials rarely participated in village life, so only a few villagers were involved in gift giving with low-rank officials; for the majority of villagers, officials belonged to an unapproachable world.

After the 1949 Revolution, especially during the collective era (1956–82), a new social hierarchy was established that quickly replaced the dominant role of kinship in social life. Through its agents (the cadres) at the grassroots level, the power of the party-state penetrated every corner of village society and turned the previous social order upside down. As mentioned in Chapter 2, social life during the collective era was far from "egalitarian," and the collectives were no less hierarchical than the prerevolutionary communities. The socialist hierarchy system in Xiajia village consisted of six status groups, with the cadres at the top and the so-called four bad elements at the bottom, those who were assigned the labels of landlord, rich peasant, counterrevolutionary, and rotten element.

The most noticeable impact of this new system of social hierarchy on gift exchange was that the unilateral, upward exchange of gifts became more elaborate in public life. In contrast to prerevolution practice, this new pattern involved almost every villager, due to the intensity of state intervention in village life and the day-to-day exercise of cadre power. Unilateral gift giving took three forms: (1) from villagers to cadres; (2) from lower-rank cadres to their superiors; and (3) from villagers to their urban relatives. It is this new pattern of asymmetrical gift giving that attracted my attention.

Unilateral Gift Giving in the Socialist Hierarchy

Many informants recalled that when the cadres hosted family ceremonies, almost all the villagers went to show their respect by presenting gifts, even though not everyone had previous gift-exchange
relationships with the leaders. But when the villagers hosted ceremonies, only those who were close to the cadres or enjoyed higher
social status could expect a return gift. Many ordinary villagers
could only hope to have the cadres attend the after-ceremony banquets without expecting to receive gifts. Given the much lower standard value of gifts during the collective era (0.5 to 1 yuan), it seems
to me that cadres mostly cared about the significance of receiving
rather than the economic value of the gifts.

Upward, unilateral gift giving during the collective era was not
compulsory, and subordinates appeared to present gifts to superiors
of their own free will. The secret was that in most cases villagers
(and, as we shall see below, cadres in lower positions) would not
send invitations to their superiors when the former hosted weddings
or other celebrations, regardless of the gifts they had given previously to the latter. By so doing, they helped their superiors avoid the
obligation of returning gifts. In a close-knit rural community, information about family ceremonies cannot be missed, and superiors
can easily learn about such events. If a superior wants to develop a
more intimate relationship with a subordinate, he or she may come
to present a gift even without an invitation. In other words, the
mechanism is designed to protect the face of superiors at the expense
of ordinary villagers.

Moreover, the superiors were aware of the driving force behind
this kind of gift giving and did not think of themselves as being in
the position of debtor. Unlike the landlords or other patrons during
the prerevolution era, cadres often did not reciprocate gifts in any
obvious way and pretended not to know about the balance of transactions between villagers and themselves. Such a situation, discussed
in Chapter 6, was the dispute between the cook "big bread Zhao"
and the deputy party secretary Lin. Although Zhao had continuously offered gifts to Lin for years, Lin did not make any return gift

when Zhao hosted a wedding for his son. As some villagers commented, Lin probably did not take Zhao's previous contributions into serious consideration because there were so many gifts from below.[3] I once asked a friend about the obvious decrease in the number of guests (less than 30 people) recorded by the gift list of his second wedding; I wondered whether it had anything to do with the fact that it was a second marriage. He regarded my speculation as nonsense and told me that when he married in 1977 for the first time, his elder brother was a powerful cadre. Many people attended his wedding, and they had come without invitations, not for his or his father's sake, but to flatter his brother. These guests did not show up when he remarried in 1985, because his brother had fallen from power during decollectivization. When I asked how he repaid these guests' gifts, he said, "For those sycophants, I gave them shit! Who cares about them! They are not my *renqing* and I am not responsible for gifts given for ulterior motives." In this case alone several dozen people lost both their gifts and their social credit.

When I transcribed the gift lists I discovered an interesting incident of "negative reciprocity" (Sahlins 1972), by which one party received but did not fulfill the obligation of repayment. In this case, an ordinary villager presented a gift of five yuan to a cadre, which was recorded on the latter's gift list of 1979, but I could not find the return gift from the cadre in the villager's 1989 records. When I alluded to the imbalance to the cadre and his wife during an informal interview, his wife explained that since there was no previous gift-giving relationship between the two families (which implies that the villager's motivation was to flatter the leader), and since the villager's family ceremony was performed ten years later, she forgot to return the gift. Later she argued that her husband had done some favor for the villager before the gift giving, so the villager had presented a gift to express his gratitude and balance the "debt." No matter what the reason, the hidden message she conveyed was indifference, which reflects the cadres' attitude of superiority toward their subordinates.

As a result of this kind of unbalanced flow of gifts between villagers and their leaders, village cadres usually possess the largest networks of personal relations and have the most lavish celebrations. After decollectivization and other reforms, which to a great extent broke the cadres' monopoly over resources, some villagers stopped presenting gifts to their leaders. And interestingly enough, because of the changes in power relations and the political environment at large (see Yan 1995), in recent years cadres have paid more attention to cultivating good relations with the villagers and have become more mindful of returning their share in gift exchange. The difference in guest numbers remains, however, which vividly illustrates the disparity of social status and prestige between subordinates and superiors. According to my survey of gift lists in 1991, the number of gift givers in ordinary villagers' ceremonies varied from less than 100 to 200; in contrast, the number of guests attending cadres' ceremonies usually exceeded 300.

A second form of unilateral gift giving in the socialist hierarchy is found among cadres themselves. Due perhaps to the importance of political allies and the influence of superiors, upward gift giving has long been practiced within the bureaucratic system of traditional China. A folktale may well illustrate how, in popular perception, officials are engaged in upward gift giving. It is said that when a county governor's birthday was approaching, the officials in the government gathered together to discuss what kind of gifts they should present to their superior. Finally, the smartest official among them proposed: "Since the governor was born in the year of mouse, why not give him a golden mouse as a birthday gift?" They all agreed and presented a golden mouse to the governor. The governor was very happy and said: "Let me tell you a little secret. I will celebrate my wife's birthday next month. She was born in the year of cow."

Using village cadres as the reference point, we can see that gift giving among cadres goes in both horizontal and vertical directions. If a cadre wants to be active and successful, he or she has to participate in the horizontal ring of gift exchange among fellow cadres in other village offices in order to maintain a large network. As these gifts are exchanged among colleagues with similar status, balanced reciprocity is commonly practiced. Nevertheless, owing to frequent promotions and demotions, some of those who fall out of power may choose to withdraw from the exchange networks without fulfilling previous obligations. After all, these networks rely heavily on temporary political alliances. This means that there exists a strong possibility for the one-way flow of gifts among cadres with equal rank.

Unambiguous, unilateral gift giving takes place between village cadres and their superiors at the township (*xiang*) government level (and occasionally higher levels). This may take two forms. In recent years it has become an unspoken rule that lower-rank cadres present gifts to their leaders in the name of the local office and the villagers. According to my informants, in every year of the past decade, hundreds of kilograms of fish, pork, and fine rice were transported to the homes of the major leaders in the township government. This was done as a public affair and the villagers were enlisted to help deliver the gifts. The rhetoric used by the local cadres to explain this was that the masses understood how much their leaders had devoted themselves to their public duties, and therefore they wanted to express their gratitude by offering these humble gifts. In fact, as the villagers pointed out, this kind of gift giving has little to do with the masses, and the cadres' primary purpose was to cultivate a good, personalized relationship with their superiors.

This kind of gift giving is by no means limited to the grassroots level; actually, it is currently practiced at all levels of the bureaucratic system—all the way up to the central bureaus in Beijing. For instance, an official in the ministry of commerce told me that at the end of each year, trucks loaded with various kinds of food and other goods were driven into the compound of the central bureau. In his words, "Today it is a truck loaded with lamb from Inner Mongolia; and tomorrow it may be apples from Shandong province. All these gifts are tributes from the local bureaus to the Beijing bureau and they are distributed among officers as extra benefits. Don't think we are corrupt. Special gifts are secretly given even to our leaders in the ministry, and we never know what kind of gifts they receive."

The second form of vertical gift giving is found in ceremonial exchanges. As do villagers to their leaders, village cadres offer gifts to their superiors in the township government or at higher levels when the latter host family rituals, but they do not expect return gifts. For instance, the village party secretary Han, whose case was analyzed in Chapter 5, told me that in 1990 he calculated his expenditures for gift giving and found the total was over 2,600 yuan. This was extremely high in comparison with other families—the main reason being his upward gift giving. According to Han, since he had become a principal cadre in Xiajia in 1981, he had continuously presented gifts to most cadres in the township government and to fellow cadres in other villages. But when he hosted a wedding for his second son, only lower-rank cadres attended. He emphasized that he did not send invitations to cadres in the township government because he did not want to remind them of obligations from below. Yet his superiors were never remiss in letting him and other lower-rank colleagues know the dates of their own ceremonies. He recalled that he attended the wedding of the son of the current vice governor of the county, which lasted four days; the third day was reserved especially for village cadres from all over the county. During the banquet, he and several friends made fun of themselves, saying that they were called upon to endow the vice governor's family ceremony.

Sometimes, hierarchical gift giving among cadres may take a more compelling form. In a case I witnessed, Mr. Su, a retired government official who grew up in Xiajia, formally invited all five cadres in Xiajia to attend his youngest son's wedding in the town seat. According to my informant, Su had an obvious ulterior motive—to accumulate monetary gifts and to make a show of his prestige. Su had stopped maintaining gift-giving relations with most villagers in Xiajia after he left the village in the early 1950's. "This man knows nothing about *renqing*," said my informant. "He should not have forgotten his natal home and fellow villagers in the first place, no matter how big he has become. Besides, without previous interactions and good feelings with us, how could he possibly think about asking us to present gifts. But he did. It's really a shame!"

Nevertheless, in spite of all the complaints, my informant still decided to attend the wedding and make his contribution. Why? He told me that Su's second son was currently in charge of an important office in the local government. It would not be wise to refuse the invitation, because it might be taken as a sign of disrespect. "That would be the last thing I wanted. Keeping up a good relationship with your superiors is, you know, the key to keeping your rice bowl [i.e., one's job]."

This informant was not the only one to rationalize his decision—all the other village cadres did the same thing, hoping to maintain good relationships with Su's second son. It is obvious that both sides made rational calculations, taking social hierarchy into consideration. On the one hand, Su had considered his second son's influence when he sent invitations to the village cadres with whom he did not have previous relationships of gift exchange. On the other hand, the village cadres reacted in a similarly rational way by trying to manipulate the game in their favor. They took advantage of the occasion to cultivate good relationships with a superior (Su's second son). But at the same time, they complained about Su's behavior, which to a certain extent relieved them of their emotional distress and helped them to justify their actions.

In addition to villager-cadre and cadre-superior relations, there are other less visible or less frequent types of hierarchical gift giving among villagers. During radical periods of socialism when class struggle was emphasized, those who belonged to the four bad elements had serious difficulties in gift exchange. Actually, they were forced into a dilemma. On the one hand, they did not dare to offer gifts in public to villagers with good class labels or cadres because they might be accused of attempting to seduce the latter. On the other hand, they also worried that their failure to offer gifts might be interpreted as a denial of previous gift-giving relations or as a violation of *renqing* ethics. In many cases, they would deliver a message in advance, by some secret channel, to ask the host whether they should attend the ritual. This would avoid having their gifts rejected in public, especially if the host happened to be a politically radical person. In 1966, a villager whose father was a former landlord attended his patrilineal cousin's wedding; his gift was publicly rejected and he was accused by the host of trying to corrupt the revolutionary villagers. In Xiajia, a public refusal of a gift occurred only this once, primarily because of the host's willingness to demonstrate his political loyalty to the party-state. The inherent tensions in gift-giving relations have had a great impact on those who carried the bad class labels.

When these "outcasts" hosted weddings or funerals, they also worried about the political implications of their acts. They expected that some of their previous gifts would never be returned because people from revolutionary families might want to terminate any close relationships with them. As the legitimacy of performing family rituals had been put in question for people with bad class labels, few of them cared about the balance of gifts. A woman who married a landlord's son told me that when she was on the way to her husband's home during the wedding day, their wedding wagon was stopped by a huge political parade that had been organized to denounce the four bad elements. The first question that crossed her mind was whether her husband's father was among the targets and how that might affect her husband. After realizing that the group came from another village, she turned to worrying about her wedding. As she said: "At that time, all we could hope for was to have the wedding performed safely and peacefully. Who dared to think about the gifts? I was especially grateful to those who came to the wedding, but I did not blame those who did not. At least, thank heaven, no one came to disturb my wedding."

Owing to government restrictions on rural-urban migration and the great inequalities between town and country, when villagers have gift-giving relationships with urban relatives, they are also in a disadvantageous position. A villager may have urban connections in two ways: (1) by keeping good relations with one's own agnates who moved to the cities before the restrictions; or (2) by marrying one's daughters to urbanites and thus establishing affinal relationships with the latter. In either case, villagers are considered inferior to their urban relatives, and in gift-giving activities they often give more than they receive. One villager complained that he participated in his urban cousin's (father's sister's son) family ceremonies three times before he married, but the latter did not come to his wedding in 1971. He was so humiliated by this that he cut off the relationship. In another case, when a village girl married a worker in Ha'erbin, her proud parents expected this would raise their status in Xiajia. They soon discovered that they were not welcomed by their urban affines, and when they brought some local products as gifts to the latter, they were given some used clothes and household utensils— items not considered proper gifts to be exchanged between affines.

As outlined in Chapter 2, the socialist hierarchy was based on three sets of binary oppositions: cadre vs. villager, city vs. countryside, and red vs. black (in class origin). The last was abolished in 1979. While the economic reforms have eroded cadre power and reduced the inequalities between the urban and rural sectors, these two oppositions still persist in present-day China. Consequently, unilateral gift-giving patterns reflecting features of the socialist hierarchy are still alive in Xiajia community, and unbalanced reciprocity remains an important part of gift exchange.

Unbalanced Reciprocity and the Reproduction of Social Hierarchy

With regard to the issue of unbalanced reciprocity or asymmetrical exchange, anthropologists and sociologists share the following conclusion: unilateral giving eventually leads to an increase of power and prestige for the donor. Many ethnographic studies suggest that what appears to be the operation of a unilateral, asymmetric principle is in fact governed by a rule of symmetric reciprocity (see Firth 1967a; Malinowski 1984; and Mauss 1967). Sahlins (1972) offers a more general model incorporating unbalanced exchange into a continuum ranging from the generalized (unbalanced), to the balanced, to negative reciprocity according to variations in kinship distance and rank distinction. In the case of unbalanced reciprocity, gifts proceed downward toward social subordinates. "In primitive society social inequality is more the organization of economic equality. Often, in fact, high rank is only secured or sustained by o'ercrowing generosity: the material advantage is on the subordinate's side" (Sahlins 1972: 205). If a gift does not bring back a similar gift in the strict sense, there must be some invisible countergifts to restore the balance, such as political control over the recipient or a gain in prestige by the donor (see, e.g., A. Strathern 1971: 10). Thus, "the aim of the capitalist is to accumulate profit while the aim of the 'big man' gift transactor is to acquire a large following of people (gift debtors) who are obligated to him" (Gregory 1982: 51).

The tributary gifts given by commoners to chiefs, however, constitute an exceptional case of upward, one-way giving. Malinowski noticed that the chief sometimes owed a Kula gift to a commoner, but not vice versa. "In the inland Kula, the determining factor is the relative social position of the two partners. Gifts are brought to the man of superior by the man of inferior rank, and the latter has also to initiate the exchange" (Malinowski 1984: 473). But this one-way giving is, many anthropologists argue, balanced in the long run by the chief's ceremonial display and redistribution of material goods. Edmund Leach points out that "although an individual of high-class status is defined as one who receives gifts (e.g., 'thigh-eating chief') he is all the time under a social compulsion to give away more than he receives. Otherwise he would be reckoned mean and a mean man runs the danger of losing status" (1954: 163). In Sahlins's model, this is called "pooling" or "redistribution," and "*pooling is an organization of reciprocities, a system of reciprocities*—a fact of central bearing upon the genesis of large-scale redistribution under chiefly aegis" (1972: 188, italics original). So we return to the same issue: namely, with respect to gift giving, a chief's authority and status are achieved by giving rather than receiving, just as in the case of big-man society (see Gregory 1982: 55).

Most sociological studies of social exchange focus on the process by which the initial unbalanced exchange generates a differentiation of power and leads to an obligation of unilateral compliance. According to Richard Emerson (1962, 1972), exchange relationships are based on predicated dependence of two parties upon each other's resources. To the extent that A is unwilling to surrender voluntarily a resource desired by B and is able to use this resource to force, coerce, or induce compliance upon B, A is said to have power over B. As George Homans notes, "Men are powerful when many want what they, the few, are able to supply or many fear what they, the few, are able to withhold" (1974: 197). Moreover, if A can monopolize all the resources B needs, A will make B dependent on A's power in a "power-dependence relationship," as referred to by Emerson (1962). The central theme here is that unilateral giving establishes superordination, which in turn balances the initial imbalance in exchange relationships. As Peter Blau notes, "An imbalance of power establishes reciprocity in the exchange. Unilateral services give rise to a differentiation of power that equilibrates the exchange" (1964: 28). "A person who gives others valuable gifts or renders them important services makes a claim for superior status by obligating them to himself" (1964: 108).

It is precisely on this issue that the Xiajia case challenges the generalizations of the previous theories. As far as the material flow of gifts is concerned, unilateral giving in Xiajia reveals four features: (1)

gifts are given by subordinates to superiors without the expectation of an equal return; (2) due to the pyramidal structure of the social hierarchy, the number of donors exceeds that of recipients, which leads to an accumulation of gifts at the upper levels; (3) recipients remain socially superior and powerful, even though they fail to return the gifts; and (4) the repeated one-way flow of gifts creates an institutionalized imbalance in exchange values between adjacent social strata, which in turn is regarded as another sign of status differences. All these features seem to conflict with existing sociological and anthropological theories of social exchange.

An obvious and direct answer to the question of why Xiajia is so different lies in the fact that Xiajia village represents a type of society that differs from those that predominated earlier studies of social exchange. Most anthropological analyses of gift exchange are based on observations of social life in relatively "simple" societies, where the local economy and social relations have been only marginally or incompletely affected by the penetration of a political state (see Sahlins 1972: 188). In contrast, sociological theories of social exchange focus mainly on social interactions in modern, industrial societies, which are characterized by democratic political systems, social stratification based on economic classes, and a free-market economy. Obviously, Xiajia does not resemble either of these models. In the past four decades, Xiajia village, like other communities in China, has been under the strict control of a centralized state. Residents have lived under a planned economy with a system of state redistribution and have witnessed the establishment of a new, socialist status hierarchy. Thus it is not surprising that existing theories of social exchange do not fit the reality of life in Xiajia.

It has been widely recognized that under socialism the party-state's authority is based on its monopoly of resources and opportunities, maintained and reinforced by the new ruling class of cadres (Djilas 1957; Szelenyi 1978). Such a monopoly leads to citizen dependence upon officials for the satisfaction of material needs and social mobility, a phenomenon characterized as a form of "organized dependency" by Walder (1983, 1986). It is the redistribution of resources that constitutes the integrative principle of the socialist economy and establishes a vertical relationship between redistributor and producer (see Kornai 1986; Nee 1989; and Szelenyi 1978).

At the level of village society, grassroots cadres are in charge of the redistribution system and thus can compel villagers to depend on the resources under their control. By resources, I refer to those materials and services that are needed or desired by villagers, including economic, political, and social-cultural resources. During the collective era, Xiajia villagers worked under the supervision of cadres, and their basic needs were distributed annually by the collectives. In terms of economic resources, cadres controlled villagers by distributing basic grain rations, assigning daily work, supervising the development of family sidelines, and granting social welfare.[4] Government restrictions on rural-urban migration further confined villagers within the collectives and thereby increased the power of the local cadres. During the radical period, villagers also had to ask cadres for leave to attend all social activities outside the collective, such as visiting relatives or going to nearby marketplaces. Unlike the local officials or landlords in the prerevolution period, the cadres were completely in charge of people's daily lives.

In such a power-dependence relationship (Emerson 1962), the cadre's superior status ruled out the possibility of equal exchange. As a redistributor, a cadre may have felt free of the obligation to return a gift to his subordinates, who depended on the resources he controlled, and thus failure to return did not affect the mutual relationship. By the same token, a village cadre's gift did not obligate his superiors either, because the latter provided the necessary protection and connections for the former to remain in power. In other words, the obligation of reciprocal repayment, which is the basis of all forms of gift giving (Mauss 1967), was overshadowed by the existing inequality of social status between the two parties. The received structure of social relations neutralized obligations of reciprocity. As Blau notes: "Unilateral giving produces status differences between former peers, but once superior status is securely grounded in the social structure its occupant can demand unilateral services without endangering his superordinate position" (1964: 110).[5] Furthermore, because control of resources by the cadres often causes competition in upward gift giving among the dependent villagers, the latter's gifts are devalued, or, in anthropological terms, their gifts to the leaders are of a lower rank. The gifts in ceremonial situations are considered the obligatory dues villagers owe to cadres, not the po-

tential social debt that one must pay back. Gift giving in this hierarchical context works only as the passive strategy that subordinates
have adopted to protect themselves against discrimination by their
superiors.

As indicated above, upward gift giving symbolizes the subordinates' respect for and loyalty to their superiors and reflects the latter's
authority and popularity among their subordinates. Cadres often
compare with one another the number of guests who attend their
family ceremonies and take this as indicative of their authority and
achievement. Thus, one's failure to present a gift could be interpreted as an offense to the leader; because of the public nature of ceremonial exchanges, this would be taken very seriously and personally. The same is true of the relationship between village cadres
and their superiors. There are many ways by which cadres can express their anger toward those who fail to fulfill the obligation to
give gifts, such as assigning a bad job in collective work or, in the
case of the bureaucracy, withdrawing support for the cadres in inferior positions. The possibility that their relationship with their superiors will deteriorate already constitutes a negative sanction upon
subordinates and is sufficient to keep them engaged in upward gift
giving. This is why the majority of people continue to offer gifts to
leaders, even though no specific return can be expected.

The negative sanction inherent in hierarchical giving is also reflected in the cadres' reactions to guest attendance. An informant
who is a ritual specialist told me that when a small household (that
of an ordinary villager) holds a wedding or other ceremony, the host
usually takes note of every guest in attendance, and when checking
the gift list after the ritual, he or she is interested in who attended the
ritual. In contrast, a cadre or other high-status person cannot greet
every guest, due to the large number. When checking the gift list, a
cadre tries to determine who did not attend and why. My informant
commented that as a ritual specialist he has more responsibilities
when he manages ceremonies for big households, because the hosts
are only interested in entertaining the honorary guests and they leave
the rest to him and his assistants. Clearly, unlike ordinary villagers
who regard all guests' attendance as a favor (renqing), cadres (or their
superiors) take gifts from below for granted and therefore only want
to know "who has not attended the ritual."

There are some positive rewards for upward gift giving, but only when subordinates go beyond conventional gift giving to establish a special relationship with their superiors. Quite often other forms of social exchange must be involved, such as consistently providing personal services to the leaders or offering valuable instrumental gifts in return for favors. In these cases, the social superiors may use their positional power to redistribute resources in favor of these gift givers, thereby converting gift exchange into general social exchange. As in many other places in China, Xiajia residents describe this kind of social exchange as an effort to "cultivate personal connections" (la guanxi), and the term guanxi in this context has a more negative meaning than in its common usage. Two examples were often cited by my informants to illustrate how one can cultivate good interpersonal relations with the cadres.

In the first example, a man from a humble family background made many efforts after his marriage to build good relations with the cadres. This man strategically married a Xiajia woman, several years older, whose brother was a cadre, in order to get closer to the upper ranks. Like most villagers, he always offered gifts to the cadres when they had family ceremonies. But he also did a lot more than just the conventional gift giving. He provided voluntary services for the cadres and, as a self-taught local technician, took responsibility for doing various kinds of repair work for the cadres. His services were rewarded with the desirable job assignment of tractor driver, and after decollectivization he was given permission to use the remaining machines in the collectives to open a repair shop. To pay back his patrons, this man mobilized his brothers to answer the party secretary's call to transform a dry field into an irrigated rice paddy. Although the experiment was a complete failure, he won the trust of the cadres and anticipated being rewarded in the future. Obviously, what this man established with the cadres was a typical client–patron relationship in which "favors need not be immediately repaid. The balance sheet may stretch over many years" (Oi 1989: 146).

The second well-known case involves a young man who is now a schoolteacher in Ha'erbin city. In 1974, Xiajia village was asked to recommend a young villager to go to college without taking the entrance exams.[6] The proposed candidate was the head of the women's association. In order to take advantage of this good opportunity, a young man and his parents mobilized all their personal connections inside and outside the village. It was rumored that they offered valuable gifts, costing them more than 500 yuan, to all the relevant cadres and to some political activists. Finally, this man won the nomination over the original candidate and was sent to school in the autumn of 1974. After several months, the defeated candidate became mentally ill and never recovered. According to my informants, her illness occurred when she learned that she was not chosen not because of her competitor's superiority but because of his gifts to the cadres. This is a typical example of instrumental gift giving, in which the return of an upward gift is an expected favor from the leaders; locally called lubricating gifts (*shangyou*), these have become more and more popular in recent years. In another example, a village cadre from a neighboring village was removed from office for violating the population control policies after his wife gave birth to their fifth child, the long-awaited son. Less than two years later, he was promoted to the position of party secretary in the village, gaining the nickname "cow secretary." In order to be restored to office, he had offered gifts to all the major cadres in the town government, including a cow to the party secretary.

These examples are revealing in two ways. First, although the inferior's unilateral gift giving is eventually repaid by his or her superiors, it is not in kind. Rather, superiors repay the gifts by the exercise of their positional power, by arranging a job assignment or career promotion. The offering of instrumental resources, unlike donations of material gifts, does not incur a loss of resources in direct proportion to the amount given. The cadres are supposed to distribute the resources controlled by them anyway; what differs is to whom they distribute the favors and for what profits. More important, after the transaction, the previous hierarchical relations between the two parties remain and are perhaps accentuated by an increase in personal wealth on the part of the superiors.

Lebra suggests that "each culture provides mechanisms which keep within a limit the tension generated in the mutual constraint between symmetry and asymmetry" (1969: 130). The gift giver's disadvantageous position in a hierarchical context is balanced by distinguishing notions in Chinese culture. The emphasis on nominal status and role difference in Chinese culture, for example, provides unilateral gift giving with a legitimate foundation. Until the 1949 Revolution, loyalty, filial piety, chastity, and righteousness (*zhong, xiao, jie, yi*) were promoted as the most important moral characteristics for human beings in Chinese culture, and among them filial piety was particularly emphasized in village life. The display of respect, obedience, and devotion to one's parents, elder kinsmen, and social superiors was positively rewarded by village society as good behavior. By the same token, failure to be filial could ruin one's credit in other domains of social life. For instance, the Chinese believed that "an unfilial son is also a bad businessman who fails to pay his parents' old age insurance" (L. Yang 1957: 302). As a result of the glorification of filial piety and loyalty, "the mere position of a ruler or a parent guaranteed his privilege to receive respect and service from his subject or son" (L. Yang 1957: 308). After 1949, although filial piety in domestic life was severely attacked by the CCP, its extension in public life was transferred into a new political norm called "absolute compliance with the Party's leadership." As in the prerevolution era, the position of village cadre provided a legitimate basis for receiving respect and gifts from the villagers.

Second, the notion of social face (*mianzi*) plays a subtle yet important role in perceptions of unilateral gift giving. Defined as "a function of perceived social position and prestige within one's social network" (K. Hwang 1987: 961), social face is always attached to those who are in the upper ranks or higher positions. When they receive a gift from a subordinate, acceptance of the gift itself is believed to render face to the inferior gift giver. Unlike moral face (*lian*), which refers to basic moral characteristics, social face "can be borrowed, struggled for, added to, padded—all indicating a gradual increase in volume" (Hu 1944: 61). One of the ways to increase the volume of one's social face is to connect oneself with powerful and well-known people as much as possible, because personal connections are considered part of one's resources and prestige. It is common for villagers to flaunt the fact that they have attended the family ceremony of a powerful person and have started a gift-giving relationship with such a person. Although an ordinary villager cannot expect to receive a return gift from a superior recipient, the latter's acceptance of the gift can be regarded by the giver as social capital. One can increase the volume of one's own social face and then in turn enjoy respect and gifts from those of even lower status.

A typical example in this regard is the chain of upward gift giving among local cadres. When a cadre offers a unilateral, *xiaojing*-type gift to his superior, he can expect similar gifts from below (either from lower-rank cadres or ordinary villagers) as compensation. In addition, because of his close connections with his superiors, he may gain more compelling force over his subordinates. As a popular proverb has it, "The big fish eats small fish, the small fish eats tiny shrimp" (*dayu chi xiaoyu, xiaoyu chi xiami*). Such a reciprocal chain of unbalanced exchanges goes beyond the dyadic relationship between giver and recipient and involves at least a third party in the hierarchy in order to realize symmetrical reciprocity. A similar practice in Japanese society is categorized by Lebra as "lineal transferred reciprocity" (see Lebra 1975: 559–60).

To sum up, the Xiajia case demonstrates that in a hierarchical context unilateral giving does not necessarily generate power or create superiority on the part of the donor. On the contrary, the previously existing social hierarchy may overshadow the reciprocal obligation inherent to the gift and free the recipient of superior rank from falling into debt to the donor. Furthermore, when the social superior's power is based on a monopoly of resources, the subordinates' gifts become obligatory dues, with unilateral gift giving serving to express subordination and the respect of inferiors for their superiors.

Under certain circumstances, gift givers of inferior status may obtain rewards through two forms of hierarchical exchange: a patron-client relationship or by the granting of favors from one's superiors. In either form the transaction is no longer gift exchange in its original sense. Gift exchange, by definition, should be like-for-like and be more expressive than instrumental. As M. Strathern notes, gift exchange differs from barter in the sense that "people [are] exchanging things which they did not need" (1992: 169). However, if one wants to use a gift as a means of attracting other resources, one has either to make an investment in advance with ulterior motives or present a gift that is valuable and seductive to the recipient. Here, the convertibility of gifts to favors/services may balance the unequal distribution of resources between some individuals but not among the entire population. Because of this, certain individuals are able to move up the ladder of the social hierarchy while the structure of the ladder remains unchanged. In this sense, while unilateral gift giving is conditioned by the existing social hierarchy, each action of unbalanced exchange also helps to reproduce the social hierarchy.

The Prestige of Receiving and the Competition of Giving

Further questions arise: Who gains power and prestige in less hierarchical types of gift relations? Are the gift giver and recipient always affected by their respective positions in the received structure of the social hierarchy? To answer these questions, we need to review other types of gift exchange and to analyze them in the context of the involved social relations.

A dichotomy between expressive gifts and instrumental gift-giving relations is constructed in Chapter 3. In the expressive form, people exchange gifts in a like-for-like pattern, and the gifts exchanged are evaluated mainly by their symbolic, social value. By contrast, instrumental gifts are given in an attempt to attract return "gifts" which must be different from the original—mostly in the form of favors, services, or protection. Such a like-for-unlike exchange has entered into the general sphere of social exchange and a more or less market standard is applied to guide people's behavior. Moreover, these two basic types of gifts differ from each other in that the former serve to cement a long-term, existing relationship between the giver and the recipient, while the latter can be used to alter or manipulate a short-term relationship. If we take the two basic kinds of social relations—vertical and horizontal—into consideration, four categories of gift exchange are identifiable: (a) expressive gift giving in a horizontal context; (b) instrumental gift giving in a horizontal context; (c) expressive gift giving in a vertical context; and (d) instrumental gift giving in a vertical context.

With respect to expressive gift exchange in a horizontal context: as indicated in the preceding chapters, the material flow of gifts in this category manifests a salient feature of balanced reciprocity. Among social equals, such as kinsmen, friends, and neighbors, a gift always brings back a countergift, and the exchange is strictly like-for-like. As described in Chapter 4, the cycle of giving-receiving-returning may repeat itself several times each year. This feature of balanced exchange suggests that neither of the two parties gains power from the gift giving. In most cases a gift is treated simply as a return for a gift previously received, thus fulfilling a social obligation to reciprocate (see Befu 1966–67: 162). A temporary debt may exist at a given moment, but the obligation to return a gift in this context makes such a debt insignificant. The villagers in Xiajia are concerned with the impact of proper gift exchange on their relations with one another, but few feel that the gifts they give can increase their ability to control or influence others (with the exception that everyone expects to receive gifts when hosting a ceremony). In other words, the only power a gift giver can hope to gain in this context is that of accumulating potential return gifts in the future. This fact indicates that people are giving for the purpose of receiving—not vice versa. It is in the receiving that one's social networks, social face, and previous generosity are displayed. In this context the relationship between donor and recipient reverts to what it was like prior to the transaction, and neither side is deemed to be superior or inferior.

We can see several different characteristics in instrumental gift exchange in a horizontal context. A return gift in an instrumental exchange is supposed to be something different from the original gift and normally takes the form of a favor or a service. It is often difficult to judge whether this transaction of like-for-unlike is equal or not, and thus unbalanced reciprocity might well occur. In fact, many cases of instrumental exchange end up causing disagreements or quarrels between the two parties, because they may have different opinions about the fairness of the exchange. Before receiving a return gift, the giver gains a sort of power, at least in a moral sense, to influence the recipient, the latter being relegated to the position of debtor. As instrumental exchange in most cases appears to be a one-shot deal, and no previous credit can be counted upon, the power of the gift giver is short-lived, yet quite obvious and demanding. As a popular proverb says, "Eating from others, one's mouth becomes soft; taking from others, one's hands become short" (*chiren zuiruan; naren shouduan*). The previous equality in this dyadic relationship is temporarily broken, and the donor becomes superior over the recipient before the obligation of return is fulfilled. Yet, the donor's advantageous position does not derive from social prestige recognized by the local people. On the contrary, it is the recipient who gains prestige, because the exchange itself shows that he or she possesses resources that are sufficiently in demand to attract instrumental gifts.

Characteristics of the third and fourth types of gift exchange have been explored in detail in the sections above: social hierarchy and the monopoly of resources result in a pattern of one-way gift giving from subordinates to superiors; unilateral giving does not generate power or create superiority on the gift giver's side because the previously existing social hierarchy overshadows the reciprocal obligation inherent to the gift and frees the recipient of superior rank from falling into debt to the donor. Yet there is one point that should be noted. In instrumental gift giving in a vertical context, the recipient's absolute superiority is challenged by the donor, because a return, no matter what the form, is definitely expected and in most cases is made. It is in this sense that the donor gains a sort of power to influence the recipient, despite the fact that the latter remains superior. As in the horizontal context, the donor's power can last just as long as a returned favor or service is delayed, and, similarly, prestige still remains with the recipient.

But those of higher rank usually are reluctant to receive instrumental gifts directly from their subordinates, because acceptance of a gift from subordinates with ulterior motives may weaken the superiors' authority and superiority. As Schwartz notes, gift giving may impose an identity upon the giver as well as upon the recipient, for "gifts are one of the ways in which the pictures that others have of us in their minds are transmitted" (Schwartz 1967: 1). The transaction of an instrumental gift indicates both the donor's perception of the recipient as someone who can be bought off by goods and the recipient's acceptance of such an identity. To avoid the superior's loss of social face, instrumental gift giving in a hierarchical context often involves a middleman or a broker able to get access to the superior through other channels, such as kinship ties or a neighborhood relationship. It follows that instrumental gift giving in a vertical context is also preconditioned by existing social ranks. And since the

Social relation between X (gift donor) & Y (recipient)	Horizontal		Vertical	
Type of gift exchange	Expressive	Instrumental	Expressive	Instrumental
Direction of gifts	X ⟲ Y	X ⟲ Y	X → Y	X ⟲ Y
Who gains power?	X	X	Y	X
Who gains prestige?	Y	Y	Y	Y
Who becomes superior?	?	X	Y	?

NOTE: Solid arrows indicate the flow of material gifts; dotted arrows indicate the flow of non-material gifts, such as favors, services, or protection.

FIG. 2. *Power and prestige in gift-giving relations*

transaction is completed by a middleman when the gap of rank is too large, the gift giver can hardly gain any power to influence the recipient directly.

In most studies of gift exchange, it is the gift giver who is the focus of scholarly interest; however, the Xiajia case suggests that the recipient is equally important for a better understanding of gift-giving behavior. Moreover, earlier studies tend to emphasize how social-political status is generated by the power of gifts, yet the Xiajia case demonstrates that the exchange itself might be conditioned by existing power relations. The distinctive features of the Xiajia case are summarized in Fig. 2.

As Fig. 2 shows, when the social contexts and the motivational features of gift giving are taken into account, it becomes clear that the notion of superiority can be applied only to two out of the four types of exchange relations: instrumental exchange among social equals and expressive exchange in a hierarchical context. In the former, the giver becomes temporarily superior over the recipient, and in the latter, the recipient remains superior as before the transaction. As indicated in the preceding chapters, an expressive gift-giving relationship is characterized by its cycle of giving-returning, and thus those involved are indebted to each other in a permanent relationship. Giving or receiving is just a momentary mark in this endless process; neither can change previous status. Therefore, no one becomes superior over another, and social equals remain equal. Although an instrumental gift may grant power to the giver, in a vertical context the social mechanism of bridging the subordinate and the superior with a middleman prevents direct interaction between the two parties. Consequently, the giver's superiority, which by definition is limited in a dyadic relationship, is diluted by the middleman, and the recipient can escape from the compelling force of indebtedness to the giver.

Moreover, in the expressive type of gift exchange in a vertical context, all of the advantages go to the recipient, who is already in a superior position in the social hierarchy. This result conflicts with the patterns found in many other societies, where the donor gains power and prestige and the recipient acquires material advantage (see, e.g., Gregory 1982; Raheja 1988; Sahlins 1972; A. Strathern 1971; and Vatuk and Vatuk 1971).

Furthermore, in all types of gift exchange, prestige goes to the recipient instead of to the giver, an interesting phenomenon that once again violates the general rules observed elsewhere. As shown in the previous chapters, Xiajia residents pursue in their long-term, expressive gift exchange the establishment, reinforcement, and expansion of their *guanxi* networks, which constitute their local moral world. The most visible means of showing one's achievement in this arena is by the acceptance of expressive gifts in both ritualized and nonritualized situations. In other words, incoming gifts serve as an index of one's personal networks and social face as well as of previous efforts to observe the *renqing* ethics. Thereby, the more gifts one receives, the more one may gain social recognition of one's prestige. This remains true even for the short-term, instrumental gift exchanges, where the incoming gifts indicate one's ability to control and mobilize various resources.

It is not by accident that the gift lists villagers keep are records of the gifts they receive. As I indicated in Chapter 3, these gift lists serve as monuments in villagers' personal histories, and reviewing one's gift lists can produce a strong feeling of achievement. During an interview, a well-to-do non-cadre villager showed me the five gift lists he had kept since he established his own conjugal family. Pointing his finger at the total amount of gifts on each of them, he said with pride: "Look at these figures. When I built my house 23 years ago, I had only 45 guests and received less than 200 yuan worth of gifts. Have a look at the latest one—there are more than 200 guests and 3,000 yuan. It was not easy for me to have so many guests, but I made it." When his wife reminded him that all the gifts were merely returned for what had been given out previously, he said it was worth doing and shouted: "This shows that I have as much *renqing* as those big guys have. But I am a decent farmer and I worked all this out by my own hands. I am proud of myself."

It is not surprising, therefore, that all my informants preferred to talk about gift receiving rather than gift giving. Often they spent hours enumerating the guests who attended their family ceremonies in the recent past and recalling the exact amount of monetary gifts they received from each individual guest. For those who had successful ceremonies, the total amount of gifts was the most favored topic in our interviews. They compared the gifts they received with those of their kinsmen and neighbors and used the value of the gifts to judge the quality of a given ceremony. However, when asked to talk about outgoing gifts, few informants could provide me with detailed answers. Some remarked that "it is meaningless [*meiyou yisi*] to remember every gift you have given out."

If receiving is so prestigious, why do the villagers bother to give in the first place? The answer is that they give because they want to receive. For most villagers, the only way to attract incoming gifts is to give gifts to others who will return the gifts under the obligation of reciprocity. Unless one decides to renounce village society, one has to be more and more involved in this cycle of giving and receiving. So the prestige of receiving provides the permanent motivation for gift giving. If gift giving were prestigious in and of itself and people were interested only in giving gifts, then the networks of gift exchange would have become smaller and smaller over the years, due to lack of demand. The natural limitation of human lives would have eventually ended this closed cycle, since no new member would have wanted to join the game of gift exchange as a recipient.

As a result, Xiajia residents compete with each other in gift giving with the expectation of receiving, but not for the sake of giving per se. What people are competing for is an expansion of the gift-giving range and of the scope of their networks, not merely the economic value of the gift in any particular transaction. A symbol of success is an increase in incoming gifts, rather than the defeat of any individual rival in a race to offer gifts. Instead of rejection of the failures, competition as such involves more and more participants; thus, it is inclusive, constructive, and open-ended. Again, this gift-giving framework constitutes an interesting contrast to cases such as the potlatch, where gift giving is a one-on-one contest and victory is based on the value and amount of gifts an individual participant can offer (see, e.g., Boas 1897; Codere 1950). It is clear here that the competition in giving for future receiving is the reason why gift-exchange activities in Xiajia have become more and more frequent and why the scope of personal networks has become larger and larger. After all, Xiajia villagers seek not the gift itself, but the relationship that such a gift may cement or create—the cultivation of *guanxi*.

Marriage Transactions and Social Transformations

Thus far I have focused on how the system of gift exchange in China has survived four decades of socialism, despite the significant incursions and social alterations made by the party-state. As indicated in the preceding chapters, while the central values and principles, such as *bao*, *guanxi*, *renqing*, and *mianzi* remain important, Xiajia residents have adjusted their gift-giving behavior in accordance with political and social changes affecting their community. This chapter is concerned primarily with the impact of social change on patterns of gift giving, concentrating on the most popular type of gifts: bridewealth and dowry.

Anthropologists have examined systems of bridewealth and dowry in many parts of the world, but have rarely found a society in which the state has made repeated but unsuccessful efforts to restrict the practice of marriage transactions. After the 1949 Revolution, leaders of the Chinese Communist Party were determined to reconstruct the family—the very foundation of Chinese society—thereby creating a new society and, with it, a new notion of personhood (Davis and Harrell 1993: 1–10; C. K. Yang 1965). CCP leaders targeted the system of marriage payments as an area of special attention in this socialist transformation of society. The 1950 marriage law banned the exaction of money or gifts in connection with marriage (Article 2) together with concubinage and child marriage; this legal prohibition was restated in the 1980 marriage law (Ocko 1991: 320–23).

Throughout the 1950's, 1960's, and 1970's, ideological attacks on the custom of marriage payments were a frequent feature of party propaganda, condemning bridewealth as "buying and selling in marriage" and lavish dowries as "feudal extravagance." Various efforts, such as mass education campaigns and the creation of new wedding styles, were made to change marriage patterns. Despite these attempts at social engineering, however, the practice of marriage transactions never ceased, but was transformed in novel ways (Croll 1984; K. Johnson 1983; Parish and Whyte 1978; and Siu 1993: 176–80). Since the economic reforms of the late 1970's, high bridewealth and lavish dowries have reappeared all over China, and the expenses associated with marriage have escalated in both urban and rural areas. According to a 1986 survey of rural China, while villagers' income increased 1.1 times between 1980 and 1986, expenditures on bridewealth increased tenfold (*People's Daily* 1984; see also Gu 1985; Qian et al. 1988; and Zhang and Fan 1993). As we shall see below, similar changes occurred in Xiajia village.

How did the local system of marriage payments interact with state policy during four decades of socialism? Does the recent surge of marriage costs represent a resurrection of traditional patterns, thus signaling the failure of the socialist experiment? To answer these questions, I introduce the local terminologies of marital gifts and then examine changes in the content of bridewealth and dowry as well as post-exchange consumption patterns over the past four decades. Next I analyze the active role of the bride and groom in marriage transactions, with reference to the development of conjugality in village life. Exploration of new meanings attached to marriage transactions leads to the conclusion that, as a response to social changes in the larger environment, the custom of bridewealth has evolved from a form of gift giving between families to a means of wealth allocation within the family, and parallel to this development, there has been a change from indirect to direct dowry. These findings help us to understand local responses to state socialism and to pose challenges to previous theories of marriage exchange.

Thanks to the local custom of recording marriage transactions, the present chapter draws on well-documented data of 51 marriages which occurred during the period of 1950 to 1993. In Xiajia village and the surrounding areas marriage negotiations usually result in the writing of a formal bridewealth list called *caili dan* (meaning the "list of betrothal gifts"). This gift list is produced in two copies during the engagement ritual and records all monetary and material gifts in a particular marriage. I soon discovered that the best way to study marriage transactions is to collect bridewealth lists and use them to map historical changes (for the custom of making *caili dan* and other types of gift lists, see Chapter 3). Thus, an itemized bridewealth list was either collected or reconstructed for each of the 51 cases, and a structured interview was conducted in order to gather background information. Every bridewealth list was double-checked with both spouses to obtain data as accurate as possible. Dowry for each case was also recalled by my informants.[1]

Bridewealth and Dowry: Anthropological Concepts and Local Terminologies

Anthropological studies of the Indian dowry system have demonstrated that the complexity of gift content and the diverse destinations of wealth allocation are of central importance to understanding the nature of dowry as a custom (Hershman 1981; Tambiah 1989; and Vatuk 1975). Michael Herzfeld's analysis of the Greek notion *prika*, a term usually translated in English as "dowry," highlights the contrast between the legal definition of the dowry and the contextually determined nature of the village usage of *prika*. There are, Herzfeld warns, dangers inherent in simply adopting legal definitions of village terms, and thus "all we can legitimately attempt is to describe the contexts in which we encounter the village terms" (1980: 235).

In light of these views, it is clear that in order to understand the nature of marriage transactions in today's China, one must examine in detail the content of bridewealth and dowry, as well as the ultimate recipients of these gifts. Furthermore, synchronic analyses of this nature must be placed in diachronic context and be based on a better understanding of the local terminology in marriage transactions, because both the composition of marriage prestations and local perceptions of these gifts are constantly changing in response to political and economic developments (see Siu 1993). The prescriptive, abstract definitions of bridewealth and dowry in scholarly usage sometimes may obscure the rich meanings of local practice (see Comaroff 1980: 9–11; Herzfeld 1980: 233–37).

In anthropological literature, the term "bridewealth" commonly refers to the property transferred from the groom's family to the bride's family. It serves to validate both a marriage agreement and the transfer of the rights over women from one family to another. Bridewealth is often used by senior men to establish future marriages for the male siblings of the bride. In contrast, "dowry" is often considered to be the bride's share, taken with her upon her marriage, of her inheritance from the family of her birth. In highly stratified societies in Europe and Asia, dowry constitutes an important strategy to advance family status or build prestige (Comaroff 1980; Goody 1973; Harrell and Dickey 1985; Schlegel and Eloul 1988; Spiro 1975; and Tambiah 1973). In Chinese societies dowries are often subsidized through the bridewealth paid by the groom's family to the bride's family (Cohen 1976; Freedman 1979; McCreery 1976; Ocko 1991; Parish and Whyte 1978; and R. Watson 1985), a complicated practice characterized by Jack Goody as "indirect dowry" (1973, 1990). This term, in my opinion, is the best characterization of marriage exchanges in Chinese society; yet it has not been widely accepted in the field of China studies and, accordingly, the term "brideprice" is still commonly used (see Siu 1993: 167; R. Watson 1981a: 605). No matter what term is used, however, it is clear that according to existing theories, bridewealth and indirect dowry (subsidized by bridewealth) by definition must be properties transferred between the groom's and bride's families.[2]

This dichotomy of bridewealth and dowry (or indirect dowry) based on the interfamilial flow of gifts cannot accurately reflect the current practice in Xiajia village. In addition to marital prestations exchanged between two families, there are properties transferred within the groom's family—material gifts given by the groom's parents to the newlyweds as a conjugal unit. These properties are regarded by the villagers as part of the marriage transaction and since the late 1960's have been formally written into the bridewealth list.

In Xiajia village and the surrounding areas, bridewealth is called *caili*. The first character *cai* means color or colorful, indicating happiness in marriage, and the second character *li* means gifts. The term *caili* can thus be translated as "marital gifts." When I asked what constituted *caili*, villagers always came up with a quick, short answer: money and goods. But upon further inquiry, most informants said that it was not easy to give a fixed answer because the specific nature of marital gifts varied according to historical period (usually measured in decades). I will return to these specific terms, but it is sufficient at this point to note that monetary gifts were, until recently, presented by the groom's family to the bride's family. Accordingly, I will follow previous studies and call this "bridewealth." Beginning in the mid-1980's, however, all monetary gifts were subsumed under a new category: *ganzhe*. This term refers to the conversion of material goods into monetary terms. For example, if A borrowed a sack of corn from B and wants to repay B in cash for the sake of convenience, A may ask B whether it is acceptable to convert the value of the borrowed grain into a certain amount of cash. In so doing A may use the word *ganzhe* to indicate such a conversion. In the context of marriage transactions, *ganzhe* implies the conversion of all kinds of betrothal gifts given to the bride's side into sums of cash. Hereafter I will refer to this new category as converted bridewealth. The total amount of the converted bridewealth is recorded in the bridewealth list, and, more important, it is given directly to the bride herself during the engagement ritual. This fact distinguishes the converted bridewealth from all other forms of monetary gifts (which are given to the bride's parents).

Material gifts that constitute another part of the *caili* include a great variety of goods and can be classified into three subsets: (1) furniture; (2) bedding items; and (3) major appliances, *dajian* (meaning literally "big items"), such as bicycles or television sets. It is the responsibility of the groom's family to purchase all material gifts. Such items are accumulated by the groom's family but are transferred to the room of the newlywed couple before the wedding date. It should be noted that these material gifts are not given to the bride or the groom as individuals; instead they are offered by the groom's parents to the newlywed couple as a conjugal unit, or a subunit, within the larger family. Thus it might be proper to refer to these items as the direct endowment of the conjugal room.

Unlike bridewealth, dowries since the prerevolution era have usually included only material goods, such as jewelry, cosmetics, and bedroom furniture. Xiajia residents refer to the dowry subsidized by the monetary gift from the groom's family (Goody's indirect dowry) as *yangmao chu zai yangshen shang*, literally "the wool from the sheep's body." If the gifts presented by the bride's parents exceed the amount of betrothal money received, the amount in excess is called *peisong* (meaning "giving dowry at one's own expense"), which fits well the scholarly usage of direct dowry. If a bride's parents retain the entire bridewealth, or most of it, and then use it for some other purpose, the parents might be labeled "daughter-sellers." Different strategies in dowry practice are classified by villagers into three types, all of which focus on parental attitudes toward their daughters. The first type is *mai nuer* (selling the daughter) and is characterized by demands for high bridewealth coupled with the return of a very low dowry. The second is *jia nuer* (marrying out a daughter), implying that the bride's parents turn all the received bridewealth into dowry for the benefit of their daughter. The final strategy is *peisong nuer* (sending off one's daughter with economic sacrifice), which involves an extra dowry from the bride's parents' own savings. Although the names of these strategies have remained unchanged over the past four decades, Xiajia villagers, as I shall demonstrate below, have adopted different strategies during different time periods.

Considering these emic views, I would suggest that Xiajia residents have constructed a mental universe involving a tripartite division of bridewealth, direct endowment, and dowry (including indirect dowry)—rather than the standard anthropological dichotomy of bridewealth and dowry. This emic system pays special attention to the ultimate recipient of both monetary and material gifts, rather than merely focusing on the movement of bridewealth between families. In the Xiajia situation, the intrafamily transfer of wealth is also taken into consideration.

Marriage Finance by the Groom's Family: The Old and the New

From the recipient's point of view, both monetary and material gifts (bridewealth and direct endowment) can be seen as marriage finance offered by the groom's family, whereas dowry is marriage finance provided by the bride's family. Table 8 summarizes the changes in marriage finance by the groom's family.

The first category in the section of monetary gifts in Table 8 is called *liqian* by villagers, which means literally "ritual money" and can be translated as "betrothal money," since the term "ritual" in this context refers to the engagement ceremony. Ideally, the economic function of betrothal money is to subsidize the bride's parents in their preparation of a dowry for their daughter. Nevertheless, in the 1950's and 1960's it was not unusual for parents to use a daughter's betrothal money to pay for a son's marriage. The most intriguing point reflected in Table 8 is that from 1950 to 1959, marriage finance provided by the groom's family constituted only one category: betrothal money. This money was meant to cover all the expenses of the bride's natal family. Until the early 1960's, therefore, all resources were under the bride's parents' control, and it was very likely that higher bridewealth benefitted the bride's parents instead of the bride herself—thus helping to explain why earlier studies tend to emphasize bridewealth. Moreover, Table 8 reveals that *liqian* increased in a consistent yet not remarkable way. The average amount of betrothal money in the early 1950's was 200 yuan. According to my informants, at that time people were generally poor and hesitated to spend too much on marriage because they needed to invest in the land that they had just been allocated from land reform. Betrothal money increased to 300 yuan on the eve of the Cultural Revolution in the mid-1960's. Then it decreased in the second half of that decade as a result of the severe ideological attacks on traditional cul-

TABLE 8

Marriage Finance by the Groom's Family

(RMB yuan)

Years	Value of gift (RMB yuan) by gift type[a]								Total expenses	No. of cases
	BM	T	PRS	CB	F	B	MA	CE		
1950–54	200								200	3
1955–59	280								280	5
1960–64	300	100	20			50			450	4
1965–69	200	300	20			100	120		740	6
1970–74	300	300	50		70	100	150		970	6
1975–79	400	400	200		200	200	300		1,700	8
1980–84	400	700	300		500	300	500		2,700	6
1985–89				4,500	1,000	800	1,000		7,300	7
1990–93				6,500				3,500	10,000	6

NOTE: The figure in each marriage case represents the average expenditure per marriage in the given five-year period.

[a] BM = betrothal money (*liqian*); T = trousseau (*mai dongxi qian*); PRS = payment for ritual service (*zhuang yan qian*); CB = converted bridewealth (*ganzhe*); F = furniture; B = bedding; MA = major appliance (*dajian*); and CE = converted endowment (*ganzhe*).

ture led by the Red Guards. In the 1970's and the early 1980's, it again increased significantly.[3]

The second category, "trousseau money," emerged in the mid-1960's and refers to monetary gifts offered by the groom's family to the bride's family for the purpose of purchasing clothes, shoes, and other minor items for the bride. In local usage, trousseau is called *mai dongxi qian*, literally "money for purchasing goods." Trousseau money, however, was not given to the bride's parents. Instead the groom's family used the money in this category to buy items and then sent them to the bride's family to give to the bride. Later, on the wedding day, the same items were taken by the bride along with her dowry to the groom's family home, where they remained her private property. This category represents a significant change because the goods are specifically for the bride herself.[4]

The first obvious increase in trousseau money coincided with the only decrease in betrothal money, which, as shown in Table 8, took place during the radical phase of the Cultural Revolution (1966–69). My informants told me that the attack on the practice of bridewealth was intensified during that period, and many villagers were reluctant to receive large amounts of betrothal money. Nevertheless, because of economic difficulties and the increasing value of women's labor, the demand for bridewealth persisted. As an alternative strategy, some villagers started to ask for a much larger amount of money in the guise of the trousseau; and in several cases villagers simply replaced the previous category of *liqian* with the new category of *mai dongxi qian*. However, both the groom's and the bride's families understood that part of the trousseau money was actually the betrothal money and agreed that it would be given to the bride's parents directly. By so doing, villagers hoped to avoid the accusation of practicing the feudal custom of bridewealth. An unexpected result, however, was that the new category of trousseau gradually became an important part of the bridewealth and was recorded on the bridewealth list—a ritualized indicator of its legitimization as part of the marriage transaction. During the 1970's, expenditures on clothing doubled, and specific instructions regarding the style and quality of clothes could be found in the gift lists. (See the sample lists in Table 9.) By the early 1980's, as shown in Table 8, the amount designated for the trousseau exceeded that of the betrothal money and thus became the most important category of bridewealth.

During the late 1960's, a third category, called "money for filling the pipe" (*zhuang yan qian*), began to be a factor in marriage negotiations and was also recorded on the bridewealth list. Unlike the trousseau money, this monetary gift was given directly to the bride for the ritual service of filling the tobacco pipes of her senior in-laws during the wedding. In Table 8, I refer to this as "payment for ritual service" and regard it as the first basic change in the practice of bridewealth. Although it seems relatively insignificant in terms of monetary value (20–50 yuan between 1960 and 1974), it constituted, for the first time, a category of gifts given by the groom's family to the bride herself—directly and exclusively. As shown in Table 8, the amount of payment for ritual service increased considerably during the late 1970's and early 1980's, along with the rise in trousseau value. It was also during this period that the groom's family relinquished its control over the purchase of the trousseau and allowed the young couple themselves to buy trousseau items. These developments reflect the increasing importance of the bride and groom in marriage transactions.

TABLE 9

Comparison of Two Bridewealth Lists

Category	1971 gift list	1991 gift list
Betrothal money (*liqian*)	200 yuan	
Trousseau	2 pairs of polyester trousers, 1 muffler scarf, 1 pair of leather shoes, 3 pounds of wool, 8 pairs of socks, 10 meters of corduroy, 5 meters of velveteen, and 5 meters of wool fabric (250 yuan)	
Payment for ritual service	50 yuan	
Converted bride-wealth (*ganzhe*)		5,500 yuan
Furniture	a cabinet (70 yuan)	1 set of modern furniture and 1 sofa, 1 traditional cabinet (1,200 yuan)
Bedding items	2 sets (100 yuan)	4 luxury sets (1,000 yuan)
Major appliances (*dajian*)	a sewing machine (170 yuan)	a sewing machine, a woman's wrist-watch, and a washing machine (1,000 yuan)[a]
TOTAL COST	840 yuan	8,700 yuan

[a] It was agreed by both sides that the bride's family would provide a TV set as part of the dowry by the time of the wedding.

Finally, we see that all three categories—betrothal money, trousseau, and payment for ritual service—were transformed into a single new category, *ganzhe*, converted bridewealth, in the late 1980's. (See the sample gift lists in Table 9.) As indicated above, the cash from this converted bridewealth was given directly to the bride herself. According to Xiajia villagers, the first year that *ganzhe* money became popular was 1985, because it was rumored that after that year there would be no extra land allocated for the purpose of house construction. Those planning marriage at that time worried about losing the opportunity to acquire land, so many grooms suggested that their brides ask only for cash as betrothal gifts. This money was then used to buy materials for the construction of a house. The standard amount of *ganzhe* increased at this time, and in the following years it continued to climb.

Similar changes occurred in the provision of material gifts by the groom's family. Direct endowment, as noted earlier, includes three kinds: furniture, bedding items, and major appliances. As shown in Table 8, none of these material goods was part of marriage transactions during the 1950's. Bedding items, according to older informants, were to be provided by the bride's family as part of the dowry. If they were not provided, the bride had to accept whatever she was given by the groom's family (sometimes secondhand items). Neither furniture nor major appliances were provided. Owing to the extremely cold winters in Heilongjiang province and the general poverty level of the villagers, in both the prerevolution period and the 1950's, few newlywed couples had their own conjugal room immediately after their wedding. It was common that they would be given a separate heated bed (*kang*) in the same room where other family members slept. (The room was, of course, relatively big, and the heated beds were separated by curtains.) Only after they had their first or even second child were they given a tiny room inside or attached to the main house. Such a residential arrangement actually required little furniture, and few ordinary villagers could afford to buy new furniture for their sons' marriages anyway. As a result, it was up to the bride's family to provide whatever furniture the newly married couple needed; usually only a wooden cabinet was included in the dowry.

During the 1960's, demands for material goods went up, and bedding items were among the first to be written formally into the bridewealth list—a sign of their becoming a socially accepted component of marriage transfers. By the mid-1960's, a wristwatch had become the ideal gift desired by women, signaling that luxury items (by the standards of a poverty and shortage economy) began to enter villagers' perception of marital gifts. The trend to demand material goods for the conjugal unit continued to develop throughout the following two decades. As shown in Table 8, furniture became a necessary part of marriage expenses, and demands for the well-known "four big items" (bicycle, sewing machine, wristwatch, and radio) and luxury bedding items soon emerged. Although these gifts, as indicated above, were formally written into the bridewealth list, they were not given to the bride as an individual; instead, they were property owned by the bride and groom as a conjugal unit. In contrast to the relatively slow increase of betrothal money in bridewealth, the sum of cash needed to buy these material items for the conjugal room grew rapidly.[5]

More radical changes took place during the 1980's. While the four big items remained desirable, new items appeared on the gift lists, including TV sets, tape recorders, washing machines, and motorcycles. Earlier demands for quality furniture developed into aspirations for modern styles, including a set of sofas that typify urban tastes, which had begun to influence farming communities. Some requirements, such as four sets of luxury bedding, exceeded the practical needs of the new couple. This trend reached its peak by the early 1990's when the new form of transfer—*ganzhe*—began to emerge. In this new arrangement all of the expenses for buying material gifts were converted into cash and, following the example of the converted bridewealth, the cash was given to the bride, who, as understood by both the groom's and the bride's families, represented the two as a conjugal unit. Here, direct endowment was finally transformed into what I prefer to call "converted endowment."[6]

To sum up, over the past four decades marital gifts provided by the groom's family evolved from a simple, single category of betrothal money into six different ones of monetary and material gifts. These categories have, in turn, recently been transformed back into a simple, one-category form—that of *ganzhe*. These changes are summarized in Fig. 3.

The creation of every new category indicates the emergence of a new relationship in marriage transactions and thus constitutes an important step in the ongoing process of change. Moreover, it is clear that despite the party-state's severe criticism of marriage payments, the average expenditure per marriage has increased 50-fold, jumping from 200 yuan in 1950 to 10,000 yuan in 1993. However, the practice of high bridewealth does not always imply "marriage by purchase" as argued by party cadres. The bride's parents do not necessarily benefit from the rise of marriage payments provided by the groom's

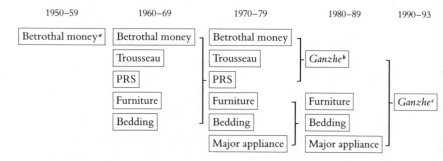

FIG. 3. *Changes in marriage finance by the groom's family, 1950–93*

[a] Terms: Betrothal money = *liqian*; trousseau = *mai dongxi qian*; PRS (payment for ritual service) = *zhuan yan qian*; major appliance = *dajian*.

[b] Here *ganzhe* refers to what I call "converted bridewealth," namely, the conversion of the three categories of monetary gifts (betrothal money, trousseau, and PRS) into a sum of cash, with the cash given to the bride herself by the groom's family.

[c] This *ganzhe* includes both the "converted bridewealth" and the "converted endowment." The latter refers to furniture, bedding, and major appliances, which are converted into a sum of cash in the form of *ganzhe*. The cash from these two kinds of *ganzhe* (converted bridewealth and converted endowment) is given to the bride herself by the groom's family.

family. In fact, the rise of marriage payments resulted mainly from the invention of new categories, which privileged the bride and groom as a conjugal unit. Furthermore, the recent innovation of *ganzhe* has completely altered the structure of marriage transfers: it is now the bride (and the groom, whose role is hidden in public) who has final control over the marriage finances provided by the groom's family. (I will return to this point later.)

Marriage Finance by the Bride's Family: From Indirect to Direct Dowry

It is rather difficult to measure changes in the practice of dowry for two reasons. First, unlike bridewealth, which is mandatory for parents who wish to have their son married, dowry is optional (see Ebrey 1991). Some families may decide not to provide any dowry at

TABLE 10

Marriage Finance by the Bride's Family
(in Contrast to Bride-price from the Groom's Family)

Years	Bridewealth received (RMB yuan)	Indirect dowry offered (RMB yuan)	Direct dowry offered (RMB yuan)	No. of cases
1950–54	200	20		3
1955–59	280	20		5
1960–64	300	30		4
1965–69	200	50		6
1970–74	300	120		6
1975–79	400	400		8
1980–84	400	400	200	6
1985–90	Converted bride-wealth (4,500)		350	7
1990–93	Converted bride-wealth and converted endowment (10,000)		600	6

NOTE: The figure in each marriage case represents the average expenditure per marriage in the given five-year period.

all, and the decision does not ruin a marriage (even though it will damage the family's social status and prestige). Moreover, there is always a socially accepted standard for the bridewealth, although the standard itself is constantly changing; in contrast, individual families have to make their own judgments about how lavish the dowry should be and what kinds of gifts will be given as dowry. Whenever I discussed the dowry custom with my informants, they resorted to the standardized bridewealth as a reference point. As indicated above, they distinguish indirect dowry from direct dowry (*peisong*) by measuring the proportion of dowries to the bridewealth received. Following this emic view, Table 10 summarizes the changing practice of dowry in contrast to that of bridewealth in Xiajia since the 1950's.

According to my informants, in the 1950's and 1960's many families withheld a significant portion of the received bridewealth and used it to pay the marriage expenses for their sons. The dowry during this period was small and usually included only a pair of mirrors, a washing basin, and two boxes of soap. A trend toward a pure bridewealth system is clearly shown in Table 10, where we can see that during the period from 1950 to 1964 only 10 percent (or less) of the betrothal money received by the bride's parents was given to the bride as indirect dowry. In the late 1960's, 25 percent of the bridewealth was returned as indirect dowry, and the 1970's saw a continuing increase of indirect dowry. Beginning in the late 1960's, my informants recalled, families allowed their daughters to take a wooden cabinet or a table, some bedding items, and clothing from their natal families with them upon marriage, the total value of which was still lower than the bridewealth received. By the end of 1970's, many families converted all the bridewealth they received into material goods given to their marrying-out daughters as (indirect) dowries. While this practice of indirect dowry was popular during the late 1970's and early 1980's, some well-to-do families began to offer dowries in excess of the bridewealth they had received. The most valuable dowry presented by a villager in 1989 included a color TV set, a compact stereo system, and a washing machine, worth more than 3,000 yuan in total. My latest survey of sixteen marriages that occurred during 1992–93 shows that more than 50 percent of the families adopted the indirect dowry strategy, less than 10 percent of the families withheld part of the bridewealth they had received, and the remaining 40 percent provided either modest or lavish *peisong*. These changes reveal a trend moving from the one-way flow of bridewealth and indirect dowry in the 1970's and finally toward the offering of lavish dowries since the late 1980's.

The case of Mr. Gao provides an excellent example of this trend. Gao, age 65 in 1991, is an ordinary farmer who has six daughters and two sons. With too many mouths to feed, Gao's family remained economically below the average in Xiajia for many years. During the 1970's, Gao was known as one of the local daughter-sellers, because he failed to use the bridewealth to prepare for his daughter's dowry, yet he requested large amounts in monetary betrothal gifts. I witnessed the marriages of two of his daughters, who happened to be around my age and with whom I had worked on the same production team for several years. When his third daughter left home on her wedding day, she carried only a small package containing some basic clothing and cosmetics. Although the fourth daughter had been given a small chest and a pair of mirrors as a dowry, her father still withheld 90 percent of the monetary betrothal gift. When I revisited Xiajia in 1989 and 1991, however, I found that Gao had let his fifth and sixth daughters take their entire monetary bride-wealth with them while he tried to raise money for his youngest son's marriage. When I discussed the change with him, he said, with a sense of humor, that he wanted to rehabilitate his reputation.

Another interesting indicator of the changing emphasis from bridewealth to dowry is reflected in the local terms for betrothal money—the monetary gift offered by the groom's family to the bride's family. As noted above, villagers refer to this monetary gift as *liqian*, which means literally "ritual money." The same character *li* also means "proprieties" and ceremonial expressions of ethical ideas. (See my discussion of the Chinese term *liwu* for "gift" in Chapter 3.) Thus *liqian* also indicates that the betrothal money is a reflection of cultural rules. One of the rules of marriage transactions is that the bride's parents should use the received betrothal money to prepare a dowry for their daughter, and, ideally, they should also offer extra gifts from their own savings. During the 1950's and 1960's, however, when most villagers withheld a significant portion of the received betrothal money for other uses, they called the cash gift *yangqian*. In this new term the first character *yang* means "to rear a child" or "to raise a domestic animal." In combination with the second character *qian* (money), the meaning is obvious: the betrothal money is paid to the bride's parents for having reared the bride. It follows that the bride's parents had the right to use this money for purposes other than preparing a dowry for their daughter. By manipulating the terms for betrothal money, the poor villagers were seemingly able to justify their failure to provide enough indirect dowry to their daughters, as in the case of Gao. The term *yangqian*, however, is no longer used by villagers and was used during the 1950's and 1960's only in conversations, never appearing on the written bridewealth list—a clear sign that it lacked cultural legitimacy.

This view is further supported by interviews with several older women. When I asked why it had been called *yangqian* rather than *liqian*, one said: "It is the money for breast-feeding my daughter and raising her up; so it should be called *naishui qian* [milk money]." Another woman added, "Unfortunately, we could not enjoy the milk money for ourselves; it was all spent for feeding other kids or marrying in a daughter-in-law." The most intriguing comment, however, was made by a third woman who was a village schoolteacher and the mother of two in a better-off family. She told me: "Don't be fooled by their answers. *Yangqian* was never a proper term; it was just made up by some parents who were afraid of being called daughter-sellers. Why is there no one calling it *yangqian* today? Because parents can now afford to give the money to their daughter or buy things for her. So *liqian* has become the correct term."

In recent years the demands from daughters have become a major factor contributing to the rise of lavish dowries. Table 10 shows that the emergence of direct dowries coincides with the new category of converted bridewealth (*ganzhe*) since the mid-1980's. As indicated above, in the new practice of converted bridewealth, the bride's parents receive nothing from the marriage finances offered by the groom's family, and therefore whatever they offer to their daughter's marriage is in the form of a direct dowry. It has now become common for a bride to negotiate with her own parents for a higher dowry and, in many cases, the bride submits part of the converted bridewealth to her parents for use in purchasing dowry items. Additionally, some girls use their own savings to help their parents prepare dowries. The latest development is that by 1993 more than twenty village girls have left Xiajia to work in urban areas in the hope of earning money for more lavish dowries. Realizing that they have to provide proper dowries anyway, many parents now encourage their daughters to work outside and then let them keep part of their income. This in turn intensifies the competition for lavish dowry (indirect and direct alike).

In short, recent changes in both the bridewealth and the dowry have pointed to the increasingly active role of the bride in marriage negotiations and subsequent property transactions. Because dowry is always much less important than bridewealth in Xiajia marriage negotiations, the following analysis focuses on the couple's interactions with the groom's family in arranging the bridewealth and direct endowment.

The Bride and the Groom: New Agents in
Marriage Transactions

In discussing women's property as reflected in marriage transactions, Rubie Watson observes that Cantonese village women put great emphasis on their dowries because the presentation of the dowry defines their status as lawful wives (1991: 239–41). In most Chinese contexts a large portion of the dowry derives from the bridewealth, so it follows that women should pay attention to it, for "a woman can define herself in comparison to her peers by the quality and size of her betrothal gifts and wedding festivities" (Ocko 1991: 321). Indeed, ethnographic evidence from Xiajia village shows that brides and their mothers always try to increase the amount of bridewealth.

During the 1950's and 1960's, engaged girls were not directly involved in the process of purchasing betrothal gifts, but they tried to protect their interests by monitoring the preparation of the material gifts before the wedding date. They adopted many strategies to detect whether the groom's family kept their side of the bargain, such as sending an inspector to check the gifts before the wedding day or trying to pick out the items by themselves. If the groom's family spent too little on preparing the material goods, the bride might refuse to attend the wedding ritual.

The bride's role became even more active after the local custom called "taking engagement photos" (*zhao dinghun xiang*) emerged. Beginning in the early 1970's, engaged girls participated in the process of purchasing material goods for their own betrothal. The bride and groom made a ritualized trip to a nearby city (either the county seat or the provincial capital, Ha'erbin) to buy clothes and other personal items catalogued on the gift list. They also sat for an engagement picture in a photo studio. More important, most couples spent a night or two together at a hotel. The village office (the production brigade during the 1970's) issued them an official letter that entitled them as a couple to rent a single room in a hotel. After this trip, mutual visits continued between the young couple, and they received small gifts from each other's family during these visits (at least several times a year).

The effect of this custom on the groom's family has been twofold.

First, it gives the groom's family an opportunity to secure the marriage contract because the engaged couple stay together in a hotel room, implying sexual activity. In public opinion, a de facto marital relationship is established: as the villagers put it, "Raw rice has become cooked" (shengmi zhu cheng shufan). Second, living together for a few days gives the couple a feeling of conjugal union and naturally leads them to make plans for their future life after the wedding ceremony. This rather romantic experience is believed to create mutual affection and emotional ties between the young couple. As one informant recalled: "After the trip [for the engagement photo] my son's heart was stolen [by his bride]; he always defended the girl when we criticized them that they had spent too much during the trip. It was not a good idea to let them be together so early." It is clear that emotional ties between the young couple may develop into strong conjugal solidarity, which generally tends to be against the interests of the groom's family, especially those of the groom's mother.[7]

Along with participating in the custom of taking an engagement photo, brides gradually began to take into consideration the future of their conjugal families when they participated in the bargaining of marriage transactions. In a 1975 case in which I was among the male bride-senders, the bride made a furious protest at the beginning of the wedding. She complained to all the participants and onlookers that her in-laws had cheated her by buying fewer bedding items and furniture than were recorded on the bridewealth list. When I asked her why she was so insistent on receiving material goods, she replied, "You don't understand. That is my best chance. After the wedding, no one will allow a daughter-in-law to use the family money to buy anything." As mentioned earlier, both bedding items and furniture belong to the category of direct endowment (properties transferred within the groom's family) and are the property jointly owned by the bride and her husband as a conjugal unit. So the bride actually fought for the interests of the new conjugal unit rather than for herself exclusively, and therefore her act did not affect her relationship with her husband.

Since the new category of ganzhe emerged in the late 1980's, the bride and groom have taken control over most of the marriage finances. In a case I witnessed in July 1991, the toughest negotiator at the engagement table was the prospective bride. She insisted on a *ganzhe* gift of 5,500 yuan even though the groom's family only offered 4,000 yuan originally. As a result, 5,000 yuan was finally agreed upon by both sides, plus 500 yuan to be paid to her for performing her duty of serving cigarettes and wine during the wedding ritual. When she returned from the engagement ceremony she had 3,000 yuan in her pocket and expected to have the remaining yuan prior to the wedding.

Interestingly enough, the more money a bride received from the marriage arrangement, the less she spent buying herself personal items. I was told that since the innovation of the *ganzhe* system women have become more aggressive in demanding higher bridewealth but they have also been purchasing less clothing. This contrasts sharply with the 1970's, when not only the number of items but also the quality of clothing fabric was specified in writing (see Table 9). When I asked a newly married woman why she did not buy all the items listed on the engagement contract, she said, "Fashion changes quickly. I don't want to waste my money buying too many things which will be out of fashion soon. Besides, money can give birth to money. Why should I be silly to waste it?" The second reason she mentioned was purely economic, not aesthetic. In this case she saved 2,200 yuan of her betrothal gift and loaned the money to someone else at a high interest rate.[8]

It was very common in 1993 for engaged women to possess several thousand yuan in cash. According to my informants, more than half of the families in Xiajia village have to borrow money in order to arrange their sons' marriages, and, ironically, more than half of these families borrow the money from betrothed women. Clearly, in Xiajia village engaged women now play an active role in the arrangement and management of bridewealth. Nevertheless, this is only part of the story; the deeper motivation for a woman to pursue costly betrothal gifts is to build the future prosperity of her conjugal family, which involves not only the bride but also the groom.

My interest in the role of the groom in marriage transactions was inspired originally by a noteworthy case in 1989, when a young man encouraged the girl he had chosen to marry to demand a large amount of bridewealth from his own family. According to some informants, he told the girl: "Just be tough. Ask for 4,000 yuan in *ganzhe*, and don't bargain. Otherwise, you won't be able to extract money out of my mother's pocket." Meanwhile he stated firmly that he would marry only this particular girl. As one might expect, the girl was given everything she demanded. A few months after their wedding, the couple left the groom's family and established their own home. Some villagers gossiped that he had planned the split from his parents even before the engagement.

My informants told me that this case was not as extraordinary as it seemed, because in recent years many young men have acted in similar ways without openly declaring their intentions. An elderly friend of mine complained that in 1989 he made great efforts to marry off his eldest son, including a *ganzhe* gift of 3,000 yuan to the bride. But only three months after the wedding his son asked to live separately and, with his bride, went to Ha'erbin city to go into business, using the gift as capital. The significant point reflected in these cases is that young villagers may begin planning their conjugal family as early as the engagement period.

Among other factors, I found that the new form of family division has contributed to young villagers' (women and men alike) strong motivation to ask for high bridewealth. The key feature of family partition (*fenjia*) is that when all the sons have married, the father of the household divides the family estate equally among his sons and then lives either with a son or stays with his wife in a separate small unit. Ideally, the time of the family division should be delayed as long as possible, usually until the death of the father or after his retirement as household head. As in many areas of rural China, this traditional form of family division has been practiced in Xiajia for many generations.

Since the late 1960's, however, a new form of family division has emerged, whereby the first married son (usually the eldest) sets up a separate household with his wife soon after their marriage, leaving his parents and unmarried siblings in the old household. The second married son repeats this pattern after his marriage, and the process goes on until all sons are married. The villagers in Xiajia distinguish the latter type of family partition from the former by calling it *danguo* (meaning to live independently) instead of *fenjia*. The family estate remains undivided in his parents' home, because there are still unmarried siblings who need financial support from the family.

Usually a young couple wishing to leave by *danguo* are entitled to only their shares of the rationed grain, cooking fuel, and their personal belongings. Another local term for this form of family division is *jingshen chuhu*, which means literally "to leave the family naked" (with no family property).[9]

The *danguo* form of family partition was welcomed by young people during the 1970's and became dominant during the 1980's. Since decollectivization in 1983, the time of partition has been moved up considerably. According to my informants, nearly one-third of the newly married couples in Xiajia established their own households before they had children, and more than 40 percent did so right after the birth of their first child. The earliest case reported was seven days after the wedding ritual. Prolonged big families can be found only among the poor, because they cannot afford to build new houses for their married sons.[10]

Danguo has had a profound impact on the system of marriage transactions in two ways. It encourages the female party (the bride's parents and recently the bride herself) in a marriage negotiation to request a large amount of bridewealth, because the bridewealth will provide the major resources for the young couple to establish their own household. All the material gifts, from bedding items to major appliances, belong to the new couple as a conjugal unit. It is natural that the bride would want to increase these resources as much as possible, and such attempts to do so are certainly supported by her future husband under *danguo*. Moreover, since sons gain little from the family estate under the *danguo* form, grooms encourage their brides to claim their share of the family property during the negotiation of the bridewealth. A good example of this is the above-mentioned case where the young man goaded the girl to squeeze money from his own mother. In another striking case in 1990, a bride wanted the grain-processing factory of the groom's family to be included in her bridewealth list. The groom in this case had an unmarried brother, and in the end, the factory was divided into two, with each son receiving half.

In earlier patterns of marriage, one family gave bridewealth to another in order to endow a bride, whose (indirect) dowry would eventually endow her husband and herself as a conjugal branch or a subunit in the groom's parents' family. This branch would not gain independent status, however, until the end of the natural cycle of family development, which was at the time of family partition. It is true that in traditional Chinese society women could exercise control over their dowries both before and after the marriage. Women's "private money" has received substantial scholarly attention (see C. Chen 1985; Cohen 1976; Ebrey 1991; McCreery 1976; Ocko 1991; and R. Watson 1981a, 1984). Nevertheless, because betrothal gifts (in the form of bridewealth) went to the bride via the bride's parents, it was the bride's parents who decided what portion of the received bridewealth would be given to the bride as indirect dowry. In contrast, since the 1990's in Xiajia village, marital gifts are transferred from the groom's family directly to the bride in *ganzhe* transactions. The bride, with the cooperation of the groom, takes full control over her betrothal gifts from the very beginning of the marriage negotiations and, in the *danguo* form of family division, uses them to establish an independent conjugal family immediately following her marriage. The basic difference between the two patterns is that in the former, conjugality was not the goal of either the older or the younger generation and the individuality of the bride and groom was overshadowed by parental power and family interests; in the latter, conjugal independence has become the motivation for the young people to demand costly bridewealth and dowry and both the bride and groom (who plays a hidden role) have become active agents in marriage transactions. Hence, the balance of power within the family has been redefined.

The rise of individuality and conjugality naturally indicates the decline of patriarchy—a structural change in Chinese society. According to Fei: "As the family in our society is a corporative group, its central axis lies between the father and the son, between the mother-in-law and the daughter-in-law. This axis is vertical rather than horizontal. The conjugal relation becomes secondary" (1947: 42). In a conjugal family born from the *danguo* form of family partition, the relationship between husband and wife inevitably constitutes the central axis. The development of individuality and conjugality in Xiajia has been discussed elsewhere (Yan 1992c); here I want to emphasize that the aspirations for conjugal independence among young villagers may have made the most significant contribution to the consistently increasing demands for costly bridewealth.

It is interesting that the groom, although sharing the bride's strong desire for conjugal independence, does not dare to take the lead in the bargaining over marriage transfers or in the initiation of an earlier separation from the groom's parents' family. As shown above, it is usually the bride who, on behalf of the new couple, plays the role of a "selfish," tough fighter for higher bridewealth and direct endowment. Such a strategic arrangement results from the remaining influence of the vertical axis in the family organization, which sustains parental power and authority over sons. Actually this is also an extension of the old strategy employed by Chinese men for many generations—that is, to encourage one's wife from behind the scenes to fight for the interests of one's conjugal unit within the large family (see, e.g., Cohen 1976; Freedman 1966).

Therefore, it would be misleading to view the bride's control over bridewealth and direct endowment as a revolutionary change in women's property rights. On the contrary, the Xiajia case shows that women's claims for their personal property declined after pursuit of conjugal independence became a dominant theme in marriage transactions. A good example of this is that after the emergence of the *ganzhe* package, individual brides stopped buying and accumulating personal items for themselves. Instead they saved the money and invested it in business in order to expand the conjugal funds. One could make the argument that individual brides have never really fought for their own personal interests in marriage transactions. When they could not control the major part of the marriage finances, they had no choice but to ask for more trousseau and payments for their ritual service, in the hope of buying more for the future conjugal unit. Hence the increase in these two items during the 1970's. Such a strategy became unnecessary when the bride could directly receive all the marriage finances in the form of *ganzhe* gifts since the mid-1980's. No matter what brides requested—a personal trousseau in the 1970's or *ganzhe* money in the 1990's—they, with the support of their husbands, did so for the sake of their conjugal families. This may help explain why the groom's parents express few objections to the emergence of the *ganzhe* gift, because all the property eventually is transferred directly or indirectly into the conjugal family, which, in their eyes, is their son's family. Villagers characterize this in terms of a popular saying: *"feishui bu liu wairen tian"* (meaning literally "the fertile water does not flow into an outsider's field").

The Nature of Marriage Transactions: Payment, Endowment, and Inheritance

The active participation of individual brides and grooms in marriage negotiations and finances raises questions: What is the meaning of marriage transactions in today's Xiajia village? How does the Xiajia case relate to previous interpretations of bridewealth and dowry in China?

The practice of pure dowry is rarely found in Chinese societies; therefore theories of bridewealth are most relevant to our discussion here. As J. L. Comaroff notes, with few exceptions, anthropological theories of bridewealth have focused on the functional relationship between marriage prestations on one hand and structural arrangements of social groups, jural creation of statuses and alienation of rights, and the negotiation of affinity on the other (Comaroff 1980: 15). It is generally agreed that bridewealth represents a transfer of property between corporate groups, such as lineages or families. In the course of exchanging gifts, rights over women are also transferred, and an affinal relationship is created between the groups (Fortes 1962; Goody 1973; Schlegel and Eloul 1988; and Spiro 1975).

In line with this general framework, two theories have been developed to explain marriage transactions in Chinese society. One can be called the marriage payment theory. According to this approach, the bridewealth is interpreted as the payment made by the groom's family to the bride's family in an attempt to validate the transfer of rights over the bride's reproductivity and domestic services (Freedman 1966, 1979). Following this model, the term "bride-price" is consistently employed by many anthropologists who have worked in China, despite the fact that all or most of the bridewealth will be returned eventually to the groom's family in the form of the dowry. A modified version of this theory is employed by China specialists (see, e.g., Croll 1984; Parish and Whyte 1978) to explain the persistence of bridewealth in postrevolution China, with the emphasis on the increased value of women as producers. The concept of compensation is the core of the marriage payment theory. The emphasis on the value of women as reproducers or producers may change, but compensation must be paid by the groom's family to the bride's family. Consequently, women as brides are objectified and exchanged through the practice of bridewealth (Croll 1984; Johnson 1983) and they are incorporated fully into the groom's agnatic group when they are transferred away from their natal agnatic group (Freedman 1979: 289).

Another way to interpret marriage transactions in China is to propose what might be called a marriage endowment theory, of which Cohen's work, among others, is representative. Cohen asserts that because the bride and groom are the ultimate recipients of most wealth circulating within the marriage framework, "the wedding transactions cannot be regarded merely as 'payment' for this transfer of a woman. In most cases both sides lose money, although it is true that the greatest expenses are borne by the groom's family, but in any event the wedding allocations are geared to the endowment of a new couple" (1976: 177). This view is further developed by Chung-min Chen in his analysis of marriage prestations in rural Taiwan. He argues that because bridewealth is used to purchase indirect dowry, it can be considered the first "withdrawal" of the groom's share of his natal family's estate. "Through the process of wedding presentations, a part of his family funds is transformed into his wife's dowry. It thus becomes part of the property that he and his wife will own exclusively" (C. Chen 1985: 127). Emphasizing that neither display nor compensation is the dominant aspect of indirect dowry, Jack Goody also highlights the endowment function: "In China the allocation of wealth to the bride was in effect a way of endowing the couple, since the son had no property of his own until partition took place" (1990: 125–26).

It seems to me that both theories have a basis in fact, and their differences derive from regional variations in practice and different emphases in theoretical concerns. The marriage payment theory tends to emphasize the one-way flow of gifts to the bride's family as a compensation for their loss of a daughter; while the endowment theory, preassuming the balanced exchange of bridewealth and indirect dowry (or even direct dowry) between the groom's and the bride's families, stresses more the actual destination of the marriage gifts to the newlywed couple as a conjugal unit. The key determinants here are: What proportion of the bridewealth is returned as indirect dowry, and who controls these resources?

The marriage payment theory fits well a pattern discovered by Parish and Whyte in rural Guandong province during the early 1970's. They note that after 1949 the traditional system of indirect dowry was gradually replaced by a full bridewealth custom, with the provision of indirect dowries becoming much less important. They argue that as women gained in value as laborers in the collectives, men had to pay a higher bridewealth to compensate the bride's parents for having rights to the women transferred to them (1978: 185). A balanced exchange of bridewealth and dowry was found in south China by Wolf in the early 1980's that clearly favors the marriage endowment theory. According to Wolf, "Bride price and dowry are both present and, according to the complaints I heard, have increased at an equal rate. I have no doubts about the uses to which the bride price was put: it was plowed back into the dowry, and parents claimed much more was added besides" (1985: 179). More interestingly, what Kay Johnson reports from a north China village is just the opposite of what Parish and Whyte find in the south: "Bride prices seem to have diminished to a level of relative insignificance, while dowries continue to be significant and perhaps fairly high in cost" (1983: 211).

My study of the Xiajia case suggests that, in addition to regional variations, timing might be another important element for our understanding of the complex mix of bridewealth and dowry. It is clear that in the 1950's and early 1960's the practice of marriage transfers could be explained in terms of the marriage payment theory, given that only 10 percent of the received bridewealth was put into the indirect dowry. Beginning in the mid-1960's, material gifts (direct endowment), such as bedding items, furniture, and major appliances, were formally included in the marriage negotiations, and consequently the endowment function of marriage transactions has been increasingly clear and important. Subsequent changes in the 1970's and 1980's all developed in favor of the interests of the newlyweds: betrothal gifts were given to endow a conjugal unit rather than pay for transfer rights over the bride. Recent developments in Xiajia, therefore, provide more evidence to support the marriage endowment approach.

To understand better the complexity and diversity of marriage transactions in socialist China, one must appreciate two factors: the flexibility of the indirect dowry system and the impact of the dramatic changes in the larger social environment. Indirect dowry, by definition, is typologically intermediate between bridewealth and dowry, containing features of both. According to a general scheme elaborated by Alice Schlegel and Rohn Eloul, indirect dowry systems prevail in societies characterized by differences in social status (class or rank) and wealth, absence of urban centers, and some degree of social mobility. More important, social status is negotiable, and fortunes can change rapidly due to natural disasters or social disorder. "Under such conditions, status competition becomes fierce, and neither the groom's side nor the bride's side can afford to lose face by receiving more than they give. Indirect dowry solves that problem" (Schlegel and Eloul 1988: 303). In reality the exchange of the bridewealth component and dowry component, however, may not always be kept in balance. Anthropological studies of marriage exchanges in other parts of the world, such as Egypt and Turkey, have demonstrated that it is not unusual to find indirect dowry systems that maintain direct dowry with only token bridewealth added, as well as the converse—substantial bridewealth with a token dowry (1988: 304).

Marriage transactions in Xiajia fit well into this model of indirect dowry. As shown in Table 10, even during the 1950's when most villagers withheld for other purposes the major part of the bridewealth received, they still returned 10 percent of the betrothal money as indirect dowry, or with a "token dowry" as Schlegel and Eloul refer to it. By contrast, in a recent case of a lavish dowry in 1989, the family offered a direct dowry of 3,000 yuan in excess of the 7,000 yuan bridewealth (which was given to the bride herself in the form of *ganzhe*). And this family, which was among the wealthiest households in Xiajia, was as demanding as others when negotiating the sum of bridewealth with the groom's family. This case shows that all villagers share the same ideal model, namely, the provision of a proper dowry to balance the bridewealth received, but they have to make practical adjustments in accordance with their own needs and family situations.[11]

It is precisely this flexible nature of the indirect dowry system that enables Xiajia villagers to cope with rapid changes in the outside world. Using property ownership, class rank, and social stratification as the major variables that determine one's strategies in marriage transactions, we can see that Chinese villagers have experienced dramatic changes in the past four decades. After the 1949 Revolution, land reform eliminated differential landholding as a basis of inequality, and the previously advantaged groups were deprived of privilege and wealth. The collectivization of agriculture and the legal ban on rural-urban migration in the 1950's further reduced opportunities for social mobility. During the 1960's and 1970's many of the socialist experiments originally aimed at social equality ultimately resulted in the creation of new forms of inequality based on political qualifications and concentrations of power in the hands of officials (see Chapter 2; J. Watson 1984; and Whyte 1981). The economic reforms from the late 1970's once again reversed many people's fortunes and led to another wave of structural changes in the existing socialist hierarchy (Yan 1992a: 1–15). By the early 1990's, the renegotiation of social status had become a salient feature of everyday life in both urban and rural China, with people repositioning themselves in the newly emerging system (Yan 1994). It is not difficult to comprehend the villagers' tendency to make frequent modifications in their strategies of marriage finances, given how quickly the society changed. More important, what we have seen in the Xiajia case is not the coexistence of different patterns operating for different classes/ranks or social groups, such as in the Indian case (see, e.g., Tambiah 1973, 1989); instead the same villagers are involved with all of these changes. Those who adopted the bridewealth alternative in the 1960's and 1970's later provided some of the most lavish dowries in the 1990's. For this reason, neither the marriage payment theory nor the endowment theory alone can explain the complexity and diversity of marriage transactions in socialist China.

Furthermore, the Xiajia case also enables us to discern the active role played by the bride and groom in marriage transactions, an important change that has received little scholarly attention. Comaroff's review (1980: 4–29) shows that there have been three major approaches in the anthropological literature on marriage transfers: the structural-functional, the Marxist, and the structuralist, with the first being the most influential. Given differences in ethnographic and regional emphases, scholarly interests center on several major themes. There are scholars who emphasize the logic of exchange in marriage prestations, be it economic (Spiro 1975) or symbolic (Lévi-Strauss 1969). Others stress the function of marriage gifts in realizing the rights and duties inherent in the creation of a conjugal bond (Fortes 1962). Still others emphasize the redistribution of family property at marriage (Goody 1973) or the correlation between marriage payments, social stratification, women's property rights, and modes of production (Goody 1973, 1992; Harrell and Dickey 1985; and Tambiah 1973, 1989). Marriage payments are also seen as a means of social domination and as a mechanism for reproducing social systems (Meillassoux 1981).

There has been a general tendency among anthropologists to treat marriage payments as family strategies employed by the parents of both the bride and groom, as "ways in which households attempt to adjust labor needs, the transmission of property, and status concerns" (Schlegel and Eloul 1988: 305). This view, in turn, reflects the received wisdom that marriage in "traditional" societies is not a personal affair between two individuals; instead it involves two kin groups (lineages or families) and thus constitutes a community (public) event. Accordingly, the bride and groom are absent in most discussions of marriage payments, because their role has been considered insignificant—if not irrelevant—in marriage negotiations and arrangements.

It is precisely on this latter point that my analysis of the Xiajia case, which places special weight on the role played by the bride and groom in transacting their own marriage, may shed new light on anthropological discussions of marriage transactions. As shown above, since the late 1960's couples in Xiajia have gained more independence in and control over the financial arrangements of their own marriages. By the early 1990's, the bride and groom had assumed full control over the disposition of the bridewealth and dowries. Interestingly, new and unconventional items have become targeted betrothal gifts in recent years, such as a plot of farming land, a family grain-processing factory, or a dairy cow. Many of these new bridewealth items are means of production and thus can generate more wealth, further indicating that the ultimate intention of the bride and groom is to accumulate a productive fund for their conjugal family.[12] As a result, it is no longer sufficient or accurate to view the transfer of marriage gifts as a strategy employed by parents; instead it is now quite common for the groom to encourage his bride to request a higher bridewealth from his family, in the hope of extracting more family wealth for the establishment of a new conjugal family. This is a significant alteration in the marriage transaction complex, and in this new transaction the bridewealth might be considered, to follow Goody's approach, a form of wealth devolution for the groom who seeks to claim his inheritance rights.

In his analysis of the dowry system, Goody argues that in India there is a bilateral transmission by which parental property devolves vertically on both sexes. He argues that dowry—the property that a woman takes with her into marriage to form a conjugal fund—"can be seen as a form of pre-mortem inheritance to the bride" and, as such, part of a woman's property complex (1973: 17). It is true that this generalization, as McCreery (1976) correctly points out, may not apply to the dowry custom in pre-1949 China, because Chinese women had no legalized property rights (see also R. Watson 1984; Ebrey 1991). The Xiajia case shows, however, that the *ganzhe* gift has enabled the bride and groom to control all property transferred in a marriage. Village men, who doubtless enjoy inheritance rights to their families' property, have taken advantage of the *ganzhe* gift to transfer family property to their conjugal families. As a consequence, the system of marriage transactions is no longer a cycle of gift exchange between two families, but has become a way of distributing wealth from one generation to the next or a new form of premortem inheritance for marrying sons. Accordingly, the pursuit of conjugal independence by individual brides and grooms is replacing parental concern about the interests of the larger family as the major determinant in the negotiation and arrangement of marriage transactions.

Here the implication of the Xiajia case is that, when studying marriage transactions in complex societies, especially those undergoing rapid change, we might reconsider the units of analysis and pay special attention to the role of the young in their own marriages. The "African" form of marriage transactions—bridewealth—has dominated scholarly discussion in anthropology for several decades, and most theories of marriage payments are based on work done in Africa and Oceania where lineages predominate as analytic units. Coinciding with the change of interest in anthropology from structure to process during the 1960's, the dowry systems in Eurasia began to serve as the main model, and accordingly the family/household has replaced the lineages as the focus of analysis (Schlegel and Eloul 1988: 299–300). Nevertheless, since the decline of parental power, the increase of freedom in mate choice, and the development of courtship among the young have emerged as general trends in many societies (see Goode 1963), it is logical that studies of marriage transactions should refocus on the roles played by individual brides and grooms. Recent developments in Xiajia village may, at the surface level, conflict with William Goode's classic model of the family (1982: 184), which predicts a declining significance of marriage payments in the modern world. However, examination of the ultimate destination of marital gifts reveals that the surge of marriage transfers results mainly from young people's increasing demands for higher bridewealth and lavish dowries, in order to build up a larger conjugal fund. This trend, in turn, conforms to the general trend toward conjugal family development in the modern world (Goode 1982: 180–85).

My aim in this chapter has been to reconstruct major changes in one local system of bridewealth and dowry, with an emphasis on the transformation of marital gifts into a form of property inheritance. Further analysis of the underlying causes of these changes remains a subject for future research. It is sufficient to say that before this transformation, bridewealth and indirect dowry, in my view, were generational and obligatory gifts presented by the groom's and bride's parents to both the bride and the groom as a potential conjugal unit. As in other situations of gift exchange, a reciprocal return was expected from the recipient: in this case the couple had to support the groom's parents in their old age and perpetuate the household by reproduction. This reciprocity may not have been realized immediately, but a delayed return was guaranteed by certain cultural expectations, such as the moral value of filial piety, the delayed time

of family partition, and the superior importance attached to patriarchy (parentalism might be a more accurate term) instead of conjugality.

These traditional expectations were either destroyed or altered
during China's four decades of socialism. The collective ownership
of the land and other important means of production in the 1960's
and 1970's reduced the sons' motivation to remain together in the old
household and thus resulted in earlier family partitions and the innovation of the *danguo* system. Ideological attacks by the party-state
on the traditional Chinese value system undermined the notion of
filial piety and encouraged young people to escape from their parents' control. Under the collective system, individual labor was the
primary source for creating wealth, and this fact also encouraged the
independence of young people. Furthermore, increased opportunities to work outside the family and new customs related to marriage, such as that of taking engagement photos, encouraged couples
to develop mutual affection and emotional ties. Conjugality became
an increasingly dominant (and conscious) ideology, and the conjugal family finally emerged as an objective goal (see Cohen 1992;
K. Johnson 1983; Parish and Whyte 1978; Selden 1993; Wolf 1985;
and Yang 1965). As a consequence, the marriage transaction is no
longer a cycle of gift exchange between two families, but has become a means of claiming one's share of family property employed
by individual brides and grooms in their pursuit of conjugal independence.

Finally, let me return to the question raised at the beginning of
this chapter: How shall we assess the recent surge in marriage transfers all over China? According to Harrell, the increasing demands
for bridewealth and dowry payments in the 1980's should be seen as
a conservative change with a modern twist: "People are reverting to
pre-collective-era patterns, but at much higher levels of expenditure, reflecting the greater availability of cash resources" (Harrell
1992: 335). Siu argues that the practice of marriage payments in a
south China community has been changing since the beginning of
this century, resulting from active responses to political and economic changes in the larger social environment. Therefore, "family
dynamics and the related terms of marriage today cannot be seen as

a restoration of what had been put on hold since the late 1950s" (Siu 1993: 187).

My analysis of the Xiajia case suggests a conclusion closer to that of Siu. The current pattern of increased expenditures on marriage transactions is by no means a simple return to "traditional" Chinese culture. On the contrary, it represents the latest phase of an ongoing change in the system of marriage transfers. The old framework remains applicable, but the meaning and function of marriage gifts have changed completely. In other words, people may still speak the same ritual language, but their actions convey new messages in response to changes in the larger social setting. The Xiajia case, therefore, demonstrates that the practice of socialism has indeed caused a social transformation in China, although not in the way originally intended by the leaders of the Maoist state. As in other aspects of social life in China, careful scrutiny enables one to find many old bottles filled with new wine.

Conclusion: Socialism, *Guanxi*, *Renqing*, and the Gift

Three conclusions emerge from the preceding chapters: First, gift exchange in Xiajia village follows procedures that challenge accepted anthropological theories. Second, the cultivation of *guanxi* networks and conformity to *renqing* ethics are characterized by the combination of both interest and disinterest, expressivity and instrumentality, the voluntary and the constrained. Third, the current practice of gift giving and *guanxi* cultivation can only be understood in relation to China's four decades of socialism. In this concluding chapter, I will discuss these three themes in an attempt to show how the Xiajia case is relevant for a general understanding of social exchange in Chinese culture. I start with the issue raised at the outset of this book: How does the Chinese system of gift exchange as shown in the Xiajia case relate to those systems found in other societies? Next, I discuss the nature of *guanxi* and *renqing* as exemplified by the Xiajia case and draw a distinction between what might be called the primary and extended forms of these emic concepts.

Finally, I demonstrate how the system of gift exchange not only survived four decades of socialism but interacted with the social changes brought on by socialism in China.

The Gift and the Chinese Gift

When I speak of the "Chinese system" of gift exchange, I do not mean to imply that Xiajia represents, or stands for, Chinese society as a whole. Obviously it does not. I would maintain, however, that much of what I have encountered in this small community in northeast China can also be found in many other parts of the country (and in Hong Kong and Taiwan as well). Cultural diversity and regional differences have long been recognized by China specialists, and, in a strict sense, all ethnographic case studies are typical as well as atypical of Chinese society. Nevertheless, when we compare gift exchange in Xiajia village with Indian or Melanesian gift exchange, it is possible to discern the main features of these ethnographically distinct cases. This, in turn, allows us to draw comparisons at a cross-cultural level, while de-emphasizing the specific particularities of each case at the microcultural or subcultural level. All anthropological theories of the gift are based on case studies of particular ethnic groups; it is only at the higher levels of generalization that we can begin to see what is unique and interesting about a given culture.

With regard to comparative studies of gift exchange, recent studies by Jonathan Parry and James Carrier are noteworthy. Parry shows that Maori and Hindu ideologies of gift exchange represent fundamentally opposite types: the former requires the reciprocity of every gift given and the latter denies reciprocity. In India, as described by Parry, it is believed that the gift of *dana* contains an evil "spirit" and may transfer inauspiciousness from the donor to the recipient (Parry 1986: 460–61; see also Raheja 1988). In contrast to the Maori case, where the *hau* is believed to punish anyone who fails to reciprocate a gift, in India, "under no circumstances, and on pain of terrible supernatural penalties, is the gift resumed" (Parry 1986: 461). However, the Maori gift and the Indian gift have one thing in common, namely, the absence of an absolute disjunction between persons and things. The separation between persons and things is, according to Parry, a product of Christian cosmology: "Christian-ity—with its notion that all men are fashioned equally in the image of God—has developed a *universalistic* conception of purely disin-terested giving" (Parry 1986: 468, italics original).

According to Carrier, the ideology of the pure gift prevailing in American society is based on two popular conceptions: (1) the gift is immaterial, and its material value is beside the point; and (2) the gift is unconstrained and unconstraining—"it is a pure expression from the heart that does not bind giver and recipient" (1990: 20–21). In line with Parry's view, Carrier argues that "the ideology of the gift is shaped by the rise of industrial capitalism. Free and disinter-ested givers and recipients who transact unobligating expressions of affection come into cultural existence with the shift of production out of the affective and substantial relations that exist in the house-hold to the impersonal relations of wage labor and capital" (1990: 31). This ideology, however, does not always work as a guide for behavior. In practice, according to Carrier, the gifts often "are not spontaneous expressions of sentiment but are recurrent, pre-dictable and socially regulated" (1990: 19; see also Caplow 1982: 389–91, 1984: 1308–16). Thus the gift relations characterized by Mauss for traditional societies also exist in capitalist societies, "even though the dominance of commodity relations means that gifts in these societies have different meanings from those in societies of the gift," as Carrier points out elsewhere (1991: 131).

The implication of Parry's and Carrier's work is that, although gift exchange exists in all human societies, the form varies greatly depending on the particular culture within which it is rooted. Hence we may find multiple forms of the gift—the Indian gift, the "Indian gift" (Parry's term for the Melanesian and Polynesian gift), the Jap-anese gift, the English gift, the Chinese gift, and so on. Part of the analytic power of Parry's and Carrier's work is that it incorporates European/American social models, which, as will be shown later, help us to see what has been missing in previous anthropological studies of the gift.

All forms of the gift are, of course, cultural constructions—or ideologies, as Parry and Carrier prefer to call them. The theoretical significance of the Chinese gift as exemplified by the Xiajia case lies in the fact that it provides its own answers to the three fundamental issues in the anthropological study of the gift: the principle of reciprocity, the spirit of the gift, and the relationship between gifts and commodities.

Reciprocity and the Material Aspect of the Gift

Although the model of reciprocity established first by Malinowski has been consistently criticized (see Lebra 1969, 1975; MacCormack 1976; Parry 1986; Schieffelin 1980; and Weiner 1980, 1985), it remains the dominant approach to date in anthropological studies of gift giving, primarily because it is based on economic rationality and thus has a long history in Western thought (Weiner 1992). The core element of this model is the notion of equivalent return or balanced exchange, which can be realized in various forms, ranging from material goods, to political power, to symbolic reward. A possible negative effect of the reciprocity model is that gift exchanges are reduced to essentially dyadic transactions between self-interested individuals. As M. Strathern notes: "The curiosity is the extent to which that view of gift exchange in fact continues to deploy the barter model of value. For it locates social interest in terms of the respective values that persons exchange with one another, measured through the worth of what they transfer, in the same way as bartered items are measured against one another" (1992: 170). In other words, pushing the reciprocity model further, one will see that in the end it is still the material aspect of the gift that accounts for everything generated by the exchange: status, prestige, power, and, of course, wealth.

Applying the model of reciprocity to the Chinese gift, we see a less clear result. On the one hand, the principle of reciprocity does play an important role in the Chinese system of gift exchange; and in the long run, most exchange relations are sustained by fulfillment of the obligation to reciprocate the received gift. On the other hand, the Chinese case also poses two difficulties for the Malinowskian model of reciprocity, namely, variations in reciprocity and the absence of reciprocity.

First, as discussed in Chapter 6, there are four operating rules of gift giving among Xiajia villagers, each of which reflects the principle of reciprocity in a different way. Under certain circumstances, these rules may conflict with each other, and one must choose among them. In such a case Xiajia villagers rely on *renqing* ethics because gift giving is, at bottom, a means of expressing *renqing*. The implication here is that reciprocity itself is deeply rooted in underlying cultural premises and thus may manifest itself differently not only in different cultures but also in different contexts of the same culture. It is therefore necessary to explore the relationship between reciprocity and its cultural premises, which, in the Chinese case, are the patterns of *renqing* ethics.

Second, ethnographic evidence presented in Chapter 7 shows that in hierarchical contexts gifts are given unilaterally on the ladder of social status—and no equivalent return is expected. The recipients remain socially superior even though they fail to return the gifts. Moreover, receiving rather than giving is regarded as the symbol of prestige. These features place the Chinese gift in sharp contrast to two basic elements of the reciprocity model: (a) gifts always obligate the recipients to repay; and (b) unilateral giving generates power and prestige on the donor's side. The absence of return gifts is also found in the Indian case of *dana* (Parry 1986; Raheja 1988; and Vatuk and Vatuk 1971), where gifts are given by social superiors to their subordinates and such unilateral giving helps to maintain caste dominance (Raheja 1988; Werbner 1990: 271–72). Reasons why this type of Chinese gift differs from those found in other societies also are discussed in Chapter 7. Both the Chinese gift and the Indian gift demonstrate that gift giving does not always involve reciprocal returns. (The differences between these two systems are examined elsewhere; see Yan 1991.) The principle of reciprocity alone is not enough to generate a universal theory of the gift; there is always something about gifts that cannot be explained in terms of economic rationality. This realization leads to an alternative approach, one that emphasizes the spirit of the gift and the inalienability of objects from their owners.

Inalienability and the Spiritual Aspect of the Gift

As discussed in Chapter 1, the spirit of the gift—the classic theme in Mauss's book—was revitalized during the 1980's. Following Mauss, Parry interprets the absence of reciprocity in the Indian *dana* in terms of the "evil spirit" of the gift. But by so doing, he actually denies Mauss's original argument that the spirit of the gift elicits a return gift. Realizing this difficulty, Parry writes: "Where we have the 'spirit,' reciprocity is denied; where there is reciprocity there is not much evidence of 'spirit.' The two aspects of the model do not hang together" (1986: 463). A perfect solution is found in studies of the Pacific, where one can see both the spirit and the obligation to return. Rather than accepting Mauss's interpretation of the Maori *hau*, many anthropologists have employed the notion of inalienability to explain the existence of spiritual, nonutilitarian ties between giver and recipient (see Damon 1982, 1983; Gregory 1980, 1982; and Liep 1990). Weiner's recent book (1992) is an exception in that she asserts Mauss is right about the Maori *hau*. Weiner argues that there is a close connection between the *hau*, the person, and valuables (*taonga*) such as cloaks, fine mats, and shells; because of this connection, valuables gain their own identity and become inalienable possessions (1992: 46–56). Her conclusion is quite close to Mauss's original proposition: "The taonga given to someone should return because it is inalienable, but the hau can be detached from an object so that another taonga may carry the original 'semblance' of the person" (Weiner 1992: 63).

Although this theory of inalienability avoids reducing gift exchange to a simplistic form of dyadic exchange between self-interested individuals, it cannot adequately explain the practice of gift giving among Xiajia villagers. For them the gift is alienable and does not have any supernatural power in and of itself. A noticeable feature of gift exchange among the Chinese is that money plays an important role (see Chapter 3). Moreover, most material gifts are consumer goods, such as wine, cigarettes, and canned food—all of which must be purchased with cash. Except for situations involving a high degree of intimacy, such as exchanges between lovers or close neighbors, food gifts should be purchased rather than homemade. In contrast to the Melanesian and Polynesian cases, which involve the endless circulation of valuable shells, fine mats, or cloaks, the objects exchanged among Xiajia villagers are rarely recycled as return gifts. Instead, it is expected that gifts will be consumed by the recipient soon after their acceptance. It is quite common for a host who runs out of cash during a ceremony to use the monetary gifts he or she has just received. Material gifts such as wine and cigarettes may also be consumed immediately under similar circumstances. When making a return gift, villagers always try to avoid the impression of repaying a debt; thus a return gift is always slightly different from the original one—another kind of material gift or a different sum of money. Therefore in the Chinese context a gift is not only alienable, it *must* be alienated; to return the same gift would be considered a gesture of insult and rejection.

Unlike the Melanesian *taonga* or the Indian *dana*, the Chinese gift itself does not contain any supernatural qualities. Nevertheless, it serves as one of the most powerful and popular vehicles to convey spiritually significant messages, such as care, affection, moral concern, and emotional attachment. Accordingly, the gift creates a spiritual connection between the giver and the recipient, which is generally categorized as *renqing* by the villagers. This is why Xiajia residents always look at how much *renqing* exists between two parties and insist that the offering of gifts be determined by previous *renqing* and *guanxi* (see Chapter 6). In other words, it is not the spirit of the gift but the spirit of the people that ties the gift transactors together; it is not the object but the *renqing* expressed by the object that is inalienable. Therefore, one's *renqing* debt eventually should be paid and ideally be paid by oneself, because a *renqing* relationship is inalienable. (I will discuss further the nature of *renqing* and *guanxi* below.)

The Chinese case does not deny the significance of the spiritual aspect of the gift; on the contrary, it may help to elaborate Mauss's original theme to suggest that both the spirit and the inalienability of the gift can be understood on two levels. The theory of inalienability elaborated by Weiner, among others, can be seen in the Melanesian case where the gift is believed to contain *hau* or another spiritual essence and thus cannot be disposed of freely by the recipient. Mauss bases his argument on this empirical evidence even though these observations may not hold for other societies. However, the theoretical theme Mauss derives from the Melanesian data is that the bond between individuals or groups can be created through the association of persons with things. Therefore, the key issue in any society is to determine what people think about the message conveyed by the gift: love, friendship, caring, obligation, or a supernatural spirit. In this sense, it may not be appropriate to speak of the spirit *of* the gift if one wants to address this issue beyond the Pacific island context, because it may revolve around the spirit *conveyed by* the gift or, as I suggest above, the spirit of the gift transactors. When research is conducted in complex state societies, the spirit and inalienability of the gift are often understood in this broader sense. For instance, in his attempt to apply Mauss's theory of the gift to Western societies, Carrier notes: "Because the degree of association between object and person will vary according to situations and societies, however, inalienability does not mean that the giver always has the right to reclaim the object or that such a right could be exercised in practice" (1991: 125). Examining gifting practices among Pakistani immigrants in Britain, Werbner writes: "Gifts, by contrast, are inalienably imbued with the *spirit of their givers,* and thus objectify social relationships which precede them" (1990: 282, italics mine).

Instrumentality and the Commercial Aspect of the Gift

A pertinent achievement in the debate regarding the opposition between gifts and commodities is the recognition of their coexistence under certain circumstances (see Carrier 1991; Godelier 1977; Morris 1986; and Parry and Bloch 1989). With some qualifications, the interchangeability of gift and commodity is also acknowledged, especially the dual role of money as a gift/commodity (see Gregory 1980; Kiernan 1988; and A. Strathern 1979). Since "the categories of 'pure gift' and 'pure commodity' may be difficult to find empirically in the economies anthropologists most often study" (Feil 1982: 342), some scholars have suggested that the distinct contrast between gift and commodity should be eliminated (see Appadurai 1986a: 11–13; Parry and Bloch 1989: 8–12).

Although a revisionist view is emerging, most studies of the gift focus on how commodities can be converted into gifts and, after the transformation, how the objects perform their new role in gift relations. If we consider that the gift economy is embedded in a commodity economy in most contemporary societies, and that gifts in many cases are actually purchased items, two further questions arise: First, is the reverse conversion—gifts into commodities—also possible? Second, when a commodity is transformed into a gift or the other way around, will the transformed object make any impact on the relational contexts previously represented by gifts or commodities? Werbner gives a positive clue to the former but seemingly denies the possibility for the latter: "In some instances, notably in the case of cash and gold, the valuables passed as gifts are also commodities and are sometimes used as such; in other words, they may be reconverted. At the same time women, as 'person-gifts,' may be commoditised, although this may be regarded as a perversion of the system. In such cases the system is distorted and the gift economy comes to be conceived of by transactors primarily in commodity terms" (Werbner 1990: 282). In other words, even though the gifts and commodities are interchangeable, gift relations and commodity relations remain essentially unchangeable and mutually exclusive.

Building on Werbner's observations, I show in my study of the Xiajia case what might be called a gray area between gift relations and commodity relations. In this area a particular type of Chinese gift, the instrumental gift, plays a role in merging these two opposing sets of relations. Following Befu's dichotomy of expressivity and instrumentality of the gift (Befu 1966–67, 1977a), I distinguish instrumental gifts as the means by which to attain utilitarian ends (involving the manipulation of interpersonal relations in the short term) from expressive gifts that are ends in and of themselves—thus reflecting long-term relationships. Instrumental gifts are given in exchange for favors or services, and the recipients in turn repay the donors by exercising their positional power or providing resources that are under their control. In China this practice is the well-known phenomenon of "going through the back door," and its main feature is to channel commodity transactions, from purchasing consumer goods to starting private businesses, in a highly personalized way. The most illuminating examples are those that involve gift giving to promote the development of private enterprises (see Wank 1995; and M. Yang 1989, 1994).

Given the central importance of personal networks in social life, the Chinese case might be more obvious, but it is by no means unique. Instrumental gift giving is reported in modern Japan (Befu 1968), and efforts to personalize commodity relations can be found in typical commodity societies as well. For instance, among the petty dealers of stolen goods in London's East End, people do not always seek maximum economic advantage when buying and selling; rather, they want to secure a long-term, personalized exchange relationship. As a result, the "goods that [are] given have been de-materialized and the transaction has been personalized" (Mars 1982: 173). The merger of personal favor and commodity exchange is also found in the widespread use of credit in small shops where credit can be both social and financial (see Johnson 1985, quoted in Carrier 1992). As Carrier notes: "In such a relationship, buying a tin of milk was not an impersonal exchange of equivalents. It was a re-creation of a durable personal relationship, recalling previous transactions and anticipating future ones" (1992: 202). The relationship of buying and selling thus resembles that of gift exchange.

The intriguing point here is that because of the instrumentality inherent in the gift, it can be utilized as a means to cultivate personal relations and produce a twofold result. On the one hand, the instru-mentalized gift is transformed into a quasi-commodity, because it is transacted only for maximizing personal interests and is reciprocated by another similarly instrumentalized return (goods, favor, service, or whatever) rather than a gift. On the other hand, the instrumental-exchange relations facilitated by the gifts in turn become personal-ized to some extent, and further commodity transactions can be ar-ranged through the "back door" by mutually trusted, more or less dependent partners. Hence a gray area is created between the poles of gift relations and commodity relations, in which the commodi-tization of the gift leads to the personalization of commodity ex-changes. Although at first this dynamic appears to be paradoxical, it may prove to be true in many contexts: the internal structure of the gift is not immutable, and in a world of commodities, the gift may have gained a commercial aspect.

Sentiment: A Neglected Aspect of the Gift

Finally, I would like to address an issue that is by and large absent from anthropological discourse on the gift: How shall we assess the role of sentiment or emotional response in systems of gift exchange? The Xiajia case shows that emotional attachment is an important part of *renqing* ethics and gives meaning to everyday interpersonal transactions. Villagers regard gift giving as a means to express both their moral obligations and feelings such as concern, affection, grat-itude, and sorrow. Gift giving may also express disaffection or anger. Moreover, in addition to institutionalized gifts exchanged between families, there are individualized gifts that pass between individuals who are bound by both social ties and emotional attachments. One example is the gift exchanged between lovers (for further consideration of such gifts, see Chapters 3, 4, and 6). These personal gifts, which are very similar to their counterparts in American society, and the sentimentality generated by such gifts have attracted little scholarly attention in anthropological literature. Why?

When I read ethnographic accounts of gift exchange in other parts of the world, I am puzzled by the absence of such discussion. Most studies are preoccupied with discovering either the economic rationality or religious beliefs of the local people. We have detailed descriptions of the patterns of economic transactions, the working principles of reciprocity, the relations between gift giving and cosmology, or the interconnection between persons and things. Few studies have touched upon the emotional world of ordinary people and the role that gifts play in expressing emotions. Weiner's recent book (1992) is no doubt the most radical departure from the rational model of reciprocity and the most thorough effort to date to explore the spiritual aspect of the gift. Nevertheless, it is still difficult to determine whether the gifts exchanged in Melanesian and Polynesian societies involve sentiments, even though it is logical to expect some sort of emotional response.

There are two possible answers to this puzzle. First, gift giving does not serve to express personal emotions in these societies; therefore, sentiments are simply absent in gifting behavior. Second, in order to emphasize the uniqueness of the local system of gift exchange, ethnographers may omit the element of sentiment because it is not deemed to be as significant as other issues—for example, equivalent return or inalienability. Taking the dominant ideology of the gift into consideration, I assume the latter proposal is likely to be correct.

As mentioned above, in contemporary Euro-American ideology, the gift is construed as a pure, disinterested, unconstrained "present," which is nothing more than a voluntary, spontaneous expression of the real inner self and inner feeling (see Carrier 1990: 20–23, 30–32; and Parry 1986: 466–68). Because of this emphasis on the spontaneous, emotional nature of the gift, David Cheal suggests that the gift economy in Western societies is actually part of a culture of love (see Cheal 1987: 150–69, 1988: 40–55, 106–20). The strong influence of this ideology on the practice of gift giving can be seen in one of the rules regarding the selection of Christmas gifts. "The economic values of any giver's gift are supposed to be sufficiently scaled to the emotional values of relationships that, when they are opened in the bright glare of the family circle, the donor will not appear to have disregarded either the legitimate inequality of some relationships by, for example, giving a more valuable gift to a nephew than to a son, or the legitimate equality of other relationships by, for example, giving conspicuously unequal gifts to two sons" (Caplow 1984: 1313). In fact, gift recipients are scaled in terms of their social/kinship distance or status in relation to the donor, and that gift exchange is not based on a neutral sense of "natural feelings" between two parties. Interestingly enough, however, the concern with social distance is translated as the "emotional value" of the relationship.

The implication here is that the Euro-American ideology of the pure gift may exaggerate the role of sentiment, thus obscuring the fact that gift exchange in such societies is also regulated by many rules and serves to deal with "relationships that are important but insecure" (Caplow 1982: 391). Furthermore, this ideology may also lead people to overlook the existence of sentiment in systems of gift exchange in non-Western societies where expression of personal feeling is thought to be similar and thus adds nothing new to the study of the gift. For instance, I have long been puzzled by a problem in Trobriand ethnography: Why are the personal gifts exchanged between Trobriand spouses, originally categorized by Malinowski as the "pure gift," either interpreted as a means "to maintain a profitable alliance" (Mauss 1967: 71) or redefined by Malinowski himself as the payment from a husband to his wife for sexual services (Malinowski 1962: 40–41). Is it not possible that a Trobriand husband offers a gift to his wife simply because of affection between them (not to mention the loaded term "love")? If the answer is negative, then why are Trobrianders so different from other people? If the answer is affirmative, why has the existence of such sentiment been overlooked in discussions of the Trobriand gift system?

In a recent article, Roger Keesing warns anthropologists against a popular focus on what is strange in another culture, or the "quest for the exotic." He challenges all of us by asking two questions: "When we rummage through our field notes to find something worth writing about, do we select the most exotic materials to characterize and essentialize Otherness? And if so, do we leave what seems mundane—or simply familiar—undescribed?" (1989: 459). With regard to the study of the gift, Carrier (1992) claims that a straightforward reading of Mauss's *The Gift* by many anthropologists has led to both the Orientalization of an alien "Other" and the Occidentalization of the modern West. As a result, "the model that had focused on difference between us and them, ignoring similarity, became a definition that denied or elided similarity" (Carrier 1992: 204). Whether these criticisms can be applied to all anthropological pursuits is empirically questionable. My own study of the Chinese case demonstrates that the sentimental aspect of gift giving in non-Western societies has often been ignored, perhaps because it has been perceived as too commonplace to warrant comment.

Rethinking Guanxi *and* Renqing: *Primary and Extended Forms*

In this concluding chapter I would like to explore further the meaning of two key notions upon which the Chinese gift is culturally constructed: *guanxi* and *renqing*. As indicated in Chapter 5, Xiajia villagers regard their personal networks—*guanxi*—as the "society" (*shehui*). A man who has built an elaborate *guanxi* network locally is called "a person in the society" (*shehui shang de ren*); one who is not successful in this aspect of social life is called a "dead door" (*si menzi*). These indigenous perceptions indicate that *guanxi* provides Xiajia villagers with the very social matrix in which one learns to be a social person and to interact with others in a socially accepted way. Given that the influence of kinship organizations in Xiajia has greatly diminished in the postrevolutionary era, structurally one's *guanxi* network constitutes one's social universe—the immediate form of social organization—outside the family yet within the village society as a "local world," to borrow Arthur Kleinman's term (1992).

According to Kleinman, a local world is constructed on social experiences defined as "an interpersonal, intersubjective realm of engagements, transactions, communications, and other social activities" (1992: 128). One of the keys to the study of social life in such a local world is to determine how individuals interact with one another and with the community as a whole. The Xiajia case reveals that *guanxi* networks serve as an intermediate form between acting individuals at one pole and the local world at the other, an organizational form that fits into the concept of a "quasi-group" (Boissevain 1968) in network analysis theories.

Dissatisfied with the group-oriented approach prevalent in anthropological studies, especially in structural-functionalism, some scholars have developed a network analysis approach to study interacting individuals (see Mitchell 1974: 280). Personal strategies of network building, individual manipulation of human resources, and the influence of personal affection on interpersonal relations have become a focus of scholarly attention. As Banck points out, "The shift in emphasis from group to individual means such a change in level of abstraction. And we must expect that what is analytically beautiful and elegant at the group level may be clumsy and refractory at the level where social individuals are under scrutiny" (1974: 38). According to the theoretical approach underlying network analysis, a given ego is connected to a person's network of people either by a single-stranded relationship, such as kinship, or by multi-stranded relationships, such as a combination of kinship, colleagueship, and friendship (see Mitchell 1969; Whitten and Wolf 1974). As networks by definition imply egocentric connections, people within the same network usually have independent relationships with the given ego but rarely interact among themselves (see Mitchell 1974).

Guanxi networks in Xiajia village are characterized by both a high rate of multiplexity in relational configurations and a high density in interpersonal transactions. Most people in a given *guanxi* network are also members of the same community and interact with each other in everyday life. In addition to exchanging gifts in various situations, they also cooperate in agricultural production, support each other in village politics, and spend recreational time together. It is in this sense that *guanxi* distinguishes itself from the common form of personal networks in network analysis studies; *guanxi* assumes a stronger organizational form as a quasi-group in village society.

Such a group, as defined by Boissevain, "[is] a coalition of persons, recruited according to structurally diverse principles by one or more existing members, between some of whom there is a degree of patterned interaction and organization. . . . It has a structural form which is given by the regular and often purposive interaction that takes place" (1968: 550).

As a quasi-group in everyday life, *guanxi* is not a monolithic entity; rather, its structure is highly stratified in terms of distance of kinship and friendship, and its scope varies greatly depending on individual villagers' inheritance in kinship ties and achievement in friendship ties. As shown in Chapter 5, a villager's *guanxi* network is comprised of three relational zones: the personal core, the reliable zone, and the effective zone, based on the degree of reliability in interpersonal relations. Although the kinship ties that one acquires from parents and parents-in-law form a prominent part of one's *guanxi* network, my analysis of the Xiajia case reveals that friendship acquired through individual efforts plays an equally important role. Actually, it is the increase in friendship ties that marks one's social achievement.

More important, the moral and emotional aspects of local worlds should not be overlooked. As Kleinman notes: "They [local worlds] are to be understood as moral worlds, for what precedes, constitutes, expresses, and follows from our actions in interpersonal flows of experience are particular local patterns of recreating what is most at stake for us, what we most fear, what we most aspire to, what we are most threatened by, what we most desire to cross over to for safety, and what we jointly take to be the purpose, or the ultimate meaning, of our living and our dying" (1992: 129). The moral characteristics of Xiajia village as a local moral world are reflected in *renqing* ethics.

In Chapter 6, I argued that the fundamental principle of interaction and communication at the individual level is encapsulated in *renqing* ethics, which should be understood as first and foremost a set of moral norms that guide and regulate one's behavior. *Renqing* is also the socially accepted pattern of emotional responses in the sense that one takes others' emotional responses into consideration. As the examples in Chapter 6 demonstrate, one's failure to fulfill the obligation of reciprocity, refusing to share resources with those within

one's *guanxi* network and ignoring other people's face are regarded
as immoral acts and thus violations of *renqing* ethics. Or, as villagers
put it: "So-and-so doesn't know *renqing*" (*budong renqing*). The same
accusation is made of those who have shown no consideration of
others' feelings and emotional responses.

Furthermore, *renqing* serves as an important standard by which
villagers judge whether one is a proper social person. In other words,
renqing gives meaning to everyday engagements, interactions, and
transactions between villagers. Without *renqing*, life is less meaningful and people are dehumanized. As Uncle Wang, the ritual specialist
who showed me both the complexity and simplicity of *renqing* (see
Chapter 6), put it: "Just think about the word *renqing* itself. It is
called *renqing* [literally, human feelings] because only human beings
[*ren*] have *renqing*. My dog doesn't understand *renqing*, and my pig
doesn't either. But my little grandson does. When my wife took him
to a wedding banquet several months ago, he asked: 'Grandma, we
must present a gift, right?' You see, he is learning *renqing* even
though he is only six."

The issue raised by Uncle Wang's grandson is actually quite common among children of his age. Older men and women like to bring
children with them to attend ceremonial banquets, telling the children that they are going to someone's home to present a gift (*sui li*)
and then to have a banquet (*zuoxi*, literally to sit at the banquet table). Every child in the village knows that one cannot attend a ceremonial banquet unless one first offers a gift. It is interesting to note
that during banquets a child has the full rights of an adult—he or she
must be given a formal seat at the table, even if there is a shortage of
seats, and must be properly served all the dishes. The reason, according to my informants, is that a child is also a person who comes
to celebrate the change in the host's life. It would be extremely in-
auspicious for a child not to be given a seat at a banquet, because refusal of a seat symbolically means being rejected as a person. Additionally, this rejection is considered a serious insult to the child's
parents. Given the prevalence of this custom, there has never been a
single case in Xiajia where a child has intruded on a banquet unac-
companied by a parent or a gift. Uncle Wang points out the above
as a telling example of how *renqing* works.

Gift-giving activities indeed embody the otherwise abstract notion of *renqing* in everyday life and further engender the educational and regulating power of *renqing* in the cultural construction of personhood within village society. As demonstrated in the preceding chapters, gift giving is one of the key means by which villagers maintain and expand their *guanxi* networks. In turn, most expressive gifts are exchanged within existing *guanxi* networks. So gifts are also framed by the wider moral context of social relations, namely, *guanxi* under the governance of *renqing*.

To summarize the relationship between the gift on the one hand and *guanxi/renqing* on the other, I suggest that the gift can be seen as a sign, or a vehicle, which conveys *renqing* against the social matrix of *guanxi*. Yet the gift is more than a sign; it is also a material object or substance in and of itself, with use value and exchange value. Thus the endless process of gift transactions, including banquets or family ceremonies, constitutes a gift economy in its own right. In this sense, the gift can be regarded as a relationship in a moral economy; nevertheless, the meaning of this gift relationship derives from the larger contexts of *guanxi* and *renqing* in a local moral world. Within the boundaries of this local moral world, the pursuit of personal interest mingles with the fulfillment of moral obligations, and the value of the gift lies mainly in its role to sustain a long-term order of social life rather than a short-term personal benefit. Consequently, *guanxi* and *renqing* are characterized by moral obligations and emotional attachments in interpersonal relations and by the stable mutuality between people within networks over a long period. These two features define the primary form of *guanxi* and *renqing* in village society.

But this local moral world is by no means the only arena within which villagers play their social roles. On the contrary, as a result of economic development, villagers find themselves more and more often dealing with people from the outside world. When villagers encounter outsiders, they tend to use what they know best, that is, *renqing* ethics and *guanxi* networks. This use leads not only to the expansion of old *guanxi* networks, but also to the cultivation of new short-term and instrumental personal connections. When many instrumental connections are recruited in *guanxi* networks, and when people have to utilize the gift as a means to get things done, *guanxi* and *renqing* are transformed into what I prefer to call extended forms. In this new form *guanxi* becomes a means of entering "back doors," and *renqing* is regarded mainly as an exchangeable resource, something that is primarily instrumental and less sentimental or moral. *Guanxi* and *renqing* in their extended forms are reflected in the types of instrumental gifts described in Chapter 3, along with the examples discussed in Chapters 4 and 6.

As I compare my findings in Xiajia with previous studies of gift exchange and interpersonal relations in Chinese society, it becomes clear that most scholarly accounts have focused on the extended form of *guanxi* and *renqing*, and thus individual pursuits of interest and exchanges of scarce resources are interpreted as the ultimate purposes of *guanxi* cultivation (see, e.g., Gold 1985; Jacobs 1979; Walder 1986; and M. Yang 1989). As Kwang-kuo Hwang puts it, "The individual's reason for employing such power [*guanxi*] to influence other people lies in a desire to obtain one or more social resources controlled by them. Likewise, the reason why the other consents to succumb to the individual's influences is that the allocator foresees that this strategy will in turn bring a certain reward or help in evading some kind of punishment" (1987: 947). It is true that the role of good feelings (*ganqing*) in *guanxi* cultivation and *renqing* maintenance has been recognized, but only to the extent that good feelings are used as a strategy to improve the quality of particularistic ties (Jacobs 1979), to develop a trusted business partnership (De Glopper 1978), or to establish the necessary connections for obtaining desirable resources (Walder 1986; M. Yang 1989).[1] In other words, the disinterested, expressive aspects of *guanxi* and *renqing* are understood not in their own right but as another outcome of rational calculation, another means to pursue personal interest. The hidden message behind these interpretations remains: "No one does anything for nothing."

In my opinion, the use of personal connections in political alliances or in business transactions constitutes an extended form of *guanxi* and *renqing*, and these activities are more often conducted outside the village community. In fact, most studies of the current phenomenon of manipulating personal connections (*guanxixue*) in China are based on observations of urban life. As my analysis of the Xiajia case shows, within the close-knit village community, the cultivation of *guanxi* is more a way of culturally constructing oneself rather than a strategy to exchange resources with others, and *renqing* is more a part of a person's moral world than an exchangeable resource. This primary form of *guanxi* and *renqing* is a consequence of residential stability (or lack of social mobility) in rural communities—where most of the residents live as close neighbors throughout their lives. In such contexts expectations of reciprocity and pursuit of personal interest can be realized by cultivating long-term, stable relationships. This may explain the differences between my findings and those reported in earlier studies.

Furthermore, the Xiajia case contributes to a better understanding of the complexity of interpersonal relations in Chinese society. The primacy of personal connections has long attracted scholarly attention, and the most illuminating analysis is offered by Fei (1947). He characterizes Western social structure as a mode of group configuration, in which individuals are bound together by group membership and related rights and obligations. By contrast, Chinese society is characterized by a mode of differentiated configuration (*chaxu geju*), in which a person is related to others by various role relations, and these relations are differentiated in accordance with the degree of intimacy attached to that person (Fei 1947: 26–27). With such a structural mode of differentiated configuration, Chinese society is based not on discrete organizations but on overlapping personal networks, namely, *guanxi*.

While Fei's interpretation of *guanxi* is based mainly on rural society, King and Hwang try to establish a model of *guanxi* and *renqing* that can be applied to urban China as well. King distinguishes preordained interpersonal relations (such as the father-son relationship) from voluntarily constructed relations, and he maintains that *guanxi* and *renqing* play an important role only in the latter relations (1988: 89; 1991: 66–67). Hwang offers a tripartite division of all interpersonal relations: the expressive tie, the mixed tie, and the instrumental tie (1987: 949–53). The expressive tie is composed of family members and close friends and can render feelings of affection and attachment. The instrumental tie stands in opposition to the expressive tie and represents a professional patron-client relationship, such as that between a salesperson and customers in a shop or between a doctor and patients in a hospital. In the middle is the mixed tie that occurs among relatives, neighbors, classmates, and colleagues. "A mixed tie is a relationship in which an individual seeks to influence other people by means of *renqing* and *mianzi*" (Hwang 1987: 952).

The most enlightening part of King's and Hwang's models is that they also pay attention to social relations in which *guanxi* and *renqing* are not important. They both examine the mechanism of avoiding *renqing* and discuss how and why the Chinese want to observe universalistic rules (see King 1991: 75–79; Hwang 1987: 963–67). But in their efforts to compartmentalize personal relations they also run the risk of ignoring the expansion of *guanxi* across the domain of personal relations and thus underestimate the applicability of *renqing* ethics to people in other groups. For example, the Xiajia case shows that even among brothers and closest relatives, gift exchange is maintained to perpetuate good relations (good *guanxi*), and *renqing* ethics are observed as moral norms. This situation challenges both King's and Hwang's views that primary personal relations do not need to involve *renqing*. Furthermore, Xiajia villagers' efforts to establish instrumental personal connections, such as offering gifts to someone in exchange for a favor, lie outside the boundary of the mixed tie as defined by Hwang. The instrumental tie is turned into an extended form of *guanxi*. Actually, most activities designed to cultivate particularistic ties (*la guanxi*) take place in areas where personal relations are supposed to be professional and instrumental, including in the well-known phenomenon of "going through the back door" (*zou houmen*). In this connection, the distinction between the primary and extended forms of *guanxi* and *renqing* can help us to understand both the internal dynamics of *guanxi* cultivation and the potential of *renqing* ethics to embrace all kinds of personal relations.

The Gift Economy and Socialism: Restoration or Transformation?

I shall conclude by assessing the interactive relationship between the system of gift giving and social changes brought on by four decades of Chinese socialism. It is well known that both gift giving and *guanxi* cultivation existed long before the 1949 Revolution. Does the current practice of gift giving represent the simple resurrection of traditional culture? Ethnographic evidence from Xiajia village suggests that this is not the case. During the past four decades Xiajia villagers never ceased in their devotion to gift exchange. But they adjusted their behavior and network cultivation in response to the social-political changes affecting their community. As a result, the system of gift exchange did not die, even during the most radical periods of socialism; rather, the system has undergone complex changes and multiple transformations. The best example in this respect is the transformation of marriage transactions over the past four decades, which has been examined in detail in Chapter 8. In the following pages, I will summarize several features of the interactive relationship between gift giving and social changes in Xiajia society.

The Creation of New Rituals

One apparent development is that several ritualized situations of gift exchange have been either created or developed on the basis of traditional rituals. For instance, the gift-giving ceremonies for abortion and female sterilization were created in response to the implementation of the one-child policy in rural areas. In Xiajia village, the first large-scale gift-giving ceremony for sterilization took place immediately following the campaignlike mobilization for birth control in 1982. It is believed that when a woman undergoes a sterilization operation, her *qi*, that is, the essence of her body, will flow out, and she will lose both her reproductive abilities and her physical strength at the same time. In fact, many women who have undergone the operation have complained that for a time thereafter they felt much weaker and easily became ill. From an objective point of view, this could have been due to malnutrition or to lack of rest. But in any case, the local belief system motivated the villagers to do something to compensate the women.

Moreover, both men and women regard female sterilization as akin to male castration. They use the word *qiao* to indicate female sterilization, which usually is used only for gelding and spaying animals, especially pigs. The medical term for both male and female sterilization is *jueyu*, but ordinary villagers do not refer to it in this way.[2] The fact that villagers insist on using the term *qiao* indicates that female sterilization causes a great deal of anxiety and discontent.

A compensation ritual, therefore, was created by women for other women, and this ritual was supported by men. According to my informants, large-scale gift giving began when a woman fell seriously ill after being sterilized, and from that time all women who were sterilized began to receive gifts. Thus a new ceremony was created.

Some other gift-giving ceremonies were developed on the basis of private rituals, such as childbirth, house construction, or engagement celebrations. Prior to 1949, these were all minor ceremonies celebrated within a close circle of agnates and affines. Social changes during the collective era resulted in the elaboration of the childbirth celebration. As villagers worked collectively, all earning their income from the same collectives, relational distances among them were shortened. As a villager explained: "If one's wife gave birth, most of his team members would go to congratulate him, because people were eating from the same big rice pot every day and were thus related to each other." The house construction ceremony is a recent innovation designed to elicit monetary gifts from a wider group of social connections. When I lived in the village during the 1970's, only close kinsmen brought housewarming gifts, mostly red banners, to the host, while the others contributed their free labor (of course the host had to provide meals for the laborers). In the 1990's, free labor cannot be expected, and it is possible to earn wages for constructing one's relatives' or neighbors' houses while also presenting gifts to maintain good mutual relationships.

Village cadres generally have not been enthusiastic about the elimination of traditional ritual life; on the contrary, they seemed to enjoy the solemn ceremonies even more than the ordinary villagers, when the political atmosphere allowed them to do so. It is said that the practice of receiving monetary gifts during engagement rituals started in 1982, when a production team leader performed a ceremony for his son's engagement and set up an accounting table to receive gifts. According to some informants, the idea of presenting gifts was proposed by several men who wanted to flatter their team leader, as a result of which the engagement rite subsequently was upgraded to a major ceremony, characterized by the writing of a gift list and a large banquet.

It is interesting that the villagers' creation of gift-giving rites has had its own standard of selection. For instance, a form of ancestor worship ritual called *shaoxiang* (literally, "burning incense") was not resumed by the villagers after the 1949 Revolution. The ritual had usually been performed in the courtyard of the host on a selected date; ancestor scrolls were displayed on a long altar and incense was burned. A group of musicians and singers were invited to perform folk drama. The ritual lasted for three days, and throughout the final day, members of the host family would kneel in front of the ancestral shrine. Guests and visitors were welcomed, and a banquet was prepared. As one might expect, an accounting table was also set up to receive gifts from the guests.

Beginning in the late 1970's, visits to ancestral tombs during the Qingming Festival and worshiping of ancestors at home during the lunar New Year period gradually reemerged in many households.[3] But up to 1991 no one in the village has tried to resume the *shaoxiang* ritual. On the contrary, some informants even avoided talking about this rite during my interviews, and when the subject came up they always added a standardized footnote: "It was a superstitious, feudal custom." Such hesitation may have had something to do with the CCP's severe attacks on lineage organization and ancestor worship during the early 1950's. Still affected by the social memory of that period, Xiajia villagers would rather test the party's tolerance in other domains, such as the birthday celebration, instead of the dangerous and sensitive rite of *shaoxiang*.

Changes in the Content of Gifts

Another new feature in ceremonial gift giving is that the content of gifts has been constantly changing, a result of the villagers' effort to negotiate with state authorities about the legitimacy of traditional exchange patterns. A 74-year-old ritual specialist recalled that ceremonial gift giving prior to the revolution was much more sophisticated and less materialistic. The accounting station (*zhangfang*) for receiving gifts was always decorated with red cloth (a symbol of good luck) and accompanied by fine music. People expressed their good wishes to the host when they presented their gifts, the value of which was generally much lower than it is currently. In certain circumstances, gifts were given under the direction of the ritual specialist, and thus the exchange itself was a rite.

The ritual specialist's account was confirmed by many older villagers, and they all insisted that in the past people paid more attention to the proper ways of gift giving and to the good feelings conveyed by the gifts rather than to the monetary value they embodied. "When I was young, people respected proprieties and manners of gift exchange. The gifts were treated seriously as tokens of a person's heart," said a 79-year-old folk musician, who repeatedly emphasized this point during our conversation. Despite the obvious possibility that these senior villagers may have been nostalgic about and idealizing past practices, it is clear that traditional patterns of ceremonial gift exchange were characterized by elaborate proprieties and differentiated usages of monetary and material gifts.

Traditional patterns of gift giving were altered a great deal during the early postrevolution period. The CCP strongly criticized traditional ceremonies and tried to transform them primarily for three reasons: (1) the rituals were considered superstitious practices; (2) the rituals played a role in supporting the authority of the local elite and lineage elders; and (3) the performance of rituals wasted time and money in nonproductive activities (see Parish and Whyte 1978: 248–50). The CCP tried to label the ritual specialists "religious and superstitious practitioners" and to impose a government ban on their performances. Consequently, although ritual life has remained, it has been modified and simplified to a great extent, and ceremonial gift giving has also become much less elaborate. For example, the traditional speech during the gift offering in a wedding context has been abandoned and replaced with an official testimony by the cadres. Prayers during house construction ceremonies and birthday celebrations have also been abandoned. The accounting station, the key place for gift giving, is no longer decorated with red cloth, and gift lists are written in notebooks with pens rather than on traditional red paper with a calligraphy brush.

In an effort to adjust to the new social-political environment, villagers have also adopted new forms of gift giving. During the collective era, people often presented collective gifts—that is, several people bought a gift together and shared the costs. Their names appeared collectively on the gift list as either a "Maoist study group," a "branch of the CCP," or in the case of one I collected, simply "the commune members from the third production team." According to my informants, the collective gift had a double effect: it reduced the individuals' costs of gift giving considerably; but it also helped to bring more people into the cycle of gift exchange. It was difficult for a person to refuse an invitation to participate in collective gift giving because it would alienate him or her from the group. During the heat of the Cultural Revolution, gifts increased somewhat in revolutionary content. A small book of Mao's quotations or a poster with revolutionary slogans might seem a perfect gift for a newly married couple. However, this practice did not become popular or last long. My informants could remember no more than five such cases, and in all of them the gifts were exchanged between radical young activists, namely, village Red Guards.

Although additional situations for gift giving have been created in the past collective period, ritual performances have remained simple and less refined. The traditional, sophisticated etiquette of gift exchange has not reemerged, even though ritual specialists have begun to be active again and the significance of gift exchange in maintaining social connections has increased. Many older villagers have attributed this change to the fact that the younger generations lack an interest in the old proprieties and complain that current practice has increasingly placed emphasis on the material rather than the spiritual value of gifts. Since decollectivization in 1983, ceremonial gift giving has seen a rapid increase in the value of gifts due to inflation, improvement of living standards, and the influence of the marketization of the rural economy. In addition, new ways of cultivating interpersonal relations have been introduced into village life, such as giving cash payments for labor assistance during house construction. These trends have made the content of gifts more oriented toward exchange value than toward symbolic value.

Socialist Destratification and the Intensification of Gift Exchange

The quest for social equality was surely one of the most powerful political impulses in the CCP's effort to transform Chinese society. Beginning with the land reform movement, previously advantaged groups were deprived of privileges, prestige, and other favorable mobility opportunities. Egalitarian ideals, such as "getting rich together," were encouraged throughout the collective era. Neverthe-less, socialist egalitarianism ironically stimulated ordinary villagers' incentives to participate in the contest of gift exchange and made the exchange more pronounced.

Prior to the 1949 Revolution, not everyone had the ability to host an elaborate ritual. At that time, only well-to-do families could af-ford to hire professional musicians and to offer a large, costly ban-quet. For ordinary villagers, celebrations of family rituals were lim-ited to the most important rituals (such as weddings or funerals), and the social scope of gift exchange was much smaller than is presently the case. According to older informants, the obligation of gift giv-ing applied only to close agnates and affines. The number of guests normally ranged from 30 to 50 for ordinary villagers, and only land-lords or the local elite would have more than 100 guests. An elderly villager, Wang, whose father was a tenant, but who also owned a lit-tle private land, told me that 37 guests attended his wedding in 1945, including his father's brothers, mother's brother and sisters, his sis-ters' husbands, a few cousins, several neighbors, and two honored guests representing the landlord for whom his family was working. Significantly, Wang's mother recounted this story to me several times when I lived in the village. It is clear that both Wang and his mother were proud of that wedding, because the number of guests was considered large among his class at that time.

After land reform even the poorest villagers wanted to perform solemn ceremonies, and the social scope of gift exchange soon ex-panded to a much larger group. For instance, when an informant married in the winter of 1947 (during the land reform campaign in this region), despite economic constraints, his family managed to host a banquet and perform the wedding in style, to show that they had really become "masters of the society." Because he worked as a local activist during land reform and thereafter became a cadre, 102 guests attended his wedding.

The key factor here is that land reform and the subsequent polit-ical campaigns altered the previous system of social hierarchy, thus raising the hopes of ordinary villagers. The previous social gap be-tween the rich and the poor was diminished, and the difference be-tween the life-style of the elite and that of the commoners was dras-tically reduced. Although the distribution of life chances was still far from equal, every villager (except for the "four bad elements") could claim to have an equal right to social achievements in ritual life. Hence, performing family ceremonies in style was perceived as a necessity for nearly everyone. While becoming more simplified in its performative aspects, gift exchange actually intensified in terms of its frequency and social scope. For instance, birthday celebrations were performed only by the local elite prior to the 1949 Revolution. In the three decades following land reform, birthdays were rarely celebrated, and the younger generation was not even familiar with the custom. However, in 1979 a wealthy resident of Xiajia held a ceremony for his mother's sixtieth birthday; many others soon followed his example. As an informant put it: "We are all forced to marry our children in style and to have large celebrations for house construction. Because we all work in the same collectives, nobody wants to be the underdog in these affairs. So I have to keep up by doing the same as the next person."

Socialist Restratification and the Instrumentalization of Gift Exchange

It is generally recognized that in countries dominated by state socialism experiments originally aimed at social equality ultimately result in the creation of new forms of inequality and new concentrations of power. This irony has been referred to as a movement from destratification to restratification (see J. Watson 1984: 2; and Whyte 1981: 309). In Xiajia village, social life during the collective era was far from "egalitarian," and the collectives were no less hierarchical than prerevolution communities (see Chapter 2). With regard to gift giving, as discussed in Chapter 7, the socialist system of hierarchy created a new kind of dependence relationship between cadres and ordinary villagers, in which the cadres' superior status and power eliminated the grounds for balanced gift exchange. As a redistributor, a cadre may feel free of the obligation to return a gift to his subordinates, because the latter depend on the resources controlled by the cadre and, thus, the failure to return the gift cannot possibly sever the relationship.

Reciprocity was once the core of gift exchange in rural life. It is the redistributive nature of the socialist economy that has encouraged the unilateral, upward process of gift giving from villagers to cadres, because of the latter's control over the former's life chances. This has led to the instrumentalization of gift giving, whereby villagers present gifts in exchange for favors or protection. The prolonged shortage of material goods during the first three decades of socialism further underlined the necessity of developing instrumental personal connections. Hence the extended form of *guanxi* and *renqing* (*guanxi* as particularistic ties and *renqing* as exchangeable resources) became more important in village society. Interestingly enough, this kind of instrumentality plays a similarly significant role in other countries where state socialism has prevailed. It is known as *blat* in the former Soviet Union (Grossman 1983: 105–8), *dojscie* in Poland (see Wedel 1986), and *protekcio* in Hungary (Róna-Tas 1990: 119).

Although decollectivization reduced the dependence of villagers on local cadres, it also forced individual villagers to cultivate networks on a larger scale and to interact with state agents who control redistributive resources outside the village boundary. As independent farmers, they have to deal with all kinds of problems of agricultural production, from the purchasing of seeds to the selling of grain. Cadres at all levels in the state sector still hold redistributive powers, which means that instrumental personal connections have gained in importance during the postreform era. Mutual assistance during the busy season, financial aid from private loan sources, and social connections outside the village are essential in order to pursue a better life. Moreover, a larger web of personal relations can provide protection to ordinary villagers when they come into conflict with village cadres or agents of the local government. All these demands for personal connections have encouraged the development of gift exchange and the cultivation of *guanxi* networks, which, for most villagers, is still the most common way to expand their personal contacts. Not surprisingly, gift giving has accelerated since the collectives were dismantled, and the role of networks has become increasingly significant. As a result, by 1991 Xiajia villagers had built up networks of unprecedented complexity, as revealed in Chapters 4 and 5.

In a study of popular rituals in south China, Siu (1989b) argues that the practice of socialism has destroyed most of the social bases for traditional rites and that these bases have been replaced by polit-ical functions. Rituals related to individual life cycles were stripped of their wider social linkages and confined within the household. As a result, the current practitioners of rituals are most concerned with the mundane affairs of everyday life, such as network building, where the power of the socialist state has long been internalized. Thus, the spectacular flourishing of rituals, according to Siu, is a re-construction of the 1980's rather than a restoration of the traditional culture. "The resurgence of these rituals in their transformed state represents cultural fragments recycled under new circumstances" (Siu 1989b: 134).

The system of gift exchange in Xiajia constitutes a similar process of "recycling tradition," rather than a revitalization of tradition. To cope with four decades of socialism, Xiajia villagers have consis-tently adopted new patterns of gift giving, redefined their percep-tion of *guanxi* networks, and adjusted their methods of conform-ing to *renqing* ethics. Because socialism in China of the 1990's is undergoing its most critical transition, and a new form of social life rooted in a market economy is in the process of formation, what I have presented in the preceding chapters must now be read as an eth-nographic account of the past. If residents in Xiajia continue to in-teract with the outside world as they have in recent decades, the sys-tem of gift exchange, together with the cultural complex of *guanxi* and *renqing*, will no doubt be transformed in interesting, and as yet unpredictable, ways. The only certainty in all of this transformation is that gifts and gift giving will continue to play a central role in the lives of Xiajia villagers.

Reference Matter

Notes

O N E. Introduction

1. Unfortunately, at the time of completion of the final version of this manuscript, I was able to read only the two concluding chapters of Mayfair Yang's 1994 book, which she kindly forwarded to me in advance of publication. Thus my summary here certainly does not do justice to the contents of the entire work.

T W O. Xiajia Village

1. The eight-banner system was created by Nurhaci, the founder of the Manchu empire, between 1601 and 1615. Using the original basic social unit—the clan—Nurhaci divided his followers into standardized fighting units of up to 300 adult males. These units were further combined into eight larger groups designated as banner units, each distinguished by the color and border of the unit flag: plain yellow, bordered yellow, plain white, bordered white, plain red, bordered red, plain blue, or bordered blue. After the Manchus assumed power at the national level, Mongolian and Chinese soldiers were incorporated into the system as the Mongol eight banners and the Chinese eight banners. This was a military and political system as well as a socioeconomic one, and the Manchus were able to boast that they had the most efficient mechanism of social mobilization known at that time (see Kessler 1976: 6–14; Oxnam 1975: 119–21).

2. At the time of the land reform in the late 1940's, there were nine landlords and six rich peasants in Xiajia. Land concentration was a social phe-

nomenon commonly found in northeast China. After the 1911 Revolution, previous Manchu and royal land was sold at low prices, and the buyers were mainly powerful local elites and officials.

3. An interesting footnote to this story of the local hero is that a few years later he was kidnapped by a group of local communists, and the Wang lineage had to pay a large ransom to get him back. One of the kidnappers, who is currently a cadre in the neighboring county government, recalled that the kidnapping was a good way to show the people that no one could resist the communists.

4. To date, C. K. Yang's *A Chinese Village in Early Communist Transition* (1965) remains the best ethnographic account of the land reform in a village setting. See also relevant chapters in Friedman, Pickowicz, and Selden 1991; Hinton 1966; Potter and Potter 1990; and Siu 1989a. For a detailed explanation of class labels, see Kraus 1977. These labels were officially abolished in 1979 when economic reforms were launched nationwide.

5. In Xiajia village, the average per capita income was 528 yuan in 1988 and 616 yuan in 1990; the national average in those years was 545 yuan and 623 yuan, respectively.

6. Along with the development of rural reforms, the number of cadres decreased considerably; by spring 1989 there were only five cadres left in village service.

7. According to Cohen, the term *nongmin* entered Chinese in association with Marxist and non-Marxist perceptions of the peasant, "thereby putting the full weight of the Western heritage to use in the new and sometimes harshly negative representation of China's rural population" (1993: 156). And this Chinese concept of peasant (*nongmin*) in turn has had impact on Western scholars who work on China (1993: 160). In the light of Cohen's views, I use the word "peasant" (*nongmin*) in this study only in administrative contexts, that is, to indicate a person's residential status. In other contexts, I use more specific terms, which are not ideologically charged, such as villager or rural resident.

8. During the early period of the rural reforms, a primary concern among the Chinese leaders was whether the *si shu hu* would become poor. To justify the reforms, active reformers made great efforts to demonstrate that the *si shu hu*, like other peasants, actually benefitted (see, e.g., Y. Chen 1990).

9. The hand/mouth ratio in a family (and the life cycle as well) is certainly another contributing factor to intravillage inequality during the collective period. Because it plays the same role as in most societies and thus cannot be seen as a unique feature of socialist hierarchy, however, I will not discuss it in the present study, even though I am fully aware of the impor-

tance of able-bodied laborers for a family's prosperity. For relevant studies, see Parish and Whyte 1978; and Selden 1985.

10. Elsewhere, I have discussed in detail the rise and development of the notion of conjugality and its impact on the family in Xiajia village. See Yan 1992c.

THREE. World of Gifts

1. I am grateful to M. Cohen for alerting me to the cross-cultural existence of gift-recording customs and to the Gamble and Bestor sources. In a recent communication Cohen told me that in 1991 he found gift lists being compiled in suburban Shanghai, Hebei, and Sichuan provinces. It remains unclear although interesting whether the prevalence of this custom in China, Taiwan, Hong Kong, Japan, and Korea indicates a basic cultural element that spread from China to other parts of East Asia.

2. For analysis of the ritual aspects of Chinese weddings, see, e.g., Freedman 1979; R. Watson 1981a. Cohen offers a detailed account of gift exchange and other forms of property allocation within the wedding framework, with a focus on the formation of new family organizations as property-owning units (see Cohen 1976: 165–85).

3. When I lived in Xiajia, I joined the *yangge* team. But I was not a dancer, and my duty was to carry all the cigarettes the team leader received as gifts. I was considered the best candidate for this job by my teammates because I did not smoke.

FOUR. Gift Economy

1. In an important article on this subject, Ambrose King supports Qiao's suggestion that the Chinese term *guanxi* must be introduced as a conceptual instrument for social studies, "if a new science of relationships is going to be developed, *kuan-hsi* [*guanxi*] is a concept that could hardly be excluded" (King 1991: 63).

2. See Chapter 3 for a detailed explanation about the local distinction between expressive and instrumental gift-giving activities, namely that between *suili* and *songli*.

3. The questionnaire consists of 22 questions on attitudes toward gift giving and accounts of gift-exchange activities. The survey was based on stratified samples. As the intensity of gift-giving activities is closely associated with the developmental cycle of family organization, I decided to take the age group as the basic standard for selection of the sample. A total of 100 samples were selected according to age, sex, marital status, and economic

position. Ninety-three questionnaires were returned and were used for further analysis.

4. This is an unusually large amount even for the party secretary. Because he had been trying to arrange an urban household registration for his second daughter for the past two years, he had spent more than usual on instrumental gift giving. According to both him and his wife, under normal conditions, their expenditures would have been somewhere between 1,000 and 1,200 yuan.

5. However, Liu can expect to receive a reciprocal return from this friend later, perhaps in the form of a special certificate to buy chemical fertilizer, as the latter is in charge of the local department store. For a detailed discussion of gift-giving relations in their hierarchical context, see Chapter 7.

6. Unfortunately, the 1959–61 famine, which caused at least 30 million deaths (Ashton et al. 1984: 614), remains a largely understudied topic, mainly due to the lack of accurate data and the CCP's tight control over information. However, at least one book-length report was published in Chinese in 1989, entitled *Thirty Years in the Countryside: A Chronology of Social-Economic Development in Fengyang County, 1949–1983.* Based on local government files, conference records, and nonpublished surveys, it is a valuable collection of historical data. With regard to the Great Leap Forward and the subsequent famine, one finds detailed records about mass mobilization, public dining halls, iron smelting, deep plowing, high grain procurement, famine, starvation, and even 63 cases of cannibalism (see Wang et al. 1989, especially 164–203).

7. According to my informants, this is one of the three cases that can be directly attributed to prolonged hunger. There were, however, more than a dozen deaths due to various diseases caused by hunger or malnutrition.

F I V E. *Guanxi*

1. In a general review of exchange theories, Befu makes a distinction between structural and motivational approaches. The former is primarily associated with anthropologists, and the latter is found mostly among sociologists and social psychologists (see Befu 1977: 206–7).

2. The Chinese word *shehui* originally referred to (1) performances in ceremonial situations or (2) a small group formed by people who share a common interest. See the Chinese dictionary *Ci Yuan*, p. 1228. The modern term *shehui*, however, comes from Japan, where it was adopted from classical Chinese, and translates as the English word "society."

3. Urban/rural inequalities have been a focus of interest among China

scholars. For a detailed anthropological analysis, see Potter and Potter 1990, chap. 15; for a general review, see Walder 1989: 405–24.

4. The only exception here seems to be those in the category of *lianqiao*, because their gifts are quite moderate. But these men are in fact Xu's wife's remote cousins' (her father's sibling's daughters and mother's sibling's daughters) husbands rather than full *jiefu* (sister's husband), for Xu's wife does not have any full sisters.

S I X. Reciprocity and *Renqing*

1. To the best of my knowledge, Ambrose King is one of the first scholars to regard *renqing* as a crucial term conceptualizing Chinese social life (see King 1988a [1981]: 77–79). Recently, Hwang has offered a more elaborate definition, proposing a *renqing* rule to guide social behavior in Chinese society (Hwang 1987: 953–57). My first three definitions have been discussed by both King and Hwang.

2. When I participated in gift-giving activities in the village, I was particularly cautious about offering large gifts, because I did not want the recipients to fear that they could not afford to make return gifts to me in the future. Usually I followed the local standard for gift exchange between friends and kept the value of my presents at average. However, when I visited my old landlady, I felt freer to present whatever gifts I wanted. She had provided me with free housing for seven years during the 1970's, and my gifts to her should definitely have corresponded to our previous good relations. In this case, the third rule of gift giving overrides the fourth.

3. Actually, Du's case is quite typical for Chinese villagers. For instance, it has become a cultural tradition along the southeastern coast of China that those who emigrated to America or other countries returned years later to help their relatives and friends at home (see, e.g., J. Watson 1975: 132–54). Another good example of sharing is the education fund supported by lineage organizations. In traditional China, villagers in a kinship group often united to support a few talented youths in their pursuit of higher education. If the youths were successful, the whole group would benefit in the future (see Freedman 1966).

4. The phrase "thick-skinned face" is an indirect accusation that a person does not care what society thinks of his or her character and conduct. A person with a thick-skinned face will seek personal interests in defiance of moral standards, and therefore is hard to deal with. For a further explanation of the phrase, see Hu 1944: 54.

5. According to Jacobs, "Many Matsu informants note the word *kan-ch'ing* [*ganqing*] can also be used to describe love between man and woman,

but they say this type of *kan-ch'ing* is not the same as the *kan-ch'ing* we are presently analyzing" (1979: 260, n. 67).

6. The propaganda of the CCP always stresses that the party and its leaders, especially Mao Zedong, granted the greatest *enqing* to the Chinese people by establishing the socialist system. For instance, one of the most popular songs during the 1960's begins with the lines, "Both Heaven and Earth are smaller than the *enqing* of the CCP, both father and mother are not as good as Chairman Mao." The cultural code put the Chinese people in debt forever, legitimizing the CCP's rule forever.

7. The Japanese notion *on* is also characterized by lifelong indebtedness of the recipient to the donor. According to Befu, "In the eyes of the Japanese, an *on*-receiver, the debtor, cannot repay the debt completely by giving gifts to the *on*-giver, since material gifts and the favors or services which caused to create the *on* relation are not quite comparable, and the latter is immeasurably more valuable than the former. . . . It [the gift] is an expression of the gratitude of the debtor to the creditor for the *on*, and it in fact has the effect of reinforcing the existing hierarchical relationship" (Befu 1966–67: 169). Such a relationship of indebtedness can last even longer than one's lifetime, and the descendants of the *on* recipient continue to pay respect to and reciprocate the donor for the previous *on* (see Lebra 1969: 129–38). It should be noted that the term *on* is the Japanese pronunciation of the Kanji, read in Chinese as *en*. Both relate to the shared popular Confucian ethics.

S E V E N . Power and Prestige

1. However, elders offer gifts to juniors in the form of *yasui qian* (the "Happy New Year gift") during the lunar New Year period, but the recipients must not be adults, or at least be unmarried. For a more detailed description, see Chapter 3.

2. The landlord-tenant relationship can involve warmth and intensity as well as other emotional responses, namely, *ganqing*. Fried regards the well-developed, personalized interactions between landlords and tenants as an "institutionalized technique by which class differences are reduced between non-related persons" (1953: 101).

3. It is interesting to note that some villagers blamed Zhao for sending the invitation in the first place because they believed it should have been completely up to the cadre to decide whether a return gift would be made.

4. For a detailed discussion of how cadres in the collectives controlled villagers by controlling and redistributing resources, see Oi 1989, especially 132–42.

5. Interestingly, Blau makes this statement to explain tributary gifts to

the chief, which, in his perspective, constitute upward, one-way gift giving. But in order to support his general assumption that giving generates power, he takes this as "a notable exception to the principle that unilateral giving establishes superordination" (1964: 110).

6. This was called "college students from workers, peasants, and soldiers" (*gongnongbing daxuesheng*), a part of the radical education reforms during the Cultural Revolution.

E I G H T. Marriage Transactions

1. My informants regarded all 51 cases as representative because the worth of monetary gifts and material goods involved was deemed to be average. More important, the new trends in marriage finances, as I shall argue below, are best reflected in gift category changes rather than in the actual amount of wealth transferred. It is a common practice for individual families to negotiate the amount of bridewealth and dowries, but they always follow accepted categories of marriage gifts. In this sense, we may say that every betrothal gift list is "representative" in indicating the structure of marriage transfers. During my research, I also found that villagers, especially women, have surprisingly long memories about the details of their marriages. Women usually can recall every betrothal gift, but sometimes exaggerate the size of their dowries. When this happens, husbands often correct the inaccuracies.

2. It should be noted that several scholars who work on China (Cohen 1976; Ebrey 1991; McCreery 1976; and R. Watson 1991) have pointed out that indirect dowry has involved an intergenerational transfer of family properties: monetary and material gifts went from the groom's family (in the form of bridewealth) and the bride's family (in the form of indirect dowry) to the newlywed couple and eventually became the conjugal fund when the couple formed their own household. However, as I shall argue, little attention has been paid to the properties transferred within the groom's family, which are used to endow the new conjugal room directly instead of being exchanged between families.

3. From the late 1950's to the early 1980's, the Chinese currency, *renminbi* (or RMB), was stable. Alterations in betrothal gifts resulted mainly from changes in local economic conditions and living standards, not from inflation. However, since 1983–84, inflation has become a problem in China, and fear of inflation reinforces current trends calling for large betrothal gifts.

4. How long a married woman can hold private property is still an issue of considerable debate in China studies. I will not touch upon this issue in the present study. Cohen suggests that a woman can control her private

money only as long as she and her husband remain part of a larger family (1976: 210–11). R. Watson argues that women living in both joint and conjugal families can have their own private money, even though the private funds of the former are probably larger than those of the latter (1984: 6).

5. This development parallels what Parish and Whyte discovered in south China: "Items that in many areas used to be part of a dowry (such as furniture and bedding for the bridal room) are now the sole responsibility of the groom's family" (1978: 184).

6. Since the 1980's the provision of a new house for one's son's marriage has become more popular and, for those families with several sons, housing is definitely the basic condition to be considered by any prospective bride. Nevertheless, housing is not yet regarded as part of the marriage transaction and has not entered the bride-price list in Xiajia village. Thus I do not include housing in the present discussion of marriage transfers. In many other areas of rural China, housing has become a necessary part of marriage transfers. See Cohen 1992; Potter and Potter 1990: 209; and Siu 1993: 166.

7. It is widely recognized that in Chinese families, conflicts between a mother-in-law and a daughter-in-law have much to do with the mother's efforts to keep her son closer to herself rather than to his wife. The most elaborate interpretation of this psychological and social complex is Margery Wolf's theory of the "uterine family." See Wolf 1972, chap. 3.

8. In many parts of traditional China, it was not unusual for Chinese women to increase their personal funds by making cash loans to other villagers or to invest their savings in local businesses (see, e.g., Cohen 1976: 179–90; R. Watson 1984: 5).

9. Cohen calls this a new form of "serial division." He has found it in three villages of north, south, and west China (1992: 371). A similar dichotomy in the form of family division is also reported by Shu-min Huang in a village in southeast China. See Shu-min Huang 1989: 159–61.

10. S. Potter and J. Potter (1990) report a similar trend from a Cantonese village. They find no joint households whatsoever, and stem households exist only temporarily. The peasants maintained that "early separation was desirable, and increasing economic prosperity made it possible to form a separate household sooner." And in the village, "joint family residence would imply that the family was too poor to afford a new house for each married son. This would tend to reduce rather than to enhance their status" (1990: 219).

11. The relationship between bridewealth and dowry is a complicated issue, which cannot be elaborated on in the present study. R. Watson (1985) suggests class status as the major variable that determines people's different strategies in a Cantonese village in Hong Kong, with the landlord-merchant

class offering lavish dowries and poor farmers tending to practice a bride-price system. Helen Siu (1993) observes that town residents provide their daughters lavish dowries while villagers in the surrounding hamlets customarily demand a high bride-price. Thus the provision of a dowry serves to mark differences between social groups. Cohen suggests that there are two large areas of traditional belief and value regarding family life: ultimate aspirations and practical management (Cohen 1992: 362). It is clear that most villagers in Xiajia would like to make every effort to realize their ultimate aspirations, such as a lavish dowry, when economic conditions allow them to do so. The implication here is that economic conditions might be an important factor that determines the villagers' preference for either high bride-wealth or a lavish dowry or the changing of the ratio of the bridewealth portion to the dowry portion in the indirect dowry system.

12. Arguing that the dowry in traditional China cannot be seen as a form of one's daughters' inheritance rights, R. Watson points out that the most valuable part of the dowry is often jewelry, which cannot generate wealth like the property men inherit, such as land or shops (1984: 8). It is an interesting development that in the 1990's women can demand income-generating property as part of the converted bridewealth (*ganzhe*), which in traditional practice would have been turned into their dowries.

N I N E. Conclusion

1. In her latest, book-length study of the *guanxi* complex, M. Yang has developed a new theory to explain the relationship between *guanxi* and *renqing* (1994: 312–20). She argues that in rural areas the expressive *renqing* rules, more than the instrumental *guanxi* rules, tend to govern villagers' behavior. Hence there is a contrast between the rural *renqing* gift economy and the urban art of *guanxi* (1994: 319). In addition, she also suggests that women more than men are more influenced by *renqing* ethics. Thus, "we can also detect a gender distinction between a more 'feminine' art of renqing and a more 'masculine' art of guanxi" (1994: 320). As I explained in note 1, Chapter 1, I was not able to read Yang's forthcoming book at the time of completion of the final version of this manuscript. So I can only refer to her new arguments in a footnote.

2. It should be pointed out that the sterilization operation is actually tubal ligation. I am grateful to Arthur Kleinman for indicating that the operation does not include oophorectomy (removal of the ovaries); it is merely contraceptive and does not ablate the woman's sexual hormonal secretion (personal communication from Kleinman). Nevertheless, Xiajia villagers do not make such a distinction, and they insist that the sterilized women

have been castrated. For popular attitudes concerning tubal ligation in Taiwan during the 1960's, see Kleinman 1980.

3. Domestic ancestor worship also involves gift exchange between the
living and the dead. The various offerings can be seen as gifts to ancestors,
and in return, ancestors grant good luck, wealth, and descendants to the living (see Ahern 1973: 98; A. Wolf 1974).

Bibliography

Ahern, Emily. 1973. *The Cult of the Dead in a Chinese Village*. Stanford: Stanford University Press.

Anderson, E. N. 1988. *The Food of China*. New Haven: Yale University Press.

Appadurai, Arjun. 1986a. "Introduction: Commodities and the Politics of Value." In A. Appadurai, ed., *The Social Life of Things*, pp. 3–63. New York: Cambridge University Press.

———. 1986b. "Theory in Anthropology: Center and Periphery." *Comparative Studies in Society and History* 28 (2): 356–61.

Appadurai, Arjun, and Carol A. Breckenridge. 1976. "The South Indian Temple: Authority, Honor and Redistribution." *Contributions to Indian Sociology* (n.s.) 10 (2): 187–210.

Ashton, Basil, Kenneth Hill, Alan Piazza, and Robin Zeitz. 1984. "Famine in China, 1958–61." *Population and Development Review* 10 (4): 613–45.

Baker, Hugh. 1966. "The Five Great Clans of the New Territories." *Journal of the Hong Kong Branch of the Royal Asiatic Society* 6: 25–48.

———. 1968. *Sheung Shui: A Chinese Lineage Village*. Stanford: Stanford University Press.

Banck, Geert A. 1973. "Network Analysis and Social Theory: Some Remarks." In Jeremy Boissevain and J. Clyde Mitchell, eds., *Network Analysis Studies in Human Interaction*, pp. 37–44. The Hague: Mouton.

Befu, Harumi. 1966–67. "Gift Giving and Social Reciprocity in Japan." *France-Asie* 21: 161–77.

———. 1968. "Gift-Giving in a Modernizing Japan." *Monumenta Nipponica* 23 (3–4): 445–56.

————. 1977a. "Social Exchange." *Annual Review of Anthropology* 6: 255–81.

————. 1977b. "Structural and Motivational Approaches to Social Exchange." In K. F. Gergen, M. F. Greenberg, and R. H. Willis, eds., *Social Exchange: Advances in Theories and Research*, pp. 194–214. New York: Wiley.

Bernstein, Thomas B. 1984. "Stalinism, Famine, and Chinese Peasants: Grain Procurement During the Great Leap Forward." *Theory and Society* 3: 339–77.

Bestor, Theodore C. 1989. *Neighborhood Tokyo*. Stanford: Stanford University Press.

Betteridge, Anne H. 1985. "Gift Exchange in Iran: The Locus of Self-Identity in Social Interaction." *Anthropological Quarterly* 58 (4): 190–202.

Blau, Peter M. 1964. *Exchange and Power in Social Life*. New York: John Wiley and Sons.

Boas, Franz. 1895. "The Social Organization and the Secret Societies of the Kwakiutl Indians." *Report of the U.S. National Museum* (1894–95): 311–738.

Bohannan, P. 1955. "Some Principles of Exchange and Investment Among the Tiv." *American Anthropologist* 57: 60–70.

Boissevain, Jeremy. 1968. "The Place of Non-groups in the Social Sciences." *Man* (n.s.) 3: 542–56.

Bourdieu, Pierre. 1977. *Outline of a Theory of Practice*. New York: Cambridge University Press.

————. 1989. "Social Space and Symbolic Power." *Sociological Theory* 7 (1): 14–24.

Burridge, K. 1969. *Tangu Traditions*. Oxford: Clarendon Press.

Caplow, Theodore. 1982. "Christmas Gifts and Kin Networks." *American Sociological Review* 47 (3): 383–92.

————. 1984. "Rule Enforcement Without Visible Means: Christmas Gift Giving in Middletown." *American Journal of Sociology* 89: 1306–23.

Carrier, James G. 1990. "Gifts in a World of Commodities: The Ideology of the Perfect Gift in American Society." *Social Analysis* 29: 19–37.

————. 1991. "Gifts, Commodities and Social Relations: A Maussian View of Exchange." *Sociological Forum* 6: 119–36.

————. 1992. "Occidentalism: The World Turned Upside-Down." *American Ethnologist* 19 (2): 195–212.

Chan, Anita, Richard Madsen, and Jonathan Unger. 1984. *Chen Village: The Recent History of a Peasant Community in Mao's China*. Berkeley: University of California Press.

Chan, Anita, and Jonathan Unger. 1983. "The Second Economy of Rural

China." In G. Grossman, ed., *Studies in the Second Economy of the Communist Countries*. Berkeley: University of California Press.

Cheal, David. 1987. "'Showing Them You Love Them': Gift Giving and the Dialectic of Intimacy." *The Sociological Review* 35: 150–69.

―――. 1988. *The Gift Economy*. London and New York: Routledge.

Chen, Chung-min. 1985. "Dowry and Inheritance." In Hsieh Jih-chang and Chuang Ying-chang, eds., *The Chinese Family and Its Ritual Behavior*, pp. 117–27. Taiwan: Institute of Ethnology, Academia Sinica.

Chen Yizi. 1990. *Zhongguo: shinian gaige yu bajiu minyun (China: The ten-year reforms and the pro-democracy movement of 1989)*. Taipei: Lianjing Press.

Chen Zhizhao. 1988. "Mianzi xinli de lilun fenxi yu shiji yanjiu" (Theoretical analysis and empirical study of the face issue). In Guo-shu Yang, ed., *Zhongguoren de xinli (The psychology of the Chinese)*, pp. 155–238. Taipei, Taiwan: Guiguan Press.

Chen Hansheng. 1989 [1929]. "Heilongjiang liuyu de nongmin yu dizhu" (Peasants and landlords in the Heilongjiang valley). In Chen Hansheng, Xue Muqiao, and Feng Hefa, eds., *Jiefang qian de zhongguo nongcun (Rural China before liberation)*, pp. 50–54. Beijing: Zhanwang Press.

―――. 1989 [1930]. "Zhongguo dongbei de liumin" (The migration of refugees to northeast China). In Chen Hansheng, Xue Muqiao, and Feng Hefa, eds., *Jiefang qian de zhongguo nongcun (Rural China before liberation)*, pp. 63–77. Beijing: Zhanwang Press.

Codere, Helen. 1950. *Fighting With Property: A Study of Kwakiutl Potlatching and Warfare, 1792–1930*. New York: Augustin.

Cohen, Myron L. 1970. "Introduction." In Arthur Smith, 1970 [1899], *Village Life in China*. Boston: Little, Brown.

―――. 1976. *House United, House Divided: The Chinese Family in Taiwan*. New York: Columbia University Press.

―――. 1990. "Lineage Organization in North China." *Journal of Asian Studies* 49 (3): 509–34.

―――. 1992. "Family Management and Family Division in Contemporary Rural China." *The China Quarterly* 130: 357–77.

―――. 1993. "Cultural and Political Inventions in Modern China: The Case of the Chinese 'Peasant'." *Daedalus* 122 (2): 151–70.

Comaroff, J. L. 1980. "Introduction." In J. L. Comaroff, ed., *The Meaning of Marriage Payments*, pp. 1–47. New York: Academic Press.

Croll, Elisabeth. 1984. "The Exchange of Women and Property: Marriage in Post-Revolutionary China." In Renee Hirschon, ed., *Women and Property—Women as Property*, pp. 44–61. London: Croom Helm.

Dalton, George. 1966. "'Bridewealth' vs. 'Brideprice'." *American Anthropologist* 68: 732–37.

Damon, F. H. 1980. "The Kula and Generalised Exchange: Considering

Some Unconsidered Aspects of *The Elementary Structures of Kinship.*" *Man* (n.s.) 15 (2): 269–92.

———. 1982. "Alienating the Inalienable." Correspondence, *Man* (n.s.) 17 (2): 342–43.

———. 1983. "What Moves the Kula: Opening and Closing Gifts on Woodlark Island." In Jerry Leach and Edmund Leach, eds., *The Kula: New Perspectives on Massim Exchange*, pp. 309–42. Cambridge, Eng.: Cambridge University Press.

Davis, Deborah, and Stevan Harrell. 1993. "Introduction: The Impact of Post-Mao Reforms on Family Life." In Deborah Davis and Stevan Harrell, eds., *Chinese Families in the Post-Mao Era*, pp. 1–25. Berkeley: University of California Press.

De Glopper, Donald R. 1978. "Doing Business in Lukang." In Arthur Wolf, ed., *Studies in Chinese Society*, pp. 291–320. Stanford: Stanford University Press.

Diamond, Norma. 1969. *K'un Shen: A Taiwanese Village.* Case Studies in Cultural Anthropology. New York: Holt, Rinehart and Winston.

Diaz, May N., and Jack M. Potter. 1967. "Introduction: The Social Life of Peasants." In Jack M. Potter, May N. Diaz, and George M. Forster, eds., *Peasant Society: A Reader*, pp. 154–68. Boston: Little, Brown.

Ding Shu. 1989. "Jiyi ren ai e; liang qian wan siwang" (Hundreds of millions in starvation, twenty million dead). *Jiu Shi Nian Dai* (*The nineties*) 5: 109–16.

Dirks, Robert. 1980. "Social Responses During Severe Food Shortages and Famine." *Current Anthropology* 21: 21–44.

Djilas, Milovan. 1957. *The New Class: An Analysis of the Communist System of Power.* New York: Praeger.

Dumont, Louis. 1980. *Homo Hierarchicus: The Caste System and Its Implications.* Chicago: University of Chicago Press.

Ebrey, Patricia B. 1991. "Introduction." In Rubie S. Watson and Patricia B. Ebrey, eds., *Marriage and Inequality in Chinese Society*, pp. 1–24. Berkeley: University of California Press.

ECSG (Editing Committee of Shuangcheng Gazetteer). 1990. *The Gazetteer of Shuangcheng County.* Beijing: Zhongguo Zhanwang Press.

Emerson, Richard M. 1962. "Power-Dependence Relations." *American Sociological Review* 27 (1): 31–41.

———. 1972. "Exchange Theory." In J. Berger and M. Zelditch, eds., *Sociological Theory in Progress*, pp. 38–57. Boston: Houghton Mifflin.

Epstein, S. 1967. "Productive Efficiency and Customary Systems of Rewards in Rural South India." In R. Firth, ed., *Themes in Economic Anthropology.* ASA Monograph 6. London: Tavistock.

Evans-Pritchard, E. E. 1931. "An Alternative Term for 'Bride-price'." *Man* 31 (42): 36–39.

———. 1940. *The Nuer.* New York: Oxford University Press.

Fairbank, John King. 1979. *The United States and China* (4th edition). Cambridge, Mass.: Harvard University Press.

Fei Xiaotong. 1947. *Xiangtu zhongguo (Folk China).* Shanghai: Guancha Press.

Feil, D. K. 1982. "Alienating the Inalienable." Correspondence, *Man* (n.s.) 17 (2): 340–42.

Firth, Raymond. 1959. *Economics of the Zealand Maori.* Wellington, New Zealand: Government Printer.

———. 1967a. *Tikopia Ritual and Belief.* Boston: Beacon Press.

———. 1967b. "Themes in Economic Anthropology: A General Comment." In R. Firth, ed., *Themes in Economic Anthropology.* ASA Monograph 6. London: Tavistock.

Fortes, M. 1949. *The Web of Kinship Among the Tallensi.* London: Oxford University Press.

———. 1962. "Introduction." In Meyer Fortes, ed., *Marriage in Tribal Societies.* Cambridge, Eng.: Cambridge University Press.

Freedman, Maurice. 1958. *Lineage Organization in Southeastern China.* London: Athlone.

———. 1966. *Chinese Lineage and Society: Fukien and Kwangtung.* London: Athlone.

———. 1979 [1970]. "Ritual Aspects of Chinese Kinship and Marriage." In G. William Skinner, ed., *The Study of Chinese Society: Essays by Maurice Freedman,* pp. 273–95. Stanford: Stanford University Press.

Fried, Morton. 1953. *The Fabric of Chinese Society.* New York: Praeger Inc.

Friedman, Edward, Paul Pickowicz, and Mark Selden, with K. A. Johnson. 1991. *Chinese Village, Socialist State.* New Haven: Yale University Press.

Gallin, Bernard. 1960. "Matrilateral and Affinal Relationships of a Taiwanese Village." *American Anthropologist* 62 (4): 632–42.

———. 1966. *Hsin Hsing, Taiwan: A Chinese Village in Change.* Berkeley: University of California Press.

Gallin, Bernard, and Rita Gallin. 1985. "Matrilateral and Affinal Relationships in Changing Chinese Society." In Hsieh Jih-chang and Chuang Ying-chang, eds., *The Chinese Family and Its Ritual Behavior,* pp. 101–16. Taiwan: Institute of Ethnology, Academia Sinica.

Gamble, Sidney. 1968. *Ting Hsien: A North China Rural Community.* Stanford: Stanford University Press.

Gates, Hill. 1989. "The Commoditization of Chinese Women." *Signs* 14 (4): 799–832.

Geertz, Clifford. 1976. " 'From the Native's Point of View': On the Nature of Anthropological Understanding." In Keith H. Basso and Henry A. Selby, eds., *Meaning in Anthropology*, pp. 221–37. Albuquerque: University of New Mexico Press.

———. 1983. "Common Sense as a Cultural System." In *Local Knowledge*. New York: Basic Books.

Gennep, Arnold van. 1960. *Rites of Passage*. Translated by M. Vizedom and G. Caffee. Chicago: University of Chicago Press.

Godelier, Maurice. 1977. "Salt Money and the Circulation of Commodities Among the Baruya of New Guinea." In M. Godelier, ed., *Perspectives in Marxist Anthropology*, pp. 127–51. Cambridge, Eng.: Cambridge University Press.

Goffman, Erving. 1971. *Relations in Public: Microstudies of the Public Order*. New York: Basic Books.

Gold, Thomas B. 1985. "After Comradeship: Personal Relations in China Since the Cultural Revolution." *China Quarterly* 104: 657–75.

Goode, William. 1963. *World Revolution and Family Patterns*. New York: The Free Press.

———. 1982. *The Family*. Englewood Cliffs: Prentice-Hall.

Goody, Jack. 1973. "Bridewealth and Dowry in Africa and Eurasia." In Jack Goody and Stanley Tambiah, eds., *Bridewealth and Dowry*, pp. 1–58. Cambridge, Eng.: Cambridge University Press.

———. 1990. *The Oriental, the Ancient and the Primitive*. Cambridge, Eng.: Cambridge University Press.

Gouldner, Alvin W. 1960. "The Norm of Reciprocity: A Preliminary Statement." *American Sociological Review* 25: 161–78.

Gray, Robert F. 1960. "Sonjo Brideprice and the Question of African 'Wife Purchase.' " *American Anthropologist* (n.s.) 62: 34–57.

Greenhalgh, Susan. 1984. "Networks and Their Nodes: Urban Society on Taiwan." *China Quarterly* 99: 529–52.

Gregory, C. A. 1980. "Gifts to Men and Gifts to God: Gift Exchange and Capital Accumulation in Contemporary Papua." *Man* (n.s.) 15 (4): 626–52.

———. 1982. *Gifts and Commodities*. London: Academic Press.

Grossman, Gregory. 1983. "The 'Shadow Economy' in the Socialist Sector of the USSR." In *The CMEA Five-Year Plans (1981–1985) in a New Perspective*. Brussels: NATO.

Gu, Jirui. 1985. *Jiating xiaofei jingjixue* (*The economics of family consumption*). Beijing: Zhongguo caizhen jingji chubanshe.

Gulliver, P. H. 1969. "Dispute Settlement Without Courts: The Ndendeuli of Southern Tanzania." In L. Nader, ed., *Law in Culture and Society*. Chicago: Aldine Press.

Hamilton, Gary G., and Kao Cheng-shu. 1990. "The Institutional Foundations of Chinese Business: The Family Firm in Taiwan." *Comparative Social Research* 12: 95–112.

Harrell, Stevan. 1982. *Ploughshare Village: Culture and Context in Taiwan*. Seattle: University of Washington Press.

———. 1992. "Aspects of Marriage in Three South-western Villages." *China Quarterly* 130: 323–37.

Harrell, Stevan, and Sara Dickey. 1985. "Dowry Systems in Complex Societies." *Ethnology* 24 (2): 105–20.

Hershman, Paul. 1981. *Punjabi Kinship and Marriage*. Delhi: Hindustan Publishing.

Herzfeld, Michael. 1980. "The Dowry in Greece: Terminological Usage and Historical Reconstruction." *Ethnohistory* 27 (3): 225–41.

Hinton, William. 1966. *Fanshen: A Documentary of Revolution in a Chinese Village*. New York: Vintage Books.

Ho, D. Y. F. 1975. "On the Concept of Face." *American Journal of Sociology* 81: 867–84.

Homans, George. 1974. *Social Behavior: Its Elementary Forms*. New York: Harcourt Brace Jovanovich.

Hsu, Francis L. K. 1949. *Under the Ancestors' Shadow: Chinese Culture and Personality*. London: Routledge & Kegan Paul Ltd.

Hu, Hsien-chin. 1944. "The Chinese Concept of Face." *American Anthropologist* 46: 45–64.

Huang, Shu-min. 1989. *The Spiral Road: Change in a Chinese Village Through the Eyes of a Communist Party Leader*. Boulder: Westview Press.

Hwang, Kwang-kuo. 1987. "Face and Favor: The Chinese Power Game." *American Journal of Sociology* 92 (4): 944–74.

Jacobs, Bruce. 1979. "A Preliminary Model of Particularistic Ties in Chinese Political Alliances: Kan-ch'ing and Kuan-hsi in a Rural Taiwanese Township." *China Quarterly* 78: 237–73.

Jankowiak, William. 1993. *Sex, Death, and Hierarchy in a Chinese City: An Anthropological Account*. New York: Columbia University Press.

Jelliffe, Derrick, and E. F.P. Jelliffe. 1971. "The Effects of Starvation on the Function of the Family and of Society." In Gunnar Blix, Yngve Hofvander, and Bo Vahlquist, eds., *Famine*, pp. 54–61. Uppsala: Almqvist & Wiksells.

Jiang Junchen. 1989 [1932] (in Chinese). "A General Survey of the Economy in Northeast China." In Chen Hansheng, Xue Muqiao, and Feng

Hefa, eds., *Rural China before Liberation*, pp. 111–16. Beijing: Zhanwang Press.

Johnson, Colleen Leahy. 1974. "Gift Giving and Reciprocity Among the Japanese Americans in Honolulu." *American Ethnologist* 1 (2): 295–308.

Johnson, Kay Ann. 1983. *Women, the Family and Peasant Revolution in China.* Chicago: University of Chicago Press.

Johnson, Paul. 1985. *Saving and Spending.* Oxford: Clarendon Press.

Jowett, A. J. 1987. *Famine in the People's Republic of China.* Glasgow: University of Glasgow.

Judd, Ellen. 1989. "Niangjia: Chinese Women and Their Natal Families." *Journal of Asian Studies* 48 (3): 525–44.

Kao, Cheng-shu. 1991. "The Role of 'Personal Trust' in Large Businesses in Taiwan." In Gary Hamilton, ed., *Business Networks and Economic Development in East and Southeast Asia.* Hong Kong: Center of Asian Studies.

Keesing, Roger M. 1989. "Exotic Readings of Cultural Texts." *Current Anthropology* 30: 459–79.

———. 1990. "New Lessons from Old Shells: Changing Perspectives on the Kula." In Jukka Siikala, ed., *Culture and History in the Pacific*, pp. 139–63. Helsinki, Finland: The Finnish Anthropological Society.

Kessler, Lawrence D. 1976. *K'ang-hsi and the Consolidation of Ch'ing Rule, 1661–1684.* Chicago: University of Chicago Press.

Kiernan, J. P. 1988. "The Other Side of the Coin: The Conversion of Money to Religious Purposes in Zulu Zionist Churches." *Man* (n.s.) 23: 453–68.

King, Ambrose Yeo-chi (Yao-ji Jin). 1985. "The Individual and Group in Confucianism: A Relational Perspective." In Donald J. Munro, ed., *Individualism and Holism: Studies in Confucian and Taoist Values*, pp. 57–70. Ann Arbor: University of Michigan Press.

———. 1988a. "Renqi guanxi zhong renqing zhi fenxi" (An analysis of the concept of renqing in the context of interpersonal relations). In Guoshu Yang, ed., *Zhongguoren de xinli* (*The psychology of the Chinese*), pp. 319–45. Taipei, Taiwan: Guiguan Press.

———. 1988b. "'Mian,' 'chi' yu zhongguoren xingwei zhi fenxi" (Face, shame, and the analysis of behavior patterns of the Chinese). In Guoshu Yang, ed., *Zhongguoren de xinli* (*The psychology of the Chinese*), pp. 75–104. Taipei, Taiwan: Guiguan Press.

———. 1991. "Kuan-hsi and Network Building: A Sociological Interpretation." *Daedalus* 120 (2): 63–84. Republished in Tu Wei-ming, ed., *The Living Thee: The Changing Meaning of Being Chinese Today.* Stanford: Stanford University Press, 1994.

Kleinman, Arthur. 1980. *Patients and Healers in the Context of Culture.* Berkeley: University of California Press.

———. 1992. "Local Worlds of Suffering: An Interpersonal Focus for Ethnographies of Illness Experience." *Qualitative Health Research* 2 (2): 127–34.

Kleinman, Arthur, and Joan Kleinman. 1991. "Suffering and Its Professional Transformation: Toward an Ethnography of Interpersonal Experience." *Culture, Medicine and Psychiatry* 15 (3): 275–301.

Kornai, Janos. 1986. *Contradictions and Dilemmas: Studies on the Socialist Economy and Society.* Cambridge, Mass.: MIT Press.

Kraus, Richard. 1977. "Class and the Vocabulary of Social Analysis in China." *China Quarterly* 69: 54–74.

Krige, E. J., and J. D. Krige. 1943. *The Realm of a Rain-Queen.* London: Oxford University Press.

Leach, Edmund. 1954. *Political Systems of Highland Burma.* London: Athlone Press.

Leach, Jerry W. 1983. "Introduction." In Jerry Leach and Edmund Leach, eds., *The Kula: New Perspectives on Massim Exchange,* pp. 1–26. Cambridge, Eng.: Cambridge University Press.

Lebra, Takie Sugiyama. 1969. "Reciprocity and the Asymmetric Principle: An Analytical Reappraisal of the Japanese Concept of *On.*" *Psychologia* 12: 129–38.

———. 1975. "An Alternative Approach to Reciprocity." *American Anthropologist* 77: 550–65.

Legge, James, trans. 1885. *Li Ki.* In *The Sacred Books of China,* parts 3 and 4. Oxford: Clarendon Press.

Lévi-Strauss, Claude. 1965. "The Principle of Reciprocity." In Lewis Coser and Bernard Rosenberg, eds., *Sociological Theory.* New York: Macmillan.

———. 1969. *The Elementary Structures of Kinship.* Trans. J. H. Bell and J. R. von Sturner. Boston: Beacon Press.

Li, Lillian. 1982. "Introduction: Food, Famine and the Chinese State." *Journal of Asian Studies* 41 (4): 687–708.

Li Shutian, ed. 1990. *Shuangchengbao tuntian shilue (Documentary records of the settlement project in Shuangcheng).* Jilin: Jilin Wenshi Press.

Liang Shu-ming. 1963. *Zhongguo wenhua yaoyi (The essential features of Chinese culture).* Hong Kong: Jicheng Book Company.

Liep, John. 1990. "Gift Exchange and the Construction of Identity." In Jukka Siikala, ed., *Culture and History in the Pacific,* pp. 164–83. Helsinki, Finland: The Finnish Anthropological Society.

Ma Yachuan. 1990. "Manzuren de qiyuan" (The origin of bannermen). In *Shuangcheng minjian wenxue (The folklore of Shuangcheng)*, pp. 148–54. Shuangcheng: Committee of Folklore Collection in Shuangcheng County.

MacCormack, Geoffrey. 1976. "Reciprocity." *Man* (n.s.) 11: 89–103.

———. 1982. "Mauss and the 'Spirit' of the Gift." *Oceania* 52: 286–93.

McCreery, John L. 1976. "Women's Property Rights and Dowry in China and South Asia." *Ethnology* 15 (2): 163–74.

MacFarquhar, Roderick. 1983. *The Origins of the Cultural Revolution, Vol. 2: The Great Leap Forward, 1958–1960*. London: Oxford University Press.

Malinowski, Bronislaw. 1962 [1926]. *Crime and Custom in Savage Society*. Paterson, N.J.: Littlefield, Adams.

———. 1984 [1922]. *Argonauts of the Western Pacific*. Prospect Heights, Ill.: Waveland Press.

Mallory, Walter. 1926. *China: Land of Famine*. New York: American Geographical Society.

Marriott, McKim. 1976. "Hindu Transactions: Diversity Without Dualism." In B. Kapferer, ed., *Transaction and Meaning: Directions in the Anthropology of Exchange and Symbolic Behavior*, pp. 109–42. Philadelphia: Institute for the Study of Human Issues.

Mars, Gerald. 1982. *Cheats at Work: An Anthropology of Workplace Crime*. London: George Allen and Unwin.

Marx, Karl. 1976 [1867]. *Capital*. Vol. 1. Harmondsworth, Eng.: Penguin.

Mauss, Marcel. 1967. *The Gift*. New York: W. W. Norton & Company.

Meillassoux, Claude. 1981. *Maidens, Meal and Money: Capitalism and the Domestic Community*. Cambridge, Eng.: Cambridge University Press.

Mitchell, J. Clyde. 1969. "The Concept and Use of Social Networks." In J. Clyde Mitchell, ed., *Social Networks in Urban Situations*, pp. 1–50. Manchester, Eng.: Manchester University Press.

———. 1974. "Social Networks." *Annual Review of Anthropology* 3: 279–99.

Morris, Ian. 1986. "Gift and Commodity in Archaic Greece." *Man* (n.s.) 21: 1–17.

Nee, Victor. 1989. "A Theory of Market Transition: From Redistribution to Markets in State Socialism." *American Sociological Review* 54 (5): 663–81.

Ocko, Jonathan K. 1991. "Women, Property, and the Law in the People's Republic of China." In Rubie S. Watson and Patricia B. Ebrey, eds., *Marriage and Inequality in Chinese Society*, pp. 313–46. Berkeley: University of California Press.

Oi, Jean C. 1985. "Communism and Clientism: Rural Politics in China." *World Politics* 37 (2): 238–66.

————. 1989. *State and Peasant in Contemporary China: The Political Economy of Village Government.* Berkeley: University of California Press.

Oxnam, Robert B. 1975. *Ruling From Horseback: Manchu Politics in the Oboi Regency, 1661–1669.* Chicago: University of Chicago Press.

Parish, William, and Martin Whyte. 1978. *Village and Family in Contemporary China.* Chicago: University of Chicago Press.

Parry, Jonathan. 1986. "The Gift, the Indian Gift, and the 'Indian Gift'." *Man* (n.s.) 21: 453–73.

Parry, Jonathan, and Maurice Bloch. 1989. "Introduction: Money and the Morality of Exchange." In Jonathan Parry and Maurice Bloch, eds., *Money and the Morality of Exchange,* pp. 1–32. Cambridge, Eng.: Cambridge University Press.

Parsons, Talcott. 1949. *The Structure of Social Action.* New York: The Free Press.

Pasternak, Burton. 1972. *Kinship and Community in Two Chinese Villages.* Stanford: Stanford University Press.

People's Daily. 1986. "Expenditure for Bridewealth Increased 10 Times." Oct. 28.

Polanyi, Karl. 1957. *The Great Transformation.* Boston: Beacon Press.

Potter, Jack M. 1968. *Capitalism and the Chinese Peasant.* Berkeley: University of California Press.

————. 1970. "Land and Lineage in Traditional China." In Maurice Freedman, ed., *Family and Kinship in Chinese Society,* pp. 121–38. Stanford: Stanford University Press.

Potter, Sulamith Heins, and Jack M. Potter. 1990. *China's Peasants: The Anthropology of a Revolution.* New York: Cambridge University Press.

Prindle, Peter H. 1979. "Peasant Society and Famine: A Nepalese Example." *Ethnology* 18 (1): 31–60.

Qian, Jianghong, et al. 1988. "Marriage Related Consumption by Young People in China's Large and Medium Cities." *Social Sciences in China* 1: 208–28.

Qiao, Jian. 1988. "Guanxi chuyi" (A preliminary discussion of guanxi). In Guoshu Yang, ed., *Zhongguoren de xinli* (*The psychology of the Chinese*), pp. 105–24. Taipei, Taiwan: Guiguan Press.

Radcliffe-Brown, A. R. 1929. "Bride-Price, Earnest or Indemnity." *Man* 29 (96): 131–32.

————. 1965 [1940]. "On Social Structure." In *Structure and Function in Primitive Society,* pp. 188–204. New York: The Free Press.

————. 1987 [1950]. "Introduction." In A. R. Radcliffe-Brown and Daryll Forde, eds., *African Systems of Kinship and Marriage*, pp. 1–85. London: KPI Limited.

Raheja, Gloria G. 1988. *The Poison in the Gift: Ritual, Prestation, and the Dominant Caste in a North Indian Village*. Chicago: University of Chicago Press.

Redding, Gordon. 1990. *The Spirit of Chinese Capitalism*. Berlin: de Gruyter.

Rocca, Jean-Louis. 1992. "Corruption and Its Shadow: An Anthropological View of Corruption in China." *China Quarterly* 130: 402–16.

Róna-Tas, Akos. 1990. "The Second Economy in Hungary: The Social Origins of the End of State Socialism." Ph.D. diss., University of Michigan.

Sahlins, Marshall. 1972. *Stone Age Economics*. New York: Aldine de Gruyter.

Salisbury, R. F. 1962. *From Stone to Steel*. Melbourne: Melbourne University Press.

Sangren, Steven. 1984. "Traditional Chinese Corporations: Beyond Kinship." *Journal of Asian Studies* 43 (3): 391–415.

Schieffelin, Edward L. 1980. "Reciprocity and the Construction of Reality." *Man* (n.s.) 15 (3): 502–17.

Schlegel, Alice, and Rohn Eloul. 1988. "Marriage Transactions: Labor, Property, Status." *American Anthropologist* 90: 291–309.

Schwartz, Barry. 1967. "The Social Psychology of the Gift." *American Journal of Sociology* 73 (1): 1–11.

Scott, James C. 1976. *The Moral Economy of the Peasant: Rebellion and Subsistence in Southeast Asia*. New Haven: Yale University Press.

Selden, Mark. 1985. "Income Inequality and the State." In William L. Parish, ed., *Chinese Rural Development: The Great Transformation*, pp. 193–218. Armonk, N.Y.: M. E. Sharpe.

————. 1993. "Family Strategies and Structures in Rural North China." In Deborah Davis and Stevan Harrell, eds., *Chinese Families in the Post-Mao Era*, pp. 139–64. Berkeley: University of California Press.

Siu, Helen F. 1989a. *Agents and Victims in South China: Accomplices in Rural Revolution*. New Haven: Yale University Press.

————. 1989b. "Recycling Rituals: Politics and Popular Culture in Contemporary Rural China." In Perry Link, Richard Madsen, and Paul Pickowicz, eds., *Unofficial China: Popular Culture and Thought in the People's Republic*, pp. 121–37. Boulder: Westview Press.

————. 1993. "Reconstituting Dowry and Brideprice in South China." In Deborah Davis and Stevan Harrell, eds., *Chinese Families in the Post-Mao Era*, pp. 165–88. Berkeley: University of California Press.

Skinner, G. W. 1971. "Chinese Peasants and the Closed Community: An Open and Shut Case." *Comparative Studies in Society and History* 13 (3): 270–81.

Smith, Arthur. 1894. *Chinese Characteristics*. New York: Fleming H. Revell.

———. 1970 [1899]. *Village Life in China*. Boston: Little, Brown.

Smith, Robert J. 1974. *Ancestor Worship in Contemporary Japan*. Stanford: Stanford University Press.

Spiro, Melford. 1975. "Marriage Payments: A Paradigm from the Burmese Perspective." *Journal of Anthropological Research* 31: 89–115.

Stein, Zena, M. Susser, G. Saenger, and F. Marolla. 1975. *Famine and Human Development: The Dutch Hunger Winter of 1944–1945*. New York: Oxford University Press.

Storey, Robert. 1990. *Taiwan—A Travel Survival Kit*. Hawthorn, Aus.: Lonely Planet Publications.

Strathern, Andrew. 1971. *The Rope of Moka*. Cambridge, Eng.: Cambridge University Press.

———. 1979. "Gender, Ideology and Money in Mount Hagen." *Man* (n.s.) 14 (3): 530–48.

Strathern, Marilyn. 1988. *The Gender of the Gift: Problems with Women and Problems with Society in Melanesia*. Berkeley: University of California Press.

———. 1992. "Qualified Value: The Perspective of Gift Exchange." In Caroline Humphrey and Stephen Hugh-Jones, eds., *Barter, Exchange and Value: An Anthropological Approach*, pp. 169–91. New York: Cambridge University Press.

Strauch, Judith. 1983. "Community and Kinship in Southeastern China: The View from the Multilineage Villages of Hong Kong." *Journal of Asian Studies* 43 (1): 21–50.

Szelenyi, Ivan. 1978. "Social Inequalities Under State Socialist Redistributive Economies." *International Journal of Comparative Sociology* 1: 61–78.

Tambiah, Stanley. 1973. "Dowry and Bridewealth and the Property Rights of Women in South Asia." In Jack Goody and Stanley Tambiah, eds., *Bridewealth and Dowry*, pp. 59–169. Cambridge, Eng.: Cambridge University Press.

———. 1989. "Bridewealth and Dowry Revisited: The Position of Women in Sub-Saharan Africa and North India." *Current Anthropology* 30 (4): 413–35.

Thompson, David. 1987. "The *Hau* of the Gift in Its Cultural Context." *Pacific Studies* 11 (1): 63–79.

Thompson, Stuart E. 1988. "Death, Food, and Fertility." In James L. Watson and Evelyn S. Rawski, eds., *Death Ritual in Late Imperial and Modern China*, pp. 71–108. Berkeley: University of California Press.

Torry, W. I. 1979. "Anthropological Studies in Hazardous Environments: Past Trends and New Horizons." *Current Anthropology* 20 (3): 517–38.

Unger, Jonathan. 1984. "The Class System in Rural China: A Case Study." In James L. Watson, ed., *Class and Social Stratification in Post-Revolution China*. Cambridge, Eng.: Cambridge University Press.

Vatuk, Sylvia. 1975. "Gifts and Affines in North India." *Contributions to Indian Sociology* (n.s.) 9: 155–96.

Vatuk, Ved Prakash, and Sylvia Vatuk. 1971. "The Social Context of Gift Exchange in North India." In Giri R. Gupta, ed., *Family and Social Change in Modern India*, pp. 207–32. Durham, N.C.: Carolina Academic Press.

Vogel, Ezra. 1965. "From Friendship to Comradeship: The Change in Personal Relations in Communist China." *China Quarterly* 21: 46–60.

———. 1991. *The Four Little Dragons: The Spread of Industrialization in East Asia*. Cambridge, Mass.: Harvard University Press.

Walder, Andrew. 1983. "Organized Dependency and Cultures of Authority in Chinese Industry." *Journal of Asian Studies* 43 (4): 51–76.

———. 1986. *Communist Neo-traditionalism: Work and Authority in Chinese Industry*. Berkeley: University of California Press.

———. 1989. "Social Change in Post-Revolution China." *Annual Review of Sociology* 15: 405–24.

Wang Gengjin, Yang Xun, Wang Ziping, Liang Xiaodong, and Yang Guansan. 1989. *Xiangcun sanshi nian: Fengyang nongcun shehui jingji fazhan shilu (Thirty years in the countryside: A chronology of social-economic development in Fengyang county, 1949–1983)*. Beijing: Nongcun Duwu Press.

Wank, David. 1995. "Bureaucratic Patronage and Private Business: Changing Networks of Power in Urban China." In Andrew G. Walder, ed., *The Waning of the Communist State: Economic Origins of Political Decline in China and Hungary*, pp. 151–83. Berkeley: University of California Press.

Watson, James L. 1975. *Emigration and the Chinese Lineage: The Mans in Hong Kong and London*. Berkeley: University of California Press.

———. 1982. "Chinese Kinship Reconsidered: Anthropological Perspectives on Historical Research." *China Quarterly* 92: 589–622.

———. 1984. "Introduction: Class and Class Formation in Chinese Society." In James L. Watson, ed., *Class and Social Stratification in Post-Revolution China*. Cambridge, Eng.: Cambridge University Press.

———. 1986. "Anthropological Overview: The Development of Chinese

Descent Groups." In Patricia B. Ebrey and James L. Watson, eds., *Kinship Organization in Late Imperial China, 1000–1940*, pp. 274–92. Berkeley: University of California Press.

————. 1988a. "The Structure of Chinese Funerary Rites: Elementary Forms, Ritual Sequence, and the Primacy of Performance." In James L. Watson and Evelyn S. Rawski, eds., *Death Ritual in Late Imperial and Modern China*, pp. 3–19. Berkeley: University of California Press.

————. 1988b. "Funeral Specialists in Cantonese Society: Pollution, Performance, and Social Hierarchy." In James L. Watson and Evelyn S. Rawski, eds., *Death Ritual in Late Imperial and Modern China*, pp. 109–134. Berkeley: University of California Press.

Watson, Rubie S. 1981a. "Class Differences and Affinal Relations in South China." *Man* (n.s.) 16: 593–615.

————. 1981b. "The Creation of a Chinese Lineage: The Teng of Ha Tsuen, 1669–1751." *Modern Asian Studies* 16 (1): 69–100.

————. 1984. "Women's Property in Republican China: Rights and Practice." *Republican China* 10 (1): 1–12.

————. 1985. *Inequality Among Brothers: Class and Kinship in South China.* Cambridge, Eng.: Cambridge University Press.

————. 1991. "Wives, Concubines, and Maids: Servitude and Kinship in the Hong Kong Region, 1900–1940." In Rubie S. Watson and Patricia B. Ebrey, eds., *Marriage and Inequality in Chinese Society*. Berkeley: University of California Press.

Weber, Max. 1968. *The Religion of China.* Trans. Hans Gerth. New York: Free Press.

————. 1978. *Economy and Society.* Berkeley: University of California Press.

Wedel, Janine. 1986. *The Private Poland.* New York: Facts on File Publications.

Weiner, Annette. 1980. "Reproduction: A Replacement for Reciprocity." *American Ethnologist* 7: 71–85.

————. 1985. "Inalienable Wealth." *American Ethnologist* 12: 210–27.

————. 1992. *Inalienable Possessions: The Paradox of Keeping-While-Giving.* Berkeley: University of California Press.

Werbner, Pnina. 1990. "Economic Rationality and Hierarchical Gift Economies: Value and Ranking among British Pakistanis." *Man* (n.s.) 25: 266–85.

Whitten, Norman, and Alvin Wolf. 1974. "Network Analysis." In J. Honigmann, ed., *Handbook of Social and Cultural Anthropology*, pp. 717–45. Chicago: Rand McNally.

Whyte, Martin King. 1981. "Destratification and Restratification in China." In G. Berreman, ed., *Social Inequality*. New York: Academic Press.

———. 1986. "Social Trends in China: The Triumph of Inequality?" In A. Doak Barnett and Ralph N. Clough, eds., *Modernizing China: Post-Mao Reform and Development*, pp. 103–23. Boulder: Westview Press.

———. 1988. "Death in the People's Republic of China." In James L. Watson and Evelyn S. Rawski, eds., *Death Ritual in Late Imperial and Modern China*, pp. 289–316. Berkeley: University of California Press.

Wolf, Arthur P. 1974. "Gods, Ghosts, and Ancestors." In Arthur Wolf, ed., *Religion and Ritual in Chinese Society*, pp. 131–182. Stanford: Stanford University Press.

Wolf, Arthur P., and Huang Chieh-shan. 1980. *Marriage and Adoption in China, 1845–1945*. Stanford: Stanford University Press.

Wolf, Margery. 1972. *Women and the Family in Rural Taiwan*. Stanford: Stanford University Press.

———. 1985. *Revolution Postponed: Women in Contemporary China*. Stanford: Stanford University Press.

Wong, R. Bin, and Pierre-Etienne Will, eds. 1991. *Nourish the People: State Civilian Granaries in China, 1650–1850*. Ann Arbor: Center for Chinese Studies, University of Michigan.

Wong, Siu-lun. 1985. "The Chinese Family Firm: A Model." *British Journal of Sociology* 36 (1): 58–72.

———. 1988. "The Applicability of Asian Family Values to Other Socio-Cultural Settings." In Peter Berger and Michael Hsiao, eds., *In Search of an East Asian Development Model*, pp. 134–52. New Brunswick: Transaction Books.

Yan, Yunxiang. 1991. "Zhongguo de xiaojing yu Yindu de tanshi: fei duichen liwu kuizeng de bijiao yanjiu" (The Chinese *xiaojing* and the Indian *dana*: An anthropological analysis of asymmetric gift giving). In Li Zheng and Jiang Zhongxin, eds., *Essays in Honor of Professor Ji Xianlin*, pp. 789–800. Nanchang: Jiangxi Renmin Press.

———. 1992a. "The Impact of Rural Reform on Economic and Social Stratification in a Chinese Village." *Australian Journal of Chinese Affairs* 27: 1–23.

———. 1992b. "Romantic Love and the Notion of Conjugality in a Chinese Village." Paper presented at the New England Conference of the Association for Asian Studies, Boston, Oct. 10.

———. 1992c. "Socialist Transformation and Family Relations: The Rise of Individuality and Conjugality in a Chinese Village." Paper presented at the 91st Annual Meeting, American Anthropological Association, San Francisco, Dec. 6.

———. 1994. "Dislocation, Reposition and Restratification: Structural Changes in Chinese Society." In Maurice Brosseau and Lo Chi Kin, eds., *China Review 1994*, pp. 15.1–24. Hong Kong: Chinese University Press.

———. 1995. "Everyday Power Relations: Changes in a North China Village." In Andrew G. Walder, ed., *The Waning of the Communist State: Economic Origins of Political Decline in China and Hungary*, pp. 215–41. Berkeley: University of California Press.

Yang, C. K. 1965. *A Chinese Village in Early Communist Transition*. In *Chinese Communist Society: The Family and the Village*. Cambridge, Mass.: MIT Press.

Yang, Lien-sheng. 1957. "The Concept of 'Pao' as a Basis for Social Relations in China." In John K. Fairbank, ed., *Chinese Thought and Institutions*, pp. 291–309. Chicago: University of Chicago Press.

Yang, Martin. 1945. *A Chinese Village, Taitou, Shantung Province*. New York: Columbia University Press.

Yang, Mayfair Mei-hui. 1989. "The Gift Economy and State Power in China." *Comparative Studies in Society and History* 31 (1): 25–54.

———. 1994. *Gifts, Favors, Banquets: The Art of Social Relationships in China*. Ithaca: Cornell University Press.

Ye Dabing, and Wu Bingan. 1990. *Zhongguo fengsu cidian* (*The dictionary of Chinese folklore*). Shanghai: Shanghai Cishu Press.

Zhang Dingming. 1926. *Shuangcheng xianzhi* (*The gazetteer of Shuangcheng county*). Shuangcheng: Committee of Gazetteer.

Zhang Liping, and Fan Ping. 1993. "Zhuantong nongye diqu de hunyin tezheng" (Marriage patterns in traditional agricultural regions: a survey in Ling county, Shandong province). *Shehuixue yanjiu* (*Sociological studies*) 5: 92–100.

Zhu Ruiling. 1988. "Zhongguoren de shehui hudong: lun mianzi wenti" (Social interactions among the Chinese: on the issue of face). In Guoshu Yang, ed., *Zhongguoren de xinli* (*The psychology of the Chinese*), pp. 239–88. Taipei, Taiwan: Guiguan Press.

Character List

fang　房

fenjia　分家

fotuo mama　佛陀媽媽

ganqin　干親

ganqing　感情

ganqing hao　感情好

ganzhe　干折

gao guanxi　搞關係

gongren　工人

gongnongbing daxuesheng
　工農兵大學生

guahong　掛紅

guanxi　關係

guanxixue　關係學

guaxian　掛綫

gubiao xiongdi　姑表兄弟

guoli　過禮

hei zhuazi　黑爪子

hong　紅

huangong　換工

hukou zhidu　戶口制度

huo　活

ji　己

jia　家

jiefu　姐夫

jieqian　借錢

jin　斤

jingshen chuhu　淨身出戶

jiubiao xiongdi　舅表兄弟

jiuping zhuang xinjiu
　舊瓶裝新酒

jiuxi　酒席

jueyu　絕育

kaidan　開單

kang　炕

kao de zhu de　靠得住的

kouliang tian　口糧田

la guanxi　拉關係

lao yingzi　老營子

li　禮

li cong wanglai　禮從往來

li da ya si ren　禮大壓死人

li shang wanglai　禮尚往來

li shang wanglai　禮上往來

lian　臉

Lianpi hou　臉皮厚

lianqiao　連橋

lianshang bu guangcai
　臉上不光彩

lidan　禮單

lijin　禮金

liqian　禮錢

liuchan　流產

liuxu　溜須

liwu　禮物

lun　倫

luzi hen huo　路子很活

mai dongxi qian　買東西錢

mai nuer　賣女兒

mei ganqing　沒感情

mei liangxin　昧良心

meilian jianren　沒臉見人

meiyou yisi　沒有意思

mianzi　面子

minren　民人

mu　畝

naishui qian　奶水錢

neidi　內弟

nongmin　農民

peisong　陪送

qi　氣

qian neng sheng qian　錢能生錢

qiao　剿

qin　親

qingming　清明

qingtie　請帖

qingwu　情物

qinqia　親家

qiongtou　窮頭

qiren　旗人

qiu banggong　求幫工

qiu de shang de　求得上的

queli　缺禮

qun　群

ren　仁

renqing　人情

sanyan　散烟

shanggong　上貢

shangliang　上梁

shangyou　上油

shaoxiang　燒香

shehui　社會

shehui shang de ren　社會上的人

shengmi zhu cheng shufan
　生米煮成熟飯

sheyuan　社員

shizai qinqi　實在親戚

shuzhang　叔丈

si　死

si menzi　死門子

si shu hu　四屬戶

sifang qian　私房錢

sipi　死皮

sixing　死性

songli　送禮

suili　隨禮

taiqian　抬錢

tanbing　探病

tianxia　天下

tongshi　同事

tongtun　同屯

tongxiang　同鄉

tongxiang hui　同鄉會

tun　屯

tunqin　屯親

waisheng guye　外甥姑爺

wanglai　往來

wenguo　溫鍋

wu　物

wulun　五倫

xi　席

xianai　下奶

xiangqin　鄉親

xiaochan　小產

xiaohu　小戶

xiaojing　孝敬

xiaoqing　小情

xin　信

xin yingzi　新營子

xinfang　新房

xinyi　心意

xu　序

yan 閹

yangge 秧歌

yangmao chu zai yangshen shang
　羊毛出在羊身上

yangqian 養錢

yangyu zhi en 養育之恩

yasui qian 壓歲錢

yayao qian 壓腰錢

yi chuizi maimia 一錘子買賣

yiban qinyou 一般親友

yinyang 陰陽

yiren de dao, jiquan shengtian
　一人得道，雞犬升天

yisi 意思

yuan 緣

yuanqin bu ru jinlin
　遠親不如近鄰

zaiqi 在旗

zhangfang 賬房

zhanguang 沾光

zhangzhuo 賬桌

zhao dinghun xiang 照訂婚像

zheng rizi 正日子

zhong, xiao, jie, yi 忠孝節義

zhuang yan qian 裝烟錢

zijiaren 自家人

zou houmen 走後門

zou qinqi 走親戚

zoudong 走動

zuoxi 坐席

zuzhang 族長

Index

In this index an "f" after a number indicates a separate reference on the next page, and an "ff" indicates separate references on the next two pages. A continuous discussion over two or more pages is indicated by a span of page numbers, e.g., "57–58." *Passim* is used for a cluster of references in close but not continuous sequence.

274 ～ Index

Banquets, 39, 46, 48, 130, 153, 225f
Bao (reciprocity), 14, 18, 145, 176.
See also Reciprocity
Befu, Harumi, 9, 44f, 148, 170, 218
Blau, Peter M., 161, 163
Bloch, Maurice, 13, 52, 217
Bohannan, P., 8
Bossevain, Jeremy, 224
Bourdieu, Pierre, 68, 116, 119, 127
Bride and groom, 55f, 177, 184–206
passim
Bridewealth, 21, 56, 176–208 passim;
converted, 180, 185, 187, 192, 194,
199, 206. See also Marriage
payment

Cadre power, 152, 159
Cadres, 29, 31; status of, 34, 36f, 60,
71; monopoly of resources, 69,
155, 162, 168, 171; in gift exchange,
86, 89, 93, 96f, 110, 119, 121, 130;
conflict with villagers, 133–38 passim, 149; and asymmetric gift giving, 152–68, 187, 231–37 passim
Carrier, James, 13, 211f, 217–22
passim
CCP (Chinese Communist Party),
16, 29, 31, 36, 93, 167, 176f, 233f
Cheal, David, 220f
Chinese Communist Party, see CCP
Cigarettes, 47, 57–61 passim, 67, 90;
as gifts, 131ff, 140, 195, 215; and
smoking behavior, 131f
Class labels, 28f, 33, 36f, 104f, 152,
158f
Cohen, Myron, 35, 38f, 47, 50f, 201,
208
Colleague relations, 100, 109f, 116ff,
121, 134, 155, 229
Collectives, 30f; hierarchy in, 34f,
40f; era of, 41, 152f; and guanxi,
108, 118ff, 152f, 163f, 208; impact
on gift exchange, 231–36
Collectivization, 29, 31, 39f, 66, 104,
110, 204

Comaroff, J. L., 179, 200, 204
Commodity economy, 12, 217
Commodity exchange, 5, 12f, 70, 219
Commodity relations, 212, 218f
Community: of Xiajia village, 22ff,
60, 102; and individuals, 40, 42,
48f; village, 48f, 82, 100, 102, 108,
227; celebration of, 60, 71f, 82, 90,
96, 99; and guanxi networks, 100ff,
114–23 passim, 227
Community solidarity, 60, 115, 118
Conjugal family, 149f, 173, 194–99
passim, 206ff
Conjugal funds, 199
Conjugal room, 56f, 181, 186f
Conjugality, 102, 177, 198, 208
Cooperation, 42, 89, 115f, 198
Cultural Revolution, 1, 39, 94, 108,
144, 182f, 234

Damon, F. H., 10ff, 215
Davis, Deborah, 177
De Glopper, Donald R., 140, 227
Decollectivization, 31–37 passim; and
gift giving, 78, 120, 154, 234; and
guanxi, 89, 118, 237
Descent, 27, 55, 62, 114; principles
of, 115. See also Agnatic groups;
Lineage
Diamond, Norma, 115
Disputes, 86f, 96, 136ff, 153
Dowry, 177ff, 181ff, 188–92; direct
dowry, 178, 181, 189, 201, 203;
indirect dowry, 179, 181, 189ff,
198–207 passim; and bride's status,
193, 197f; role of, 200–206 passim;
in non-Chinese societies, 203, 207f;
model of indirect, 203

Eloul, Rohn, 179, 200–207 passim
Emerson, Richard M., 161, 163
Emotional attachment, 64, 109, 139–
46 passim, 216, 219f, 226
Emotional concerns, 82, 87, 143
Endogamy, see Village endogamy

passim, 74f; art of, 17f; and gift giving, 81f; function of, 86–97; cultivation of, 88, 94, 175, 210, 227, 237; local conception of, 99–105; configuration of, 100, 105, 107, 223, 228; structure of, 106, 114–20 *passim*; voluntarism and, 117, 121; and *renqing*, 122f, 133, 139; and power, 145f, 165, 175; extended form of, 210, 226f, 229, 237; nature of, 222–29, 237f; high density of, 223; multiplexity of, 223

Han immigrant, 26, 33
Harrell, Stevan, 115, 177, 179, 205, 208
Hau, Maori notion of, 5ff, 11, 211, 215f
Herzfeld, Michael, 178f
Hierarchy, 3, 10; in socialist collectives, 28, 34–37; and gift exchange, 136, 147–62 *passim*, 168–73 *passim*, 204, 235f
Hu, Hsien-chin, 133–38 *passim*, 167
Hwang, Kwang-kuo, 18f, 88, 167, 227ff

Ideology: of the gift, 8, 29, 66, 114, 208; European and American, 212, 220f
Inalienability, *see under* Gifts
India: gift giving in, 9f, 63, 65, 178, 204, 211–16 *passim*
Individuality, 198
Industrial capitalism, 212
Inequality, 34, 36, 160, 163, 204, 221, 236; rural-urban, 34, 159
Instrumental-personal ties, 17, 75
Instrumentalism, 16. *See also* Gifts, instrumental
Intentionality, 82, 88
Interpersonal relations: studies of, 13ff, 18, 227ff; primacy of, 74, 93, 98, 146f, 165, 223f, 226
Invitations, 48f, 68, 76, 82–87 *passim*,

131f, 135, 153, 157, 234; formal, 48, 82, 87; refusal of, 157

Jacobs, Bruce, 16f, 75, 139f, 145, 227
Japan: gift giving in, 9, 50, 168

Keesing, Roger M., 11, 221
King, Ambrose Yeo-chi, 14, 18f, 137f, 146, 228f
Kinship: and reciprocity, 7, 12, 91, 93f, 125f, 160, 171, 221f; in Xiajia village, 38, 40; in *guanxi* networks, 100–120 *passim*, 140f, 151f, 223f; practical, 116, 118. *See also* Patrilineal kin; Patrilineal organizations
Kleinman, Arthur, 14, 222, 224
Kleinman, Joan, 14

Land reform, 28, 33, 93, 144
Leach, Edmund, 11, 161
Lebra, Takie Sugiyama, 9, 100, 166, 168, 213
Lévi-Strauss, Claude, 6f, 205
Li, 44, 49, 67ff, 123–27 *passim*, 134f, 180, 191, 225. *See* Proprieties
Lian, 136ff, 167. *See also* Face
Liang Shu-ming, 16
Lineage, 38, 121, 200, 205, 207, 232. *See also* Kinship; Patrilineal kin; Patrilineal organizations
Lineage paradigm, 99, 114f
Loans, private, 89f, 143, 237
Local moral world, 224, 226
Love gift, 66, 220
Lunar New Year, 2, 38f, 60–63, 83, 130, 143, 151, 232

Malinowski, Bronislaw, 6, 9, 73, 147, 160, 213, 221
Manchu: in Xiajia village, 24, 26f; ethnic identity, 32f, 39f
Marriage: and gift exchange 7ff, 39ff, 53, 55, 62, 66, 79f; village endogamy, 39–42, 66; marriage revolution, 41. *See also* Bride and groom
Marriage payment, 176–209; direct

Library of Congress Cataloging-in-Publication Data

Yan, Yunxiang, 1954–
    The flow of gifts : reciprocity and social networks in a Chinese village /
Yunxiang Yan.
        p.   cm.
    Includes bibliographical references and index.
    ISBN 0-8047-2603-5 (cl.) : ISBN 0-8047-2695-7 (pbk.)
        1. Gifts—China.   2. China—Social life and customs.   I. Title.
GT3041.C6Y36   1996
394—dc20   95-34618
                                                           CIP

Original printing 1996

Last figure below indicates year of this printing:

05   04   03   02   01   00   99   98   97   96